VISIONS AND REVISIONS

Irish *Writers* in their *Time*

Series Editor: Stan Smith

This innovative new series meets the need for comprehensive, up-to-date accounts of Irish writing which combine readability with critical authority and information with insight. Each volume addresses the whole range of a writer's work in its various genres, setting its vision of the world in biographical context and situating it within the cultural, social and political currents of the age, in Ireland and the wider world. The series is not confined to any one critical approach or interpretative model but represents the diversity of recent thinking about Irish literature across the centuries, as revisited and revised by modern scholarship.

Combining monograph and edited collections, the series draws on the expertise of both established and younger critics, presented in terms accessible to the general reader. It will prove indispensable for students and specialists alike.

1. *Patrick Kavanagh*
(Editor: STAN SMITH)

2. Elizabeth Bowen
(Editor: EIBHEAR WALSHE)

3. John Banville
(JOHN KENNY)

FORTHCOMING

4. Sean O'Casey
(JAMES MORAN)

5. James Joyce
(Editor: SEAN LATHAM)

6. Jonathan Swift
(BREAN HAMMMOND)

Elizabeth Bowen

Edited by

EIBHEAR WALSHE

University College Cork

IRISH ACADEMIC PRESS
DUBLIN • PORTLAND, OR

First published in 2009 by Irish Academic Press

44 Northumberland Road,
Ballsbridge,
Dublin 4, Ireland

920 NE 58th Avenue, Suite 300
Portland, Oregon,
97213-3786, USA

This edition © 2009 by Irish Academic Press
Chapters © Individual Contributors

www.iap.ie

British Library Cataloguing-in-Publication Data
An entry can be found on request

Library of Congress Cataloging-in-Publication Data
An entry can be found on request

Printed by Biddles Ltd, King's Lynn, Norfolk

Contents

Contributors

Andrew Bennett is Professor of English at the University of Bristol. He is co-author (with Nicholas Royle) of *Elizabeth Bowen and the Dissolution of the Novel: Still Lives* (Macmillan, 1994). His recent books include *Katherine Mansfield* (Northcote House, 2004), *The Author* (Routledge, 2005), *Wordsworth Writing* (Cambridge University Press, 2007) and *Ignorance: Literature and Agnoiology* (Manchester University Press, forthcoming, 2009).

Mary Breen teaches in the English Department of University College Cork. She has published on Molly Keane and Kate O'Brien. Her main research interests are in Irish women's writing and contemporary fiction. Her current research is on late eighteenth- and early nineteenth-century autobiography.

Neil Corcoran is King Alfred Professor of English Literature at the University of Liverpool and previously taught at the universities of Sheffield, Swansea and St Andrews. His most recent publications include *Elizabeth Bowen: The Enforced Return* (Oxford University Press, 2004) and *The Cambridge Companion to Twentieth-Century English Poetry* (2007). He is currently completing a study of Shakespeare and modern poetry.

Patricia Coughlan is a Professor of English at University College Cork. Editor of *Spenser and Ireland* (Cork University Press, 1990), she has also co-edited *Modernism and Ireland: The Poetry of the 1930s* (Cork University Press, 1995) and *Irish Literature: Feminist Perspectives* (Carysfort Press, 2008). She has published on many topics, including early modern colonial discourse, Le Fanu and Maturin, Beckett and Peig Sayers. Gender representations in Irish literature, twentieth-century poetry and fiction by women, are consistent topics of investigation. Publications on these include a previous essay on Bowen and discussions of several other twentieth-century Irish writers. She jointly devised and led the state-funded research project which produced the bilingual *Dictionary of Munster Women Writers 1800–2000* (Cork University Press, 2005, ed. Tina O'Toole). She is currently engaged on a study of gender, subjectivity and social change in Irish literature since 1960.

Noreen Doody lectures in English Literature at St Patrick's College, Drumcondra, Dublin City University. Her research interests are in Irish Studies and nineteenth-century literature, focusing on the work of Oscar Wilde and W.B. Yeats. She has published widely in this area and is currently working on a book on the influence of Wilde on Yeats.

Derek Hand teaches in the English Department at St Patrick's College, Drumcondra. He is interested in Irish writing in general and has published articles on W.B. Yeats, Elizabeth Bowen and on contemporary Irish fiction. The Liffey Press published his book *John Banville: Exploring Fictions* in 2002. He edited a special edition of the *Irish University Review* on John Banville in 2006 and co-edited a special edition of the *Irish University Review* on Benedict Kiely in 2008. He is a frequent reviewer of Irish fiction for the *Irish Times*. He is currently writing *A History of the Irish Novel* for Cambridge University Press.

Vera Kreilkamp is Visiting Professor at the Irish Studies Program at Boston College, Professor of English at Pine Manor College, and Co-editor of *Éire-Ireland: An Interdisciplinary Journal of Irish Studies*. She works in the areas of nineteenth-and twentieth-century Irish fiction and visual arts. Her publications include *The Anglo-Irish Novel and the Big House* (Syracuse University Press, 1998) as well as chapters in the *Cambridge Companion to the Irish Novel* (2006) and *Ireland and Empire* (Oxford University Press, 2004).

Heather Laird is a lecturer in English at University College Cork, Ireland. She completed a doctoral thesis at University College Dublin and was the James and Mary Fox Postdoctoral Fellow with the Centre for Irish Studies at NUI Galway. She is the author of *Subversive Law in Ireland, 1879–1920* (Four Courts Press, 2005) and has published essays on popular forms of resistance during the Irish Land War. Her current research interests include law in nineteenth-century Ireland, connections between Ireland and India in the nineteenth century and contemporary Irish literary and cultural criticism.

Sinéad Mooney is the author of *Samuel Beckett* (Northcote House, 2006) and the co-editor of *Edna O'Brien: New Critical Perspectives* (Caryfort, 2006), as well as numerous essays on Beckett and Irish women's writing. She is currently working on a monograph on Beckett, translation and self-translation on a fellowship from the Irish Research Council for the Humanities and Social Sciences, She is a lecturer in the Department of English, National University of Ireland, Galway.

Tina O'Toole has been a lecturer in English at the University of Limerick since 2004. A graduate of UCD and UCC, where she took her PhD, she has held a number of research posts including an IRCHSS Post-Doctoral Fellowship, a Women's Studies Fellowship at the University of Ottawa and an Irish Studies Fellowship at Queen's University Belfast. Her work includes Irish Literature: Feminist Perspectives (co-edited with Patricia Coughlan) (Carysfort Press, 2008); Documenting Irish Feminisms, a monograph co-written with Linda Connolly on second-wave feminist activism (Woodfield Press, 2005); and The Dictionary of Munster Women Writers (Cork University Press, 2005; also available as an online searchable database at www.munsterwomen.ie). She has also published articles and chapters on the 'New Woman' writers of the fin de siecle; on gender and sexual identities in Irish culture; and on migration and regionality in Irish literature.

Julie Anne Stevens lectures on English Literature at St Patrick's College, Drumcondra. She writes on Anglo-Irish literature and the visual arts. Her recent book, The Irish Scene in Somerville and Ross (Irish Academic Press, 2007), re-evaluates nineteenth-century women writers and shows how these commentators on Irish rural life immersed themselves in Continental literary and visual traditions.

Eibhear Walshe is a senior lecturer in the Department of Modern English at University College Cork. His biography Kate O'Brien, A Writing Life was published by Irish Academic Press in 2006. He was a section editor for The Field Day Anthology of Irish Writing (Volume 4, Cork University Press, 2002); a contributor to the New Dictionary of Biography (Oxford University Press, 2004) and guest-edited The Irish Review in 2000. His other publications include the edited collections, Ordinary People Dancing: Essays on Kate O'Brien (Cork University Press, 1993), Sex, Nation and Dissent (Cork University Press, 1997), Elizabeth Bowen Remembered (Four Courts Press, 1999) and The Plays of Teresa Deevy (Mellen Press, 2003.) He co-edited, with Brian Cliff, Representing the Troubles (Four Courts Press, 2004) and Molly Keane: Centenary Essays (Four Courts Press, 2006) with Gwenda Young.

Clair Wills is Professor of Irish Literature at Queen Mary, University of London. She has published widely on Northern Irish poetry, including Reading Paul Muldoon (Bloodaxe, 1993). She was an editor of the Field Day Anthology of Irish Women's Writing and Traditions (Volumes 4 and

5,Cork University Press, 2002). *That Neutral Island: A History of Ireland During the Second World War* was published by Faber and Harvard University Press and won the PEN Hessell-Tiltman Prize for History 2007.

Foreword

Until recently Elizabeth Bowen's work had suffered relative neglect at the hands of critics and academics, a neglect distressing to her admirers. There are some senses, unfortunately, in which this can never be adequately rectified. When a writer has not been entered fully into the most sophisticated critical conversations of her own time, the inadequacy of reception creates (as it does, for instance, in the comparable cases of writers as otherwise different as, say, David Jones and Henry Green) an aura of unapproachability, a sort of endlessly repeated preliminary throat-clearing in critics who do take her up, and a lack of comparative focusing and judgement of a kind which can only develop within a sustained critical continuum. Bowen, whose work is so preoccupied with ghosts of various kinds, had herself become, as a consequence, something of a ghost at the banquet of modern critical debate.

However, in recent years, as this volume attests, the critical neglect of Bowen has ceased. While there is no prospect, or danger, yet of anything resembling a Bowen critical 'industry' on the models of Joyce and Beckett, monographs written from various critical perspectives have been published in the US and Britain and have attracted attention, and more are in the pipeline; a recent issue of a prominent American academic journal has been devoted exclusively to her work; edited volumes of uncollected stories and essays are to appear shortly from an academic press; and a volume of her letters is being prepared. This is all immensely heartening for anyone who believes that Bowen's name should be more firmly established in the firmament of twentieth-century writing. As far as I am aware, however, there are no current plans for a new biography. Such a thing is, as Pat Coughlan also intimates in her chapter in this book, hugely desirable. Apart from anything else, you don't have to dig far — only as far as I did when making a radio programme about Bowen some years ago and asked a few questions in North Cork, for instance — to discover that there is still a hugely arresting story to be told: but some of those who might tell parts of it are now of course very old. Despite the lack of a recent biography, however, *Elizabeth Bowen* from the Visions and Revisions Series, which does contain some biographical material and speculation, is a timely contribution to what is now a notable ongoing public conversation about Elizabeth Bowen's work. That the volume is written predominantly but not exclusively by critics from within Ireland and appears from an Irish academic press are matters also worthy of note, since in Ireland her reputation has been a matter of considerable and, in recent years, very public controversy.

It is worth speculating for a moment, I think, on why the twenty-first century should welcome Elizabeth Bowen more wholeheartedly than her own did, and these essays encourage such speculation. There is an element of critical fashion in this, no doubt. Academic critics, even those who argue against canons, in fact tend to follow canonic lines pretty faithfully when writing monographs; and the canon of modern writing, and more specifically of modernist writing, was established early, in part by writers immensely capable of supplying provocative advertisements for their own work and creating the taste by which they intended to be judged. For various contingent reasons – of background, geography, temperament and opportunity, for instance, and probably of gender too – Elizabeth Bowen was not such a writer. But even canonic writing can reach monographic saturation point: and it is natural, as modernism recedes into the historical background, for attention to turn in alternative directions and for closer scrutiny to be given to figures once overshadowed. If Bowen is a belated beneficiary of this process, however, she would hardly have objected: she was knowledgeable, wrote a little about sartorial fashion, and knew about trends in the market. It seems to me extremely unlikely, however, that after becoming more firmly established critically in recent times, Bowen's reputation will ever dip again. The likelihood is all to the contrary.

There has also been, I think, as I suggested in my own critical study of her, an element of class resentment or hostility, or just plain lack of interest in the doings of the moneyed upper middle classes about whom she most usually writes. As those classes, at least in their Bowenesque incarnation, pale into history or fall out of visibility, this becomes less of an issue, although it does, I think, still prejudicially persist, for reasons all too easy to understand. And there has, in addition, been her occlusion by the figure of Virginia Woolf. For a long time, it seemed, one great female modernist prose writer – and Woolf is certainly that – was enough. Bowen herself readily acknowledged Woolf's achievement and seems to have kow-towed to her a bit in private life, perhaps appearing to collude more or less readily in her own occlusion; and this could not have helped her case.

Undoubtedly, however, the recently developed vocabularies and techniques of some of the newer critical schools of postmodernism, later feminism, new historicism and psychoanalytic and queer theory have coped rather better with the sheer strangeness of her work – including what one of the essays here shrewdly calls its 'generic dislocation' – than those of some of the older criticisms; and some of the essays in this book produce readings profitably and adventurously influenced by, or indebted to, such work. Bowen's final novel, Eva Trout, in particular, seems almost to secrete within itself the knowledge that it will have to wait for the moment of postmodernity to be read adequately, even if those of us who have tried to write about it at any length must surely be distressed by the inadequacy of our own accounts. Not only in relation to this notoriously problematic novel, however, but more generally, Elizabeth Bowen requires criticism, of whatever persuasion or orientation, to be exceptionally tactful, scrupulous and hesitant. We must resist the urge on the one hand to normalize to at least a receivable or interpretable degree what is originally wild indeed in her writing and, on the other, to follow this writing so far into its own fractured and complex strangenesses and aporia as to baffle any ease of readerly reception.

Prominently in Eva Trout, but in other novels and in short stories too, Bowen is a writer capable of formidable structural and thematic daring and risk; and what she is always willing to risk is that her books might not find the absolutely alert, concentrated and attentive readers they need. There is in her work, almost always, and in different registers and tonalities as it advances, a striking combination of sureness of writerly need, an unwavering commitment to the task, and a willingness to experiment of a kind which renders the entire activity peculiarly and sometimes almost vertiginously vulnerable. In Bowen's prose the normative structures of fictional coherence, and sometimes of linguistic coherence too, are exposed in the most radically unsettling ways to a potential writerly incoherence. For me, her most arresting texts, and the most arresting moments in others, are those which most tellingly convey the impression of hesitantly following in their own footsteps, of knowing only by going where it is they have to go. This can sometimes seem, especially in the most agonistic works such as The Heat of the Day, a kind of drivenness. In this, Bowen's writing itself sometimes matches the terrifying, careering propulsion with which Mrs Drover is driven against her will at the end of 'The Demon Lover', that almost paradigmatic Bowen tale of perversely asocial desire, enforced repetition and the *Unheimlich*, or the scarifying intensity, both murderous and suicidal, of the night drive which concludes *To The North*.

Even properly to understand the plot of *Friends and Relations*, for instance, demands high effort and quite intensely close reading (and some critics who have written about the novel quite understandably get the plot wrong): but the reward is to be penetrated by a richness of subtle recognition discoverable in no other way, and to be exhilarated by the discovery. These difficulties, however, need their explicators: and for this reason too we can be glad that the Bowen shelves are starting, at last, to fill. A proper conversation is yet to begin about some of her work: *Friends and Relations* itself, maybe, and certainly her first novel *The Hotel*, which is as truly weird and wonderful a performance as anything she ever wrote. It is as though – an otherwise unimaginable thing – James, Forster and Woolf have been interpenetrated with one another and set in almost dementedly spiralling, but still just controlled, motion. The novice writer *finding a voice* doesn't come into this, really; losing, and so starting to find, a self-estrangingly writerly identity, maybe, and manifestly delighting in both the loss and the recovery, or discovery.

There are also whole movements of mind, sensibility, address and intonation in Bowen, some of which emerge from, and are illuminated by, the present collection, which we can look forward to seeing brought into further relief and clarification by this recently extended critical conversation. The quality, or qualities, of Bowen's humour, for instance, which is rarely just 'social comedy', require patient attentiveness, as does the particular quality and tone of her scepticism, which is social, ethical and, although she would hardly have had it so herself, theological. The peculiar trajectories and instabilities of sexual desire in the work – what one essay here excellently calls 'a labile form of energy in itself, for which persons are mere conductors' – have, it might seem, by now been thoroughly and rigorously scrutinized: but the deeply perturbing masochism and sadomasochism represented in, and investigated by, Bowen's work is yet to be attended to as closely as it requires. Critics, if they are anything like me, probably wince and flinch in retraction from these things which, both physical and emotional, are of a kind which can occur at the most unpredictable moments. And, while memorably insightful work has been done, and is done in this volume, on specific things in Bowen – on furniture, for example, photography and the cinema – there is plenty of scope for more.

One essay in this collection, in a mode of definition which is inevitably a mode of recognition and celebration too, says that something strikes 'the classic Bowen note'. It is now getting to the point in literary criticism and literary history where we can start to ask questions which almost, just about, expect answers. What might it be for a majority of well-read people, and especially younger people, to understand what is meant by 'the classic Bowen note'? What might it mean for the reception of twentieth-century literature more generally and particularly of literary modernism to have such a note more strongly sounded in contemporary literary criticism and for Bowen to be brought far more prominently into forms of comparative critique? And what might it be for Elizabeth Bowen to become, herself, recognized as 'a classic'? One thing this would demand – and this is even more pressingly necessary than a new biography – is a new scholarly edition of her work, of all of her work. But our final contemporary question about Bowen unfortunately hardly anticipates a positive answer and may therefore strike a plaintive note: is there no commercial or academic publisher willing to take on such a thing?

Neil Corcoran
King Alfred Professor of English Literature
University of Liverpool

Introduction

This collection of essays charts the creative life of one of the most important and successful novelists in the twentieth century, the Anglo-Irish writer, Elizabeth Bowen (1899–1973). Chapter by chapter, this study provides a comprehensive scholarly account of each of her ten novels, published between 1927 and 1969, as well as the short stories, family histories, travel writings and memoirs of this accomplished and critically respected modernist. This edited collection, part of the Visions and Revisions series on Irish writing, is structured chronologically to provide a full account of Bowen's centrality as a major novelist in the traditions of twentieth-century cultural production, modernist literature and, in particular, theories of modern Irish writing. Recent critical work on Bowen's fictions has increased significantly, as the bibliography attests. As Neil Corcoran says in his foreword to the present volume, 'This is all immensely heartening for anyone who believes that Bowen's name should be more firmly established in the firmament of twentieth-century writing'.

In the opening chapter, Noreen Doody's biographical essay establishes a critical overview of Bowen's life, her family background, writing career between London and North Cork and her position as an Anglo-Irish writer. Vera Krielkamp, in her essay on Bowen's place within the tradition of the Anglo-Irish novel, argues for her to be read as an Ascendancy modernist. Andrew Bennett uses her earlier novels to explore Bowen's modernist deployment of the novel form in the 1930s. Bowen's interest in, and success with, the short story form is of crucial interest in this study. Patricia Coughlan and Sinéad Mooney consider her stories of the 1920s and onwards, both in terms of the Gothic and also in terms of representations of gender and psychoanalysis. Derek Hand delineates Bowen's figuring of Ireland, of the Anglo-Irish, and of the Irish War of Independence in The Last September and in her Irish short stories. Elizabeth Bowen's imaginative tenure on the landscape of North

Cork, the fields and hills around her family home Bowen's Court, is central to her writing. Place, the land around her home in North Cork, loomed largest in her writings at times of war and disruption, particularly during the Irish War of Independence and again during the Second World War. In her family history, Bowen's Court, Bowen is clear-eyed about the history of colonial injustice that imposed her family as unwelcome landlords and owners on this same North Cork landscape. Her family had been settled in Farrahy for nearly 200 years by the time of her birth in 1899, and her fictions reflect this long and difficult history between landlord and landscape.

In my chapter 'Success and War', I examine Bowen's ground-breaking novels of the 1930s, in particular focusing on her commercially successful novels, The Death of the Heart and The House in Paris. The experience of living in London during the Second World War had an energizing effect on Bowen's fictions, and this chapter deals with her Blitz novel, the best-selling The Heat of the Day. Family history and memoir are central to Bowen's imaginative preoccupations and Mary Breen analyzes her use of this genre in her essay on Bowen's Court, Seven Winters and Pictures and Conversations. Bowen's post-war Irish novel, A World of Love, is the focus for Clair Wills's chapter on Bowen and Ireland of the 1950s. My second chapter deals with the changes in narrative form which occur in Bowen's last works, writings of increasing darkness and experimentation and, in particular, her travel memoir, A Time in Rome, and her last two novels, The Little Girls and Eva Trout. Bowen's final novel, Eva Trout is also analyzed in Tina O'Toole's chapter, which locates her writings within contemporary ideas about the construction of gender in literature. In the two final chapters Julie Anne Stevens provides an account of Bowen's lively and engaged critical afterlife while Heather Laird considers theoretical engagements with Bowen's writings in contemporary debates around Irish studies. Overall, this collection brings together a series of contemporary critical essays on Bowen's place in Irish studies, and in post-colonial theories of writing, and highlights her importance for feminist critical thought and for contemporary theories of the novel. The purpose of this collection is to draw together existing scholarly perspectives and competing revisions and to continue ongoing, lively and fruitful engagement with her writing.

Eibhear Walshe
University College, Cork
July 2008

Acknowledgements

In putting this volume together, I was greatly helped and encouraged and I would like to record my thanks, firstly to the general editor, Stan Smith, to all the contributors for being so professional, prompt and helpful, to Professor Neil Corcoran for the foreword and Heather Marchant for copy-editing, and in particular to Lisa Hyde of Irish Academic Press for commissioning this book and for all her support, encouragement and help.

I wish to acknowledge a UCC Arts Faculty Research Grant to help me write my own chapters. Thanks are due to President Michael Murphy of UCC and Professor David Cox, Dean of Arts, UCC for granting me research leave in 2007 to work on this project. I would also like to thank Caroline Walsh of the *Irish Times* for asking me to write on Bowen and to the Mitchelstown Summer School, and to Dr Robert McCarthy, Dean of St Patrick's, Dublin, for invitations to speak on Elizabeth Bowen in Farrahy.

For permissions, I would like to thank Belou Charlaff of Curtis Brown, acting for the Bowen literary Estate, and also the National Portrait Gallery, London, for permission to use the cover photograph. My colleagues in the English Department, UCC, in particular Anne Fitzgerald, Elaine Hurley, Graham Allen, Pat Coughlan, Heather Laird, Mary Breen and Eamon O'Carragain, were, as always, so helpful and supportive and I would also thank Carmel Quinlan, Michael Dillon and Donald O'Driscoll for interesting insights into Bowen's work. Finally, I am very grateful to Elizabeth Bowen's cousins, Veronica Hall-dare and Valerie E. P. Hone, for their kindness and hospitality to me in working on this book and for sharing their invaluable memories with me.

To the North

Reproduced with permission of Curtis Brown Group Ltd, London, on behalf of the Estate of Elizabeth Bowen
Copyright © Elizabeth D.C. Cameron, 1933

ACKNOWLEDGEMENTS

The Hotel

Reproduced with permission of Curtis Brown Group Ltd, London, on behalf of the Estate of Elizabeth Bowen
Copyright © Elizabeth Bowen, 1927

Friends and Relations

Reproduced with permission of Curtis Brown Group Ltd, London, on behalf of the Estate of Elizabeth Bowen
Copyright © Elizabeth Bowen, 1931

The Mulberry Tree

Reproduced with permission of Curtis Brown Group Ltd, London, on behalf of the Estate of Elizabeth Bowen
Copyright © 1986 by Curtis Brown Ltd, London, Literary Executors, on behalf of the Estate of the late Elizabeth Bowen.

Collected Stories

Reproduced with permission of Curtis Brown Group Ltd, London, on behalf of the Estate of Elizabeth Bowen
Copyright © 1980 by Curtis Brown Ltd, London, Literary Executors, on behalf of the Estate of the late Elizabeth Bowen.

Bowen's Court

Reproduced with permission of Curtis Brown Group Ltd, London, on behalf of the Estate of Elizabeth Bowen
Copyright © Elizabeth Bowen, 1942

The Last September

Reproduced with permission of Curtis Brown Group Ltd, London, on behalf of the Estate of Elizabeth Bowen
Copyright © Elizabeth Bowen, 1929

Introduction to the Second Ghost Book

Reproduced with permission of Curtis Brown Group Ltd, London, on behalf of the Estate of Elizabeth Bowen
Copyright © Elizabeth Bowen, 1952

The House in Paris

Reproduced with permission of Curtis Brown Group Ltd, London, on

behalf of the Estate of Elizabeth Bowen
Copyright © Elizabeth Cameron, 1935

The Death of the Heart

Reproduced with permission of Curtis Brown Group Ltd, London, on
behalf of the Estate of Elizabeth Bowen
Copyright © Elizabeth Bowen, 1938

A World of Love

Reproduced with permission of Curtis Brown Group Ltd, London, on
behalf of the Estate of Elizabeth Bowen
Copyright © Elizabeth Bowen, 1955

A Time in Rome

Reproduced with permission of Curtis Brown Group Ltd, London, on
behalf of the Estate of Elizabeth Bowen
Copyright © Elizabeth Bowen, 1959

Eva Trout

Reproduced with permission of Curtis Brown Group Ltd, London, on
behalf of the Estate of Elizabeth Bowen
Copyright @ Elizabeth Bowen, 1968

The Little Girls

Reproduced with permission of Curtis Brown Group Ltd, London, on
behalf of the Estate of Elizabeth Bowen
Copyright © Elizabeth Bowen, 1963

Pictures and Conversations

Reproduced with permission of Curtis Brown Group Ltd, London, on
behalf of the Estate of Elizabeth Bowen
Copyright © Elizabeth Bowen, 1975

'The Cult of Nostalgia', in *The Listener* (9 August 1951), p.225

Reproduced with permission of Curtis Brown Group Ltd, London, on
behalf of the Estate of Elizabeth Bowen
Copyright © Elizabeth Bowen, 1951

Chronology

1899
Elizabeth Dorothea Cole Bowen born in Dublin on 7 June, only child of Henry Charles Cole Bowen and Florence Colley Bowen.

1905–06
Henry Bowen suffers a nervous breakdown and Bowen and her mother move to the Kent coast in England.

1912–14
Henry Bowen recovers but Florence Bowen dies of cancer. Bowen sent to boarding school, Harpenden Hall, Hertfordshire.

1914
Bowen moves to Downe House School in Kent. First World War breaks out, Bowen at Bowen's Court with her father.

1918
Bowen's father remarries.

1919–21
Irish War of Independence breaks out. Bowen attends the LCC School of Art in London and then travels in Italy.

1923
Bowen marries Alan Cameron. Her first short-story collection, Encounters, is published.

1925
Bowen and her husband move to Oxford.

1927
The Hotel

1929
The Last September
Joining Charles and Other Stories

1930
Henry Bowen dies. Bowen inherits Bowen's Court.

1931
Friends and Relations

1932
To the North

1934
The Cat Jumps and Other Stories

1935
The House in Paris. Bowen and Alan Cameron move to London, where they live in Regent's Park.

1938
Her most successful novel, *The Death of the Heart*.

1939
The Second World War breaks out.

1940
Bowen volunteers for secret reporting for the Ministry of Information on Ireland and Ireland's neutrality.

1942
Bowen's Court

1943
Seven Winters

1945
The Demon Lover and Other Stories

1948
Awarded the CBE.

1949
The Heat of the Day. Hononary Degree from Trinity College, Dublin.

1950
Collected Impressions

1951
The Shelbourne. Retires to live in Bowen's Court.

1952
Alan Cameron dies.

1955
A World of Love

1956
Honorary Degree from Oxford.

1959
Sells Bowen's Court.

1960
A Time in Rome. Bowen's Court demolished.

1964
The Little Girls

1965
Buys house in Kent.

1969
Eva Trout

1973
Dies in hospital in London on 22 February. Buried in St Colman's churchyard in Farahy in North Cork, next to Bowen's Court.

CHAPTER ONE

Elizabeth Bowen:
A Short Biography

NOREEN DOODY

In a back drawing-room of a tall eighteenth-century Georgian house in Herbert Place, Dublin on 7 June 1899, Florence Isabella Pomeroy Colley Bowen gave birth to a long-awaited child. Florence had been married for nine years to Henry Charles Cole Bowen of Bowen's Court, Kildorrery, County Cork before this first and only child, Elizabeth Dorothea, was born. Elizabeth Bowen's parents had expected that their baby would be a boy and had somewhat precipitously decided to name him Robert, it being the custom to name each succeeding heir to the Bowen estates Henry or Robert. Despite her parents' expectation of a son, Bowen claimed in later life that neither of them ever indicated to her any disappointment whatsoever on grounds of gender. Her observation, however, suggests an early sensitivity to place in her awareness of having usurped the position of a preconceived male presence, setting in motion the train of displacements or occupations of marginal space that would characterize her entire existence.

The Bowens, like Elizabeth's mother's family the Colleys, were an Anglo-Irish family. The Bowens, originally the ap Owens from Wales, traced their first ancestor in Ireland back to Colonel Henry Bowen, a professional soldier who arrived in Ireland with the Cromwellian Invasion and acquired lands in County Cork officially confiscated from an Irish Catholic landowner, Garrett Cushin. Bowen brought his son from England and set up house in a semi-ruined castle on the land. It seems, however, that Colonel Henry Bowen may have encountered some trouble from the dispossessed Irish gentleman, as he made it a proviso of his son's entitlement of inheritance that he would not marry Eilis Cushin nor any of the Cushin family.[1]

Apart from this altercation and a minor confrontation with rebels in 1798 the Bowens settled peaceably into Anglo-Irish life in Ireland. In 1716 Colonel Bowen's grandson married the wealthy Jane Cole whose son, Henry, built the house on the estate, completing it in 1775. Bowen's Court was a large, solid, square structure, the type of Big House that became emblematic of the Anglo-Irish Ascendancy class across Ireland. So clearly were these houses viewed as symbols of injustice and class privilege that they became the focus of reprisals in the Irish War of Independence. 'Between 6 December 1921 and 22 March 1923, 192 Big Houses were burned by incendiaries as reported in the *Morning Post* of 9 April 1923.'[2] Bowen's novel, *The Last September*, set in these troubled times, describes the splendid isolation of the Big House looking out from its tall and elegant windows across cultivated lawns at the wild and savage countryside beyond.[3]

During the eighteenth and nineteenth centuries the Bowens, like other families of the Ascendancy class, lived a life of social privilege, visiting between Big Houses, tending their estates and in many ways insulated from, and unaffected by, the less fortunate lives of the other occupants of the island. At the height of the Great Famine in 1847, however, Elizabeth's great-grandmother, Eliza Wade, attempted to address the tragedy unfolding outside the gates of the demesne and give sustenance to famine victims by dispensing soup from the basement of Bowen's Court. Unfortunately, many starving people died at the approach to the Big House in their effort to reach the soup kitchen and were buried in the nearby churchyard in a pit purposely dug to accommodate their great numbers. Eliza Wade's response is well meaning but ill-judged and wholly inadequate, and in describing her great-grandmother's action, Bowen reveals her own astute and sensitive observation of the island's inter-cultural relations.

Elizabeth Bowen's mother's family, the Colleys, resided originally in Castle Carbery, County Kildare, but at the time of Elizabeth's birth they lived in a large Victorian house, Mount Temple, in Clontarf, Dublin. In contrast with the Bowens, who had a history of mental disorder and erratic behaviour, the Colleys were lively, bright and sociable. It was while studying law at Trinity College that Henry Bowen first met and fell in love with Florence, one of the lovely Colley sisters. Florence was the more introspective of these lively girls and according to her daughter's memoir, she and her husband, Henry Bowen, 'had in common a vague-ness as to immediate things'.⁴ Bowen further describes her parents as living in a world of their own: 'Inside this world they each ruled their private kingdoms of thought, and inside it I, their first child, began to set up my own'.⁵ From this early stage, Bowen found a mode of belonging that relied upon an independent imagination and strong sense of phys-ical place. She learnt from an early stage to cultivate a form of imagina-tive belonging but also noted the selective method of noticing employed by her parents in dealing with everyday life, a method which vaunted the notion of 'keeping the lid on things' and which would appear many times as a theme in her fiction. Not noticing was a coping mechanism often employed by Bowen's class and adroitly deployed by her in The Last September to illustrate the refusal of the occupants of the Big House to acknowledge the changing political situation in the country around them. Unfortunately, there arose a tragic circumstance in the Bowen family which was impossible to ignore: He suffered a nervous break-down which escalated in the summer of 1905 causing him to be both violent and morose. He voluntarily signed himself into a mental institu-tion just outside Dublin. The illness naturally caused great distress to the vague and pensive Florence Bowen and to his daughter, Elizabeth, who no matter how shielded she might have been, was made uneasy at the uncertainty of events surrounding her father and his bouts of unstable behaviour. These circumstances culminated for the child in her hasty removal from Herbert Street in the dark of night, bundled into a cab with her nanny to seek sanctuary in the house of her maternal grand-parents in Clontarf. The stammer that she endured throughout her life dates from this traumatic time in her early girlhood.

However unusual the circumstances of the child Elizabeth Bowen's night flight and final departure from Herbert Street, journeys and travel had always been common occurrences in her young life and would feature strongly throughout her lifetime, continuing as themes into her fiction. As early as the summer of her birth, 1899, Bowen travelled from the house by the Grand Canal in Dublin on a journey to Bowen's Court, County Cork, where she would return each summer afterwards for the next six years, journeying back to Herbert Place in Dublin for the win-ters. With the chronic onset of her father's illness, however, Bowen and her mother, on the advice of their doctors, departed for England and the

Kent coast, where they had many Anglo-Irish relatives. They moved between Folkestone, Lyminge, Seabrook and Hythe, staying in numerous seaside villas. Maud Ellmann writes that her 'fiction literally houses her experience'.[6] Bowen gives shape to her shifting context through her keen observation of place. She possesses the many places she occupies through her observation and makes them not only the imaginative landscape of her fiction but also the composite terrain of her belonging.

Bowen and her mother Florence enjoyed a close, intense relationship in their new life together in England and the little girl was also happy to be in the company of her cousins, particularly Audrey Fiennes and a young girl, Hilary, who was a neighbour in her last summer at Hythe. Bowen writes about one of her favourite activities she shared with her mother during this time; she describes how they loved to visit empty seaside villas and would contrive to avoid the presence of an estate agent, sometimes to the extent of Elizabeth squeezing in through a back window of the house and opening the front door to her mother. 'We took over wherever we were, at the first glance. Yes, what a suppositious existence ours came to be, in these one-after-another fantasy buildings, pavilions of love.'[7] Her father convalesced in Ireland and by the time Elizabeth Bowen was 12 he too spent the summer at Hythe. However, although her father's mental health had very much improved and he was no longer a cause for grave concern, in 1912 Bowen underwent another catastrophic upheaval: her mother died less than six months after she had been diagnosed with cancer. 'In the last of the villas in which it came about that we did actually live, she died.'[8]

Elizabeth Bowen's adult relations, in an effort to protect her from the grief of her mother's death, did not allow her attend her mother's funeral nor see her dead; instead Elizabeth spent the days in the company of her young friend, Hilary. In her memoir of childhood, *Seven Winters*, Bowen paints a fleeting, wistful portrait of her mother:

> The most intense moments of her existence all through her life had been solitary. She often moved some way away from things and people she loved, as though to convince herself that they did exist. Perhaps she never did quite convince herself, for about her caresses and ways with me I remember a sort of rapture of incredulity ... She explained to me candidly that she kept a governess because she did not want to scold me herself.[9]

Bowen conjures up a somewhat ephemeral picture of her mother but there is a longing in her words for some tactile connection to the woman she adored. There is an ambiguity at the centre of their relationship compacted of closeness and distance which seems to call into question the nature of reality. Elizabeth senses an aloofness in her mother's devotion, and Florence's refusal to engage on a realistic plain with the more difficult realities of rearing a child can only have complicated the child's perception of reality. Florence's forced abandonment of the child in dying and Elizabeth's imposed separation from the reality of her mother's death and its attendant rituals propels her into a landscape of isolation and uncertainty. This relationship of mother and daughter based in part on fantasy and detachment must surely have contributed to Bowen's characterization of unfulfilling relationships in her fiction. Certainly, her early lessons in the ambiguous nature of reality encouraged her imaginative growth and, as Lassner points out, 'Bowen's writing does bridge the isolation and silences which she inherited and the world of adult society and literature to which she wanted to belong'.[10]

After the death of her mother, her upbringing devolved on a seemingly vast amount of Anglo-Irish aunts living in both Ireland and England. During the last months of her life, Florence Bowen had arranged for her sister Laura to look after her daughter and following her death, Laura took Elizabeth to Hertfordshire to live with her and her brother, William Wingfield Colley, who was a curate and for whom Laura kept house. The household was subdued and dull and not altogether suitable for a young bereaved girl. However, in school in Harpenden Hall Bowen found relief for her pent-up emotions in displays of high spirits. She was one of the chief ringleaders in perpetuating various fads amongst her school friends and was among the foremost participants in a craze for the occult. The burial scene from her later novel, *The Little Girls* (1964), is based on a rite in which she took part while at school in Harpenden Hall. As described in the novel, Bowen and her friends buried some personal, if not so valuable, treasures in a box beneath the earth. The sombre little ceremony is potent in its suggestions of a symbolic enactment of filial burial rites and loss.

Her father's health was restored by now and she spent her summers at Bowen's Court. She also paid visits to her Aunt Edie's house in Clondalkin, where she enjoyed among her cousins and their parents the gregariousness and congenial sociability for which the Colleys were renowned. Bowen also spent much time during these summers reading; she was an avid reader despite not having learnt to read until the age of 8 because her mother feared that, due to some possible inherited instability from the Bowens, it might be detrimental to her mental health.[11]

Elizabeth Bowen attended Downe House School, once the home of Charles Darwin, near Orpington in Kent from 1914 to 1917. While at this school Elizabeth took a great interest in writing, particularly in the short story, and was a member of an exclusive writing group. At this time, however, she saw her future as being more in the visual rather than the literary arts and, having finished school, she enrolled at the London County Council School of Art in Southampton Row, London. Prior to this she spent some time working in a hospital for shell-shocked First World War veterans. At the end of two terms at art college, Bowen decided that she had no particular genius as an artist and that her true calling was to be a writer. She took a short course in journalism and at the age of 20 began writing in earnest, focusing on the short story. Each of these early stories was rejected in turn by the various publishers of periodicals and magazines to whom she submitted them, but she persevered and during 1919–22 she wrote all of the stories that would become her first published collection, Encounters. Bowen had the good fortune to meet Rose Macaulay who was an old university friend of Olive Willis, her headmistress at Downe House. Macaulay was a well-established critic and novelist at this stage and immediately recognized Bowen's literary talent. She put her in touch with agents and relevant people in publishing and introduced her to the London literary scene. Through Macaulay, Elizabeth Bowen's literary circle increased and the young author, always a sociable being, was delighted to find herself in the company of such literary luminaries as Edith Sitwell, Walter de la Mare and Aldous Huxley.[12]

She continued to live in England, although her father was fully recovered. Henry Bowen had remarried in 1918 and Elizabeth, who was very fond of his new wife Mary Gwynn, returned home to Bowen's Court during the summers. The situation in Ireland was tense during these years of Bowen's young adult life. From 1919 to 1921 the War of Independence raged across the country, with insurgents, British soldiers and mercenaries engaging in guerrilla warfare, reprisals and counter-reprisals. Bowen's Court was never actually burnt like so many other Anglo-Irish Big Houses, but the expectation of destruction was very real. Bowen captures this time in meticulous detail in *The Last September*. Entertainment still went on during this period in the ill-fated Big Houses and the young officers of the incumbent British army complemented the company and joined the tennis parties. Just as Lois would do in her novel, Bowen fell in love and became engaged to a young British army officer, Lieutenant John Anderson. The whole thing lasted a very short time and was entirely nipped in the bud when Elizabeth went to visit her Aunt Edie and family in Italy in a hotel in Bordighera. This hotel, together with her hapless love affair, found themselves reborn and re-imagined in her first novel, *The Hotel* (1927).

Not long after this brief infatuation, on 4 August 1923, Elizabeth Bowen married Alan Charles Cameron. She had met Cameron through Audrey Fiennes' mother, Aunt Gertrude, who was living near Alan in Bloxham, Oxfordshire. Alan Cameron was born in 1893 of Scottish and Cornish descent; he had been an army officer during the war and had been awarded the MC. When Elizabeth and he first met he was recuperating from the effects of gas poisoning, which he had suffered during the war. At the time of their marriage Cameron was Assistant Secretary for Education for Northamptonshire, but in 1925 he was promoted to Secretary of Education for the City of Oxford and the young couple moved into Waldencote, a stone-built cottage in Old Headington about a mile and a half from the city. Although many of Elizabeth's friends and acquaintances judged Alan Cameron a bluff and hearty man, something of a Colonel Blimp, their marriage lasted thirty years and seems to have been both a loving and mutually beneficial arrangement. Ellmann suggests that their love was founded on a more parental than sexual model, each succouring and supporting the other and enjoying the companionship and the satirical sense of humour that they held in common. However this may be, Bowen had an extramarital love affair in Oxford with a young don, Humphrey House, and continued with the affair after his marriage to Madeleine Church. The aptness of these last names, given her proclivity for place, can hardly have escaped Bowen's keen wit. House was not Elizabeth Bowen's only acquisition in Oxford as she soon became friendly with many of its academics and literary persons; her likeableness and gifted social skills guaranteed her centrality to any group, even the usually introverted and exclusive echelons of this foremost bastion of criticism, scholarship and learning.

During her years at Oxford, Bowen published her second novel, *The Last September* (1929), and two collections of short fiction, *Joining Charles and Other Stories* (1929) and *The Cat Jumps and Other Stories* (1934). She also wrote three novels in the 1930s: *Friends and Relations* (1931), *To the North* (1932) and *The House in Paris* (1935). Elizabeth's affair with House lasted from 1933 to 1935, the year in which he and his wife left England to spend some time in Calcutta. In 1935 Alan Cameron was appointed Secretary to the Central Council for Schools Broadcasting and Bowen and he took their leave of Oxford and went to live at 2 Clarence Terrace, Regent's Park, London.

The house in London became a centre of hospitality; Elizabeth Bowen was renowned for her talents as a hostess and entertained guests not only in Clarence Terrace but also at Bowen's Court. She had inherited the Big House in County Cork on her father's death in 1930, and she enjoyed having her friends to stay there and held lavish parties for them. Alan mostly took part in these occasions and although many of Elizabeth's lively guests found him somewhat long-winded and onerous he was a sensitive and kindly presence, particularly to the young women companions of the literary-minded males whose interest was more directed at engaging the attention of their hostess. At a summer house-party in Bowen's Court in 1936, Geronwy Rees, with whom Elizabeth was romantically involved, fell in love with Rosamond Lehmann. Like so many of Bowen's acquaintances Rees finds his way into her novels, the character of Eddie in *The Death of the Heart* (1938) being based on him. Indeed, when Rees first read the novel he was flattered by the portrait but on reflection decided he disliked it and would have sued for libel but for his friends' dissuasion. Elizabeth's disappointment in the amatory ardour of Geronwy Rees was short-lived; in 1937 she had a brief romantic encounter with May Sarton and also began an affair with Sean O'Faolain. O'Faolain admired her fiction, but writing to Elizabeth of the painful divisions in Irish society he asked if she would write a novel in which the Big House people at least acknowledge what was happening in the rest of the country. He suggested to her that it would be interesting to write about the Big House in present-day Ireland and stated that the wall between the Big House and the rest of the country was still very much in place.[13]

Among those who came to stay in Bowen's Court were Lord David Cecil, Isaiah Berlin, Rosamund Lehmann, Iris Murdoch, Cyril Connolly,

Hubert Butler, Eddie Sackville-West and Maurice Craig. Virginia and Leonard Woolf once spent a night there; however, Woolf wrote rather slightingly about the house's lack of comfort and often teased Elizabeth about her 'Irish castle'. Woolf had not been very impressed on their first meeting, considering her too conventional; however, as time went by she found Elizabeth 'improved' and a friendly relationship grew between them. Bowen thoroughly enjoyed her conversations with Woolf and spoke readily to her about her plans for her novels and even discussed with her the wartime mission she had been given to carry out in Ireland.

War was an invigorating experience for Bowen and she once declared that she wouldn't have missed being in London during the blitz for anything. It was as if war enabled her to experience the immediacy of life. She became an Air Raid Precautions warden from the outset of the war and was actively involved in bringing people into the shelters and making certain they complied with blackout regulations. Bowen wrote no novels during this time of disintegrating order; instead, holding on to a firm version of what had been, she wrote up the past in an account of her family history and a memoir of her childhood: Bowen's Court, published in 1942 and Seven Winters, published in 1943. The short story was her chosen vehicle for conveying the searing, explosive experience of life during the war: The Demon Lover and Other Stories (1945) was among the greatest records of London during this time. Elizabeth Bowen's most serious love affair took place in wartime; her lover was Charles Ritchie, a Canadian diplomat, and their deep friendship lasted beyond the affair until the end of her life. Charles Ritchie married his cousin in 1951, the year proceeding the death of Alan Cameron. Their love affair would be echoed by the wartime lovers, Robert and Stella, in the novel Bowen would publish following the end of the war, The Heat of the Day (1949).

In 1940 Bowen volunteered her services to the British Ministry of Information and was sent to Ireland to collect intelligence on the state of Ireland's neutrality. When the war began Bowen had been in some sympathy with De Valera's view that Ireland was not in a condition to take part in war and his refusal to allow British forces the use of Irish ports. However, her opinion changed as the war progressed and she stood firmly in support of England's war effort. For the length of the war she travelled between Dublin, Cork and London. On one occasion she met with James Dillon, Deputy Leader of Fine Gael, and sent a dispatch to London, describing his opposition to Irish neutrality. In later years when these dispatches became public, Dillon blamed Bowen for her abuse of his hospitality in reporting what he had thought to be a private conversation.[14]

Bowen's life during wartime took on aspects of a novel: she carried out deeds of espionage, lived on the edge of death in the London bombardments, engaged in an intense love affair, maintained a marriage and documented the story of her origins, consigning her childhood and ancestry, the historical or real, to the page. Perhaps for the first time she lived the moment while her extended writing took care of the past and her short stories were meteoric bursts of lived expression. It seems as though the context of reality had to change before it was possible for her to fully live in the context of 'real life'. Bowen's life, its affairs and experiences, which so often seem to come truly alive only when displaced into her novels, found a viable reality in the chaotic times of war.

The house in Regent's Park was bombed in 1944. When the war ended Elizabeth Bowen was awarded a CBE (1948) and the following year received an honorary degree of Doctor of Letters from her father's *alma mater*, Trinity College Dublin; a similar honour would follow from Oxford University in 1956. After Alan's retirement the Camerons moved to Bowen's Court. However, shortly after the move, Alan, whose health had been impaired by his war injuries and increasingly heavy drinking, died on 26 August 1952 and was buried in the small churchyard beside the Bowen estate. Alan had been Elizabeth's main support in life and she felt his loss dreadfully. She tried to maintain Bowen's Court for some years following the loss of Alan, but its upkeep proved too costly a burden and in 1959 she was forced to sell it to a neighbour, Cornelius O'Keefe, whom she hoped would bring the place alive with his children. However, O'Keefe was more interested in the timber from the property than the house itself. The house was demolished and much of the estate's timber cut down. She commented: 'It was a clean end. Bowen's Court never lived to be a ruin.'[15]

In 1950 Bowen had begun the practice of teaching in America for part of the summer and she continued to do this after Cameron's death. She decided to set up house in Oxford, but things had changed since the time she had lived there with her husband and she felt rather marginal and out of things. She decided instead to settle in Kent and in 1965 bought a small house in Hythe, where she had lived with her mother so long ago – a sort of return to the womb, she explained. She called the house Carbery, which was the name of the ancestral estate of her mother's people.

Her last two novels were *The Little Girls* (1964) and *Eva Trout* (1969). When Bowen died on 22 February 1973 she was writing her autobiography, which was published posthumously in 1975 as *Pictures and Conversations*. Elizabeth's great friend, Charles Ritchie, was by her side when she died of lung cancer in University Hospital, London. Elizabeth Bowen is buried with her husband, Alan Cameron, in St Colman's graveyard, Farahy, County Cork.

NOTES

1. Patricia Craig, *Elizabeth Bowen* (Harmondsworth: Penguin, 1986), p.17.
2. 'Although these attacks on the houses of the former Ascendancy can be understood as part of a political and military strategy … to Anglo-Ireland itself this must have seemed a veritable *Jacquerie* and a painful demonstration of their isolated vulnerability in an Ireland which no longer appeared to accept them.' Terence Brown, *Ireland: a Social and Cultural History 1922–2002* (London: HarperPerennial, 2004), p.99.
3. Elizabeth Bowen, *The Last September* (London: Vintage, 1998), pp.91–2.
4. Elizabeth Bowen, *Seven Winters* (Dublin: Cuala Press, 1963), p.6.
5. Ibid., p.7.
6. Maud Ellmann, *Elizabeth Bowen: The Shadow across the Page* (Edinburgh: Edinburgh University Press, 2003), p.8.
7. Hermione Lee (ed.), *The Mulberry Tree: Writings of Elizabeth Bowen* (London: Virago, 1986), pp.279–80.
8. Ibid., p.280.
9. Bowen, *Seven Winters*, p.28.
10. Phyllis Lassner, *Elizabeth Bowen* (London: Macmillan, 1990), p.19.
11. Victoria Glendinning, *Elizabeth Bowen : Portrait of a Writer* (Harmondsworth: Penguin, 1983), pp.20–31.
12. Ibid., p.44.
13. Ibid., p.120.
14. Craig, *Elizabeth Bowen*, p.101.
15. Elizabeth Bowen, *Bowen's Court* (Cork: Collins Press, 1998), p. 459.

CHAPTER TWO

Bowen: Ascendancy Modernist

VERA KREILKAMP

When a great house has been destroyed by fire – left with walls
bleached and ghastly and windows gaping with the cold sky – the
master has not, perhaps, the heart or the money to rebuild. Trees
that were its companions are cut down and the estate sold up to
the speculator. Villas spring up in red rows, each a home for someone, enticing brave little shops, radiant picture palaces: perhaps a
park is left round the lake, where couples go boating. Lovers' lanes
in asphalt replace the lonely green rides; the obelisk having no
approaches is taken away ... Life here is livable, kindly and sometimes gay; there is not a ghost of space or silence; the great house
with its dominance and its radiation of avenues is forgotten. When
spring is sweet in the air, snowdrops under the paling, when blue
autumn blurs the trim streets' perspective or the low sun in winter dazzles the windows gold – something touches the heart,
someone, disturbed, pauses, hands on a villa gate. But not to ask:
What was here?[1]

Elizabeth Bowen's inherited baggage was formidable. Through the
pressures of social caste and family history she absorbed, as if by
osmosis, a literary tradition charting Anglo-Ireland's decline from colonial ascendancy to economic and political dispossession.[2] Her fiction
reinvented the conventions of an older Anglo-Irish Ascendancy genre for
the twentieth century, in effect bridging the divide between Somerville
and Ross and later novelists of the Big House. Rather than perpetuate a
division – either Bowen as a Burkean conservative or, as recent critics
emphasize, as a cosmopolitan modernist or postmodernist – this chapter seeks to examine the relationship among the varied traditions that

her work synthesizes. The strikingly modernist sense of psychic incoherence and homelessness shaping Bowen's fiction stemmed no less
from an Irish Ascendancy sensibility than from her receptivity to twentieth-century cultural innovation.

Written from the perspective of a Protestant ruling class, the Big
House genre in Ireland emerged with Maria Edgeworth's *Castle Rackrent*
(1800), reasserting its themes and tropes throughout the nineteenth
century in novels by Charles Lever, Charles Maturin, Sheridan Le Fanu,
George Moore and Somerville and Ross. The architecture, landscape and
furniture of the eighteenth-century Georgian or Palladian mansion in
this fiction confer a bifurcated national identity on its inhabitants. In its
vulnerability to social and political pressure, the house registers the fate
of a colonial class uneasily suspended, as if somewhere above the Irish
channel, between a British and an Irish identity. Such novels, charting
fissures in the fabric and structure of heavily mortgaged and under-
capitalized rural estates, continued to flourish throughout the twentieth
century, with Bowen's *The Last September* (1929) initiating a range of new
iterations of an older form.

For all its reputation as a conservative or nostalgic genre,[3] Ascendancy
fiction might be more accurately viewed as modernist before its time,
sharing little with its English counterpart, the domestic marriage novel of
social assimilation. These Irish novels turn on the uneasy social transac-
tions of a formerly ascendant class lurching precipitously toward its
liminal role in a new nation; they chart growing isolation and social
alienation rather than assimilation. Households are typically focused
inward, cut off from the surrounding social and political landscape by
differences of religion, class, language and national loyalties. The genre's
ur-text, *Castle Rackrent*, interrogates linguistic difference and offers shifting
points of view and styles; its destabilizing irony exposes the contrast
between Anglo-Ireland's pretensions to social and cultural ascendancy
and the reality of ramshackle landowners plunging themselves into economic impotence. The performative strain of Ascendancy society – a
tough-minded adherence to the rituals of ruling-class life as the native
inhabitants of a dispossessed territory flex their political muscle – creates
a tension between class decorum (or, as Molly Keane [M.J. Farrell] puts
it, 'good behaviour') and sudden violent eruptions of disorder that all of
Bowen's novels exploit.[4]

Most canonized Ascendancy novels, both preceding and succeeding Bowen's, were written in the attack mode. Edgeworth's portrayal of her drunken, improvident or litigating Rackrents in 1800 anticipates Charles Lever's depiction of the proudly isolated landowner's irresponsibility in *The Martins of Cro' Martin* (1854), or Somerville and Ross's later portrayal of unmanned or profligate landlords in, respectively, *The Real Charlotte* (1894) and *The Big House of Inver* (1925). Bowen's undermining of her own caste is characteristically more ambivalent than that of many predecessors and successors, more insistent on registering loss, less willing to renounce a morality identified with aesthetic forms and Anglo-Irish cultural style. In *The Last September*, her first novel set in Ireland, she describes isolated landlords myopically administering their estates with benevolent condescension while armed rebels invade the demesne. Unable to comprehend the sources of their tenants' hostility, proprietors remain torn between their professed Irish identities and their dependence on an occupying British garrison whose protection they resent. Bowen's characteristic preoccupation with what must be left unsaid arises from her grasp of a siege mentality in a house with a 'disproportionate zone of emptiness', where 'things ... seem to be closing in' (TLS pp.22, 28).

Reading through her works chronologically, however, we might view Bowen as an inspired dabbler in that persistent historical Ascendancy genre with which she has been so long identified. She published her second novel, *The Last September*, which she later termed her 'fiction with the texture of history',[5] less than a decade after the destruction of three estates neighbouring her family home in County Cork. Her fictional meditation looks back to the end of Anglo-Irish society in 1920, famously culminating with the IRA's political 'execution' of the Big House through fiery holocaust. Yet throughout the 1930s and the 1940s Bowen abandoned an explicitly Irish genre in her novels, writing about upper-middle-class London society and experimenting with modernist techniques confronting the dissolution of stable identities in an unmoored post-war society. Even when she returned to an Irish setting in one relatively late novel, *A World of Love* (1955), or with a brief episode in the earlier *The House in Paris* (1935), her angle of vision shifted from losses explicitly framed within a national historical trauma. Her most nostalgically apprehended Big House, viewed as an isolated sanctuary against modern disorder, appeared in *The Heat of the Day* (1949), a novel set largely in London during the Second World War.

Alternatively, however, we might read all of Bowen's work, not just the two novels and the short stories about Ireland, but works set in England as well, as returning to central Ascendancy tropes, themes and motifs. The passage quoted as the epigraph to this chapter appears in To the North (1932), a novel exploring the lives of upper-middle-class Londoners in the decade following the First World War. Seeking an analogy to convey how a young widow negotiates a depleted life after her husband's death, Bowen turns to the destruction of an Irish ancestral home, a memory seemingly extraneous to the concerns of the novel's English characters.[6] The sustained meditation invokes the burning of two hundred Big Houses during the Anglo-Irish War (1919–21), an historical ordeal that three   years earlier The Last September had transformed into a literary trope for subsequent fiction. But To the North looks forward to post-war England, not backwards to ruling-class losses on a near-by island. Animated by Bowen's response to recent cultural movements – the influence, for example, of literary surrealism and of an emerging psychology of neurosis and neurotic styles – the novel reflects and sometimes parodies a metropolitan modernity. It focuses on lives driven by dislocating motion and speed in the post-war years; characters appear, on occasion, to be reduced to the rhythms of irrational automatons performing an unhinged interiority. Ireland plays no role in this strikingly contemporary novel; yet the image of the burning house indicates how markedly Bowen's sensibility had been shaped by her caste's recent historical confrontation with the evanescent and temporary – a confrontation leaving an ineffable footprint, a memory of loss, on all her subsequent fiction.

With a personal and caste history of loss,[7] Bowen's roles as an Irish Ascendancy novelist and as an ideologically conservative modernist attuned to a wider European cultural dispossession converge in her fiction. The scrupulously invoked domestic spaces of the novels – Anglo-Irish Big Houses, tawdry English seaside villas, French or Italian hotels, tasteless suburban retreats, a borrowed country cottage, a London townhouse or flat – offer but temporary shelter against psychic homelessness. Bowen's obsession with the formative role of the material spaces men and women inhabit has led one reader to speculate that in this fiction architecture takes the place of psychology: 'character is shaped by rooms and

corridors, doors and windows, arches and columns rather than by individual experience'.[8] An unsentimental conviction about the economic
basis of morality and a preoccupation with the shaping role of the past
can lead Bowen, more than most of her Ascendancy predecessors, to a
Burkean idealization of property as a stay against unleashed power: 'We
have everything to fear from the dispossessed', she warned in 1963.[9]
Such high valuations of the security offered by objects became most
pressing after the Second World War, but surfaced already in *The Death of
the Heart* (1938), as if presciently, before her London home was damaged
in the wartime bombings: 'these things are what we mean when we
speak about civilization ... In this sense, the destruction of buildings
and furniture is more palpably dreadful to the spirit than the destruction
of human life'.[10]

The uncanny animation of 'things' in Bowen's fiction arguably stems
from multiple sources: from her reading of Charles Dickens, from the
London blitz survivor's apprehension of irrevocable losses, as well as
from her receptivity to new experiments with literary surrealism,
wherein distinctions between the human and inhuman collapse.[11] But
the Ascendancy landowner's uneasy valuation of an increasingly vulnerable and symbolic cultural artefact also plays its role. The threatened Big
House in *The Last September* hides its face in 'fright and amazement' at the
'unloving country ... the unwilling bosom whereon it was set';[12] furniture, proclaims the moral arbiter of *The Death of the Heart*, judges a house's
occupants: 'Unnatural living runs in a family, the furniture knows it'
(DH, p.101). In *To the North*, a novel influenced by Bowen's interest in
surrealism, Cecelia is characterized as a spinning sentence-making cog-
wheel, as a 'machine of agitation' (TTN, p.120), so merged with her
telephone that she might 'vanish into abeyance' when she is not plugged
in; in the same post-First World War novel Lady Water's speech registers
as the clicking open of a filing cabinet (TTN, p.109).

Reacting against her conservative valuation of a tradition embodied
in the classical shapes and furnishings of ruling-class houses, Bowen
persistently undermines the past as providing trustworthy moral patterns for the future. In *Bowen's Court* she acknowledges that her family 'got
their position and drew their power from a situation that shows an
inherent wrong' (BC, p.453). Her presentation of history's artefacts as
sources of disruption – a ruined mill in *The Last September*, alluding to

Anglo-Ireland's failure to provide for the country it controlled; or ghostly letters of a long-dead and unfaithful landlord in *A World of Love* – suggests her persistent ambivalence before the past's stranglehold on the future. To embody such ambivalence, Bowen creates brutal emotional anarchists who are, nevertheless, erotically charged objects of desire. In 'Summer Afternoon', the adolescent Maria, upon whom a middle-aged veteran of the blitz aptly bestows the Shakespearean name Miranda, challenges neutral Anglo-Ireland's incomprehension of survival without the 'beautiful things' destroyed in the veteran's bombed-out London flat.[13] In her representation of a brave new world, Maria's ruthless assault on her community's high valuation of the 'furniture' of culture appals the narrator even as she releases a flood of desire in him. In *A World of Love* the dazzlingly beautiful daughter of the Big House begins her journey towards an exorcism of the past ('the root of all evil') with a similarly crass, yet prescient dismissal of its hold: 'this continuous tedious business of received grievance, not-to-be-settled old scores'.[14] That edgy tension between elegy and anticipation of disrupting change that Hermione Lee notes in *The Last September* characterizes most of the fiction of this Ascendancy modernist.[15]

Among twentieth-century writers, Bowen is also identified with a Gothic strand of Irish literature, a genre that she successfully revived to convey the dark terrors of her own era.[16] Her turn to a world of disembodied spirits, of the dead returning to disturb the living, responds to a Protestant Gothic tradition that had survived in Ireland throughout the nineteenth century, far longer than elsewhere in Europe. In an essay on Sheridan Le Fanu's *Uncle Silas* (1864), Bowen famously identified that Victorian 'romance of terror' was unambiguously Irish, despite its English setting:

> The hermetic solitude and the autocracy of the great country house, the demonic power of the family myth, fatalism, feudalism and the 'ascendancy' outlook are accepted facts of life for the race of hybrids from which Le Fanu sprang. For the psychological background of *Uncle Silas* it was necessary for him to invent nothing. (MT, p.101)

This guilt-ridden Ascendancy 'outlook' shaped nineteenth-century Irish fiction through the deployment of familiar Gothic motifs: irregular lines of legitimacy and inheritance; miscegenation; victimized young women; animated ancestral portraits; sudden outbursts of violence; and, always, the imprisoning mythologies of the past. As if guided by the glamour of his eighteenth-century progenitor, whose haunting portrait he so uncannily resembles, the twentieth-century heir in Somerville and Ross's *The Big House of Inver* completes the destruction of honour and property initiated by that profligate ancestor. Only four years later, in Bowen's first Irish novel, landowners 'dwindled personally' under ancestral portraits that 'cancelled time' and 'negatived personality' (LS, p.28). Guarding the myths of family honour on his deathbed, Le Fanu's nineteenth-century landlord hands over his daughter to the charge of his murderous brother Silas, who covets her inheritance. In *The Last September*, Bowen's twentieth-century landlords appear no less blindly loyal to caste honour. In their commitment to a tradition of hospitality even in the midst of revolution, proprietors welcome the British soldiers charged with their protection. Such hospitality leads inexorably to a final IRA visitation: now 'the door of the house stood open hospitably upon a furnace' (LS, p.303).

Bowen's modernist exploration of extreme psychic states, no less than her caste preoccupation with its eroding social and economic position, led her to reinvent the Protestant Gothic ghost story as a form negotiating eruptions of alienated, because suppressed, memory – those memories Freud associates with the 'uncanny'. In such ghost stories, she creates apparitions as conduits to suppressed traumatic losses in a century of violent change. In 'The Back Drawing Room' of 1926, a visitor's tale about coming upon a ghost – a dispossessed Anglo-Irish woman sobbing in the ruins of her burned-out Big House – shocks the complacency of his sophisticated urban audience discussing the latest trends in spiritualism. In the post-Second World War story 'The Happy Autumn Fields', the dream apparition of an idyllic Victorian Anglo-Irish family proves not a path to recovery, but a confirmation of irrevocable loss for a survivor of London's wartime bombings. In *The World of Love*, three women are trapped on a declining Anglo-Irish estate by their erotic enthrallment to its former landlord. Lost in the trenches of the First World War, that vampiric spirit, like the spectre of eroticized terror in 'The Demon Lover', makes imaginative demands on the living: 'He had not finished with them' (WL, p.97).

In her first novel set in Ireland, Bowen famously created and prefigured the burning house of the Anglo-Irish war as the twentieth-century's central trope for later writers of the Big House.[17] Yet in registering Ascendancy losses, this cosmopolitan author also moved from local historical trauma to the wider European catastrophe of the First World War. Although a new Irish nation's 'intentional amnesia' was to blot this war from cultural consciousness, it remained central to the historical memory of the Protestant Irish in both Ulster and the south.[18] Writing the First World War into her fiction, Bowen depicts it not only as the agent of cataclysmic cultural transformation, but as a trope of literary recurrence. The war's losses in To the North, although virtually unmentioned, shadow a post-war edginess – 'the world's apprehension, strain at home and in Europe' (TTN, p.219) – as Cecelia's mother, mourning her two fallen sons, abandons her daughter to a post-war psychic homelessness. In The Death of the Heart, the First World War veteran Major Brutt becomes a pathetic supernumerary, a living casualty to radical cultural transformation as post-war society ridicules his outdated traditionalism. The 'past' that the protagonist of The Little Girls fails to recover – a world of horse carriages and carefully repaired bits of exquisite porcelain – ends in August 1914 as the unhappily married Major Burkin Jones, embodying a restrained pre-war honour, departs silently from the woman he loves for death on the Belgian front within the month.

Although Bowen set her major 'historical' novels during the Anglo-Irish war (The Last September) or the Second World War (The Heat of the Day), she turned to the First World War in her fiction intermittently, but persistently. Such persistence created a source of continuity for succeeding novelists of the Big House, and a reinsertion of that war into Irish cultural memory. For Bowen, the First World War exists not only as a dislocating break with the past, but as the century's recurring source of the dead, the maimed and ghostly undead. The shell-shocked senior subaltern Daventry in The Last September arrives in Ireland as part of the wave of middle-class replacements for an officer class disproportionately killed on the First World War battlefields. Longing for escape from the claustrophobia of the Big House, Lois is moved not only by the passionate commitment of the rebels who invade her uncle's demesne, but also, although even more ambivalently, by Daventry, whom she describes as a satanic ghost, as 'not a man … hardly even a person' (LS, p.157).

Emptied out and dehumanized by his experiences in the trenches, he exists, like the sadistic apparition of the First World War dead in 'The Demon Lover' or like the ghostly sightings of Guy in *A World of Love*, as an insistent reminder of unfinished business, of a generation mowed down and now haunting its 'incomplete' survivors (*WL*, p.45).[19]

Echoing Bowen's Gothic apprehension of the First World War as a source of ghostly visitations, the Ascendancy narrator of Jennifer Johnston's *How Many Miles to Babylon* (1974) describes himself as already among the dead. Alex Moore speaks from a Gothic landscape of ruin, where miles of bodies lie scattered along the trenches – 'the Somme, the Aisne, Ypes, Picardy, Flanders'.[20] Sent off to war as cannon fodder, Alex faces imminent death as he awaits execution by the British for his loyalty to a working-class Irish friend. His fate fulfils and simultaneously thwarts his mother's directive that her son asserts Ascendancy loyalty by joining the British war effort. In this novel Johnston recasts Anglo-Ireland's military tradition as a form of child sacrifice, whereas in her account of her caste's military past, Elizabeth Bowen had crisply celebrated, not without irony, such sacrificial devotion to honour: 'If the Anglo-Irish live on and for a myth, for that myth they constantly shed their blood' (*BC*, p.436).

But many twentieth-century novelists of the Big House, like Bowen rather than Johnston, invoke the First World War not as the arena for protagonists' lives, but as the century's backdrop for future savagery, as its haunting initiation into bloodletting. In William Trevor's novels, the Irish 'troubles' emerge as part of an unbroken pattern of early twentieth-century violence. In *Silence in the Garden* (1988), Colonel Rolleston dies at Passchendaele, where the British sustained almost a third of a million casualties in the war's last brutal battle of attrition; in *The Story of Lucy Gault* (2002), the landlord, returning to his ancestral Big House invalided from the trenches, is greeted by an assault on his property by neighbouring IRA sympathizers, an event unleashing repercussions that destroy his family's future. In *Fools of Fortune* (1983), the murderous attack on a Big House during the Anglo-Irish war and that violence's cycle of consequences – suicide, revenge and madness – emanates from the incursions into revolutionary Ireland of the Black and Tans, brutalized veterans of the First World War, like Bowen's Daventry. Even more directly than Trevor, J.G. Farrell responds to Bowen's reinscription of the

First World War into the Irish 'troubles'. Narrated by a shell-shocked First World War survivor seeking recovery, Farrell's Troubles (1970) depicts the resurgences of irrational violence around a defamiliarized Anglo-Irish Big House within a few years of armistice. The dark Gothic taboos explored in Molly Keane's fiction, particularly her exposure of the Ascendancy's abuse of its own children, are persistently related to what Sinéad Mooney describes as 'repeated patterns of involuntary recurrence ... most notably, these "returns" to certain troubled periods in Irish history, chiefly the onset of the Great War and 1922'.[21] Keane's versions of the First World War's casualties – Cynthia French-McGraths' loss of her husband in The Rising Tide (1937) and Daddy's emasculation through the loss of a leg in Good Behavior (1981) – suggest how the war's depletions of an Ascendancy patriarchy unleash a new maternal violence on the young.

Bowen wrote of the inevitability of influence, as well as of the imperative of 'keeping going a continuity' for future authors.[22] Among the many continuities her fiction establishes with subsequent Irish novelists, none seems more arresting than the persistent focus on children and adolescents through the lens of an Ascendancy sensibility.[23] Howard Moss once observed that Bowen 'grasped early the colonial mentality from both sides, and saw, in the end, it was a mirror image of the most exploitative relationship of all: that of the adult and child'.[24] Bowen's fiction circles around parents who fail their young and orphans in search of love – around solitary and watchful children or adolescents thrust from one temporary abode to another, longing for the imagined permanence of a lost home. A Bildungsroman of a young orphan, The Last September responds to the entrapment of women described by George Moore in A Drama in Muslin (1886). Writing about political threats to the ruling class a half-century earlier during Ireland's Land War, Moore depicts an Ascendancy society that embalmed its young in the rituals of an outdated caste system, even as a disaffected peasantry pressed their faces against ballroom windows. The empty lives of Moore's martyred debutantes anticipate adolescent Lois's protests against her purposelessness in the midst of Anglo-Ireland's final political crisis. Bowen's depictions of the unmoored young reoccur throughout her fiction, most memorably in two novels set outside of Ireland, The House in Paris and The Death of the Heart.

Fusing the categories of caste memory and personal history with her fictional creations, Bowen described the life of the Anglo-Irish as 'like those of only children ... singular, independent and secretive' (BC, p.20).[25] Offering an attenuated family landscape in which marriages are generally doomed and orphaned or only children are destined for neg- lect, Bowen implies alternatives to the heterosexual marriage plot. In novels such as The Last September, To the North, The Little Girls and Eva Trout, relationships between women promise more enduring intimacy than heterosexual romance. Lois's passionate bonding with Marda in The Last September (like the more explicit depictions of lesbian desire characteriz- ing one of Moore's young muslin martyrs), anticipates Molly Keane, William Trevor and Jennifer Johnston's explorations of the celibate or homoerotic life choices of characters who respond to the failures of het- erosexual love, marriage and parenthood in the Big House.

The isolation and denial of love that is the fate of Bowen's children prefigure a range of far darker imaginings in the work of two novelists who write, as if in dialogue with her, to undermine an Ascendancy fam- ily romance. Jennifer Johnston and Molly Keane depict Big House chate- laines who respond to their reduced field of social ambitions by deco- rating their houses, snubbing their social inferiors and maiming their children. Johnston's How Many Miles to Babylon, The Captains and the Kings (1972) and Fools Sanctuary (1988), as well as Keane's The Rising Tide (1937), Good Behavior (1981), Time After Time (1983) and Loving and Giving (1988), chart how the collapse of a male-dominated culture releases new opportunities for female tyranny or neglect. Bowen's meddlesome older women, Lady Naylor in The Last September or her English counterpart, Lady Waters in To the North, are reinvented as malevolent mothers, unmoored by their freedom from patriarchal control as Big House males retreat from active roles in family or social governance. Lady Charlotte in Keane's The Rising Tide, a 'shocking despot, really swollen with family conceit and a terrifying pride of race', exercises an uncontrolled tyranny over her children and servants.[26] Like Bowen, Keane turns unsentimen- tally to the fate of defenceless children. Within their domestic arenas and plots of psychological abuse, both novelists imply larger political patterns, revealing how the exploitation of the powerless breeds new aggression. Victimized Portia's astonishing capacity for cruelty to pathetic Major Brutt in The Death of the Heart, like Aroon's solicitous murder of her mother in *Good Behavior*, indicates how Bowen and her successor grasped the dynamics of power so central to Anglo-Ireland's fate.

Bowen's aestheticized morality, her understanding of classical Ascendancy style and form as offering an alternative to modern anomie, differs from the radically subversive gaze on a decaying Big House in later novels by Molly Keane, John Banville, J.G. Farrell or Aidan Higgins. Isolated and self-deluding as Bowen's Ascendancy survivors may be, they are surrounded by the space, light and classical proportions of eighteenth-century architecture rather than, for example, the vulgarity of a 'banal' Irish castle done up by the *nouveau riche* (*A World of Love*) or by an impermanent English suburban villa that breeds traitors like Robert Kelway (*The Heat of the Day*).[27] Although *A World of Love* is set on an Irish estate so plunged into decline that neighbours assume it has been deserted, Bowen's authorial eye remains quietly valedictory. Montefort has 'gone down', but beneath the neglect survives a distinguishing 'ghost of style' (*WL*, p.9); Danielstown's fiery termination in *The Last September* denies the possibility of slow decay – that recurring trope by which nineteenth-century Ascendancy fiction signalled moral, not just physical collapse.

Most recent reinventions of Ascendancy fiction turn more emphatically from any nostalgia. If Bowen's *The Heat of the Day* envisions the isolated country estate in neutral Ireland as a moral stay against Nazi betrayal, Aidan Higgins's *Langrishe, Go Down* (1966) provides an unsparing portrayal of a Big House's abject submission to a proto-Fascist seducer. Molly Keane's savage peeling away of Ascendancy delusions in her late novels – *Good Behavior* (1982), *Time After Time* (1985) or *Loving and Giving* (1988) – is closer in spirit to *Castle Rackrent* than to Bowen's ambivalent longings for a lost aesthetic coherence. Despite her exuberant pleasure in the sensuous beauty of houses and gardens, Keane insists on their inherent corruption: 'There was too much beauty around Aragon, and too much beauty is dangerous'.[28] Postmodern Irish novelists turn to parodies of Ascendancy decline, transforming Bowen's always conflicted elegy into carnivalesque black humour. In Banville's *Birchwood* (1973), the floor around the landlord's throne-like toilet collapses, 'leaving him perched on the bowl instantly constipated, his feet and crumpled trousers dangling above the abyss'.[29] Before the final conflagration in J.G. Farrell's *Troubles*, a parodic rendition of Bowen's burning house in *The Last*

September, vicious stray cats invade a rural mansion and the conservatory's rampantly spreading vegetation undermines its very foundations. Bowen's conservative modernism prefigures yet resists the fullest subversion of Ascendancy values found in the work of her successors.

NOTES

1. Elizabeth Bowen, *To the North* (New York: Anchor, 2006), p.122, hereafter referred to in the text as TTN.
2. Bowen mentions two Irish novelists, Sheridan Le Fanu and Maria Edgeworth, as sources for her own literary tradition in *Pictures and Conversations*, ed. Spencer Curtis Brown (London: Allen Lane, 1975), p.72 (hereafter referred to in the text as PC). Hermione Lee, in *Elizabeth Bowen: An Estimation* (London: Vision Press, 1981), suggests a long list of additional Ascendancy authors as 'influences', but wisely warns against overemphasizing Anglo-Irish sources and ignoring the role of E.M. Forster, Virginia Woolf and other English contemporaries in the creation of Bowen's style and themes (pp.18–19).
3. For readings of the Big House tradition as conservative or nostalgic, see Seamus Deane, *Celtic Revivals* (London: Faber & Faber, 1985), p.31, and Joe Cleary, 'Postcolonial Ireland', in *Ireland and the British Empire*, ed. Kevin Kenny (Oxford: Oxford University Press, 2004), pp.251–88 (p.271). See Vera Kreilkamp, *The Anglo-Irish Novel and the Big House* (Syracuse, NY: Syracuse University Press, 1998), pp.1–2 for an opposing view.
4. Molly Keane [M.J. Farrell], *Good Behaviour* (London: Abacus, 1995).
5. Elizabeth Bowen, *The Mulberry Tree* (New York: Harcourt Brace Jovanovich, 1986), p.125, hereafter referred to in the text as MT.
6. Bowen again turns to the same image, culled from recent Irish history, when Emmeline imagines her soon to be abandoned rented home as if burned down, as Danielstown is destroyed in the last scene of *The Last September*: 'the door open on emptiness: blanched walls as though after a fire' (TTN, pp.207–8).
7. The mental breakdown of Bowen's father when she was 6 led to a first orphan-hood – her earliest separation not only from a parent, but also from Ireland and Bowen's Court. During this exile to England, her mother died when she was 13. As an adult, Bowen lost her London house in the Blitz and was forced to sell Bowen's Court in 1959; within a year it was unroofed and demolished.
8. Maud Ellmann, *Elizabeth Bowen: The Shadow Across the Page* (Edinburgh: Edinburgh University Press, 2003), p.42.
9. Elizabeth Bowen, *Bowen's Court* (New York: Ecco Press, 1979), p.455, hereafter referred to in the text as BC.
10. Elizabeth Bowen, *The Death of the Heart* (New York: Anchor, 2000), p.270, hereafter referred to in the text as DH.

11. For a discussion of Bowen and Surrealism, see, Keri Walsh, 'Elizabeth Bowen, Surrealist', *Éire-Ireland: An Interdisciplinary Journal of Irish* Studies, 42, 3 and 4 (Fall/Winter 2007), pp.126–47.

12. Elizabeth Bowen, *The Last September* (New York: Anchor, 2000), p.92, hereafter referred to in the text as *LS*.

13. Elizabeth Bowen, *Collected Stories*, intro. by Angus Wilson (London: Jonathan Cape, 1980), p.619, hereafter referred to in the text as *CS*.

14. Elizabeth Bowen, *A World of Love* (New York: Anchor, 2003), p.35, hereafter referred to in the text as *WL*.

15. Lee, *Bowen: An Estimation*, p.44.

16. W.J. McCormack includes Bowen's fiction as his single example of twentieth-century Gothic fiction in 'Irish Gothic and After 1820–1945', in *The Field Day Anthology of Irish Writing*, ed. Seamus Deane (Derry: Field Day, 1991), vol.2, pp.831–955.

17. See, for example, Molly Keane [M.J. Farrell], *Two Days in Aragon* (London: Virago, 1985 [1941]); William Trevor, *Fools of Fortune* (Harmondsworth: Penguin, 1983); and J.G. Farrell, *Troubles* (Harmondsworth: Penguin, 1970).

18. Although the First World War drew over 200,000 recruits from Ascendancy, Catholic and Ulster Protestant society to fight with the British army, it was written out of the south's history. See Roy Foster, *Modern Ireland 1600–1972* (Harmondsworth: Penguin, 1989), p.471.

19. For the fullest reading of Daventry's Gothic role in *The Last September*, see Neil Corcoran, *Elizabeth Bowen: The Enforced Return* (Oxford: Oxford University Press, 2004), pp.55–60.

20. Jennifer Johnston, *How Many Miles to Babylon?* (Harmondsworth: Penguin, 1988), p.138.

21. Sinead Mooney, '"Dark, established currents": Molly Keane's Gothic', in *Molly Keane: Essays in Contemporary Criticism*, ed. Eibhear Walshe and Gwenda Young (Dublin: Four Courts Press, 2006), pp.195–211 (p.197).

22. See Elizabeth Bowen, 'Sources of Influence', in *Seven Winters: Memoirs of a Dublin Childhood and Afterthoughts* (New York: Alfred A. Knopf, 1962), p.82, hereafter referred to in the text as *SW*.

23. For a full investigation of this theme, see Margo Backus, *The Gothic Family Romance: Heterosexuality, Child Sacrifice, and the Anglo-Irish Colonial Order* (Durham, NC: Duke University Press, 1999).

24. Howard Moss, *Minor Monuments: Selected Essays* (New York: Ecco, 1986), p.236.

25. For Elizabeth Cullingford, the negative political metaphor of the only child suggests 'the inbred selfishness, diminishing fecundity, and inevitable disintegration of the Anglo-Irish'. Elizabeth Cullingford, '"Something Else": Gendering Onliness in Elizabeth Bowen's Early Fiction', *Modern Fiction Studies*, 53, 2 (Summer 2007), pp.276–305 (p.290).

26. Molly Keane [M.J. Farrell], *The Rising Tide* (London: Virago, 1984), p.7.

27. Elizabeth Hardwick famously criticized Bowen for her 'theology of objects' by which 'the noble and the lost souls are defined … Peace is a well-lit drawing room

... The guilty lead an uneasy existence between the thick, dark, impersonal objects in a furnished room'. Elizabeth Hardwick, 'Elizabeth Bowen's Fiction', *Partisan Review*, 16, 11 (November 1949), pp.1114–21 (p.1116).

28. Keane, *Two Days in Aragon*, p.227.

29. John Banville, *Birchwood* (London: Granada, 1984), p.69.

CHAPTER THREE

Bowen and Modernism: The Early Novels

ANDREW BENNETT

Without exception, Elizabeth Bowen's early novels resist the narrative of romantic love, the trajectory based around the possibility of radical change, of denouement. That, fundamentally, is the function of Bowen's narratives: to take on the overweening narrative line of conventional fiction and rewrite it, dispute it, deconstruct it. All of Bowen's early novels right up to *A World of Love* (1955) resist the temptations of what, in the context of his analysis of tragedy, Aristotle calls *peripeteia* (reversal) and *anagnorisis* (recognition), terms that also help us to comprehend the standard narrative line in the traditional love story – the overcoming of a barrier to the fulfilment of romantic love, sexual understanding finally attained; a reversal, via vicissitude and suffering, of the heroine's romantic fortunes, and a recognition of the self in the other. Each of Bowen's early novels – *The Hotel* (1927), *Friends and Relations* (1931), *To the North* (1932)[1] – resists the narrative change through which the love story is structured and, in this as in other ways, each bears a strange and difficult relationship with the dominant literary movement of her century's early decades, with Modernism.

Modernism can be conceived of in terms of a response to change, or indeed in terms of the very condition of change itself, Modernism as change. The kinds of change to which Modernism responds involve the cataclysms of war and revolution, of social and political conflict and renewal, of new, unsettling scientific, philosophical and technological paradigms (Darwinian accounts of evolution, post-Newtonian physics, the increasing importance of air travel, the internal combustion engine, new telecommunications networks, and so on). One of the major cultural responses to these changes was to declare, in W.B. Yeats's resoundingly apocalyptic phrase, that 'all' is 'changed, changed utterly' ('Easter 1916', l.15), to announce (as in the title of A.R. Orage's modernist journal [1907–22]) that this is the 'New Age', or, rather more mildly but no less dramatically, that the artist or writer should 'make it new' (in Ezra Pound's programmatic phrase), or in Virginia Woolf's formulation that at some point (which, writing in 1924, Woolf pinpoints to the year 1910) 'character' itself has 'changed', that people, that personality, that the very conception of the human, has been somehow transformed.[2] The physical manifestation of change is speed: Bowen herself character- ized the early twentieth century as 'the age of speed',[3] and, as the Futurists in particular made clear in their literary and other celebrations of speed, in the early twentieth century speed is a function of new tech- nologies of travel – of trains, planes and automobiles in particular. But speed is also experienced in the uncannily speedy (as well as just uncan- ny) new technologies of telegraphy and telephony, new and troubling kinds of supplement to the letter and the voice. If Modernism is change, is a sense of, and a response to, change, a response specifically to speed and to a speeded-up world, then the early novels of Elizabeth Bowen are, at least in this respect, unequivocally 'Modernist'.

Bowen herself pointed to the sense of change as one of the predom- inant concerns of post-First World War fiction in a short book on *English Novelists* published in 1945. Bringing her historical account of the English novel up to the Modernist period, Bowen declared that there had been 'a change ... though not a break', pointing to D.H. Lawrence (1885–1930) as having helped to produce this 'shift' towards what she sees as a less character-led, more 'poetic' mode of writing which had responded to an alteration in 'English habit, feeling and thought' produced in the first place by the Great War (and reinforced, as Bowen writes, by the second great war in Europe).[4] Bowenesque Modernism, by such an account, does not involve literary revolution, the avant-garde experimentation of Joyce, or Eliot, or Pound or even Woolf: Bowen's language does not in any simple sense overtly and violently break with the decorum of traditional form. Rather, it involves the kind of 'passing beyond' convention that she remarks of Katherine Mansfield in a 1956 essay: 'Born into the English traditions of prose narrative, she neither revolted against these nor broke with them – simply, she passed beyond them' (MT, p.75).

Bowen is often compared with other prose writers of the period such as E.M. Forster, Henry Green, Rosamund Lehmann, Mansfield, even Woolf herself, Bowen's friend, mentor and, in some ways, her model as a modern, professional female author. As with these other writers of the period, Bowen's writing of the 1920s and early 1930s responds to and registers a sense that the world has changed. In particular, it is the radical alteration in feeling and experience that war in particular has produced that is explicitly referred to in The Hotel and Friends and Relations, as well as being an important part of the 'backstory' in To the North. The war is registered in all these novels in terms of the effects that it has had on the very possibility of sexual relations and (therefore) marriage for the young women that feature in them. There is a strong sense in much early Bowen, indeed, that the marriage plot that had driven the Victorian and Edwardian novel is somehow broken – because, fundamentally, marriage itself is no longer viable. In that sense, the change that Bowen records involves the possibility that there will be no change for young women, that the change that drove the Victorian and Edwardian narrative, with its ideal denouement of marriage, is not available to the Bowen heroine: the condition of such a heroine is not to change (not to change her name, nor her marital status). Getting married is what Bowen's early heroines signally fail to do. And on those rare occasions that young women do marry, they do so in a dysfunctional way. Cecilia Summers in To the North is a young woman widowed by the First World War. Friends and Relations is about the married lives of two sisters and about inter- (rather than intra-) marital, adulterous desire. And the sole function of the only other notable young married couple in these novels, the minor characters Gerda and Gilbert Bligh in To the North, is to be a pair whose marriage is in trouble and needs mending (although it remains stubbornly un-mended). Indeed, a sense of Bowen's scepticism regarding married life is apparent in the guest-list for a party thrown by Gerda, which includes, as Bowen caustically puts it, 'two young authors of novels about marriage with their placid, motherly wives' (TTN, p.127). As this might suggest, in early Bowen older women – women older than say 30 – are regularly married, even reasonably happily married or at least in settled, comfortably conventional relationships. But younger women are another matter entirely for early Bowen. Her early novels are focused unerringly on young women and concern their postwar resistance to the teleology of the marriage plot. The change, for them, is that there is, that there can be, no change. This, and the related concern that romantic love is no longer possible or viable, or the solution to the condition of being a woman, is the fundamental crisis of Bowen's early, Modernist fiction.[5]

The Hotel, Bowen's first novel, is set in an Italian Riviera hotel in the early 1920s. The narrative revolves around the intertwined relationships of the hotel's British guests during one summer, focusing in particular on an androgynously named young woman, Sydney Warren. Early in the novel we are introduced to one of the few young male guests at the hotel, the 30-year-old Victor Ammering. Largely on account of his relative youth and his bachelor status, Ammering is described as 'the principal young man of the Hotel' (TH, p.19) because he is the focus of significant interest from the young marriageable women. But Ammering is also defined almost exclusively as a casualty of war: 'having been unable to find a job since the War', Ammering is 'said to be suffering from nervous depression in consequence' (p.19). While his nervous depression is apparently the result of his inability to find employment, there is also the strong suggestion that both it and his joblessness are a function of his experience in the war itself. Although Ammering regularly goes to dances, where he 'talk[s] to his partners most beautifully about the War' (p.19), he can do little more than talk, and in this respect he seems to be ironically named: the war has left him thoroughly defeated, victorious only in his ability to pull off the oxymoron of 'beautiful' talk about war. 'War', explains one of his young admirers, generalizing from the condition of Victor, has 'come very hard indeed on our generation' (p.48).[6]

In a sense, then, it is largely on account of his rarity that Ammering is of any romantic or matrimonial interest. And in this, Bowen registers the historical predicament for many young women after the First World War: the sudden paucity of marriageable men and the consequent necessary reorientation of the narratives of women's lives – with the risk indeed that their lives will have no narrative, that there will be no change.[7] What was for many a catastrophic post-war dearth of young men is explicitly referred to in the context of the hotel itself: 'how few men there are out here', comments one of the older women at the hotel: 'They say it's the same at all these places – not a man to be had' (TH, p.53). We can construe 'all these places' as meaning all the British-inhabited hotels on the

Italian Riviera, but the phrase also points to the general decline in the numbers of eligible men in the years after the great slaughter of the First World War. This predicament is not only registered in Cecilia Summers's war-widow status in To the North but repeatedly noted at the beginning of Bowen's third novel, Friends and Relations, where there is an emphasis on the success of both Studdart daughters in securing husbands in the context of 'a summer when men were so few' (FR, p.18), when 'Girls could not all expect to marry' (p.13), and when Janet in particular in 'these difficult days' had not been expected to marry (p.15).[8]

According to Ronald Kerr, another young, male, and in this case somewhat morose, guest in The Hotel, the world war has produced for women in particular a new world, a world order in which anything can happen and in which women's lives have fundamentally, even if only potentially, changed: 'There is nothing now to prevent women being different', Kerr complains, 'and yet they seem to go on being just the same.' 'What is the good of a new world', he asks, 'if nobody can be got to come and live in it?' (TH, p.111).[9] What Kerr fails to understand (what he apparently cannot understand, as a man) is the situation in which the young middle-class and upper-middle-class women find themselves, where the conventional expectation that they will marry has been undermined by the fact that, as Eileen puts it, 'no young man, if one comes to look at it dispassionately, is worth all the fuss father expects us to make about him' (p.126). It is for this reason, perhaps, that when the avuncular Colonel Duperrier tells Eileen that 'girls' can 'do pretty much what they want to nowadays', she responds that they could, 'if we ever really wanted to do anything long enough' (p.125). The Hotel therefore revolves around the discontent that the young women feel about the fact that in this new world they have more freedom than before to do what they want, and the sense that there is, tragically, nothing that they want. In answer to Freud's question 'What does a woman want?', Bowen seems to produce the answer only that a woman wants, and wants to, desire: women want (to) want. For Sydney, at least, defined as she is by a 'strange anaesthesia' (TH, p.141), the whole project of sexual reproduction (the foundation, the raison d'être, after all, of marriage) seems to have lost its point. 'What a lot of energy is wasted', she remarks, overlooking or denying the Darwinian theory of evolution and gradual species improvement, 'in replacing one lot of people by another exactly the same' (p.141). And the concept of marriage, for Sydney, seems just as strange, as she contemplates the married guests in the hotel restaurant, as if an anthropologist amongst an alien tribe, or a biologist studying exotic animal behaviour:

> Men came in without their wives and did not always look up when these entered. Women appearing before their husbands remained alert, gazed into an opposite space resentfully, and ate with an air of temporizing off the tips of their forks. When the husbands did come in it seemed a long time before there was something to say. It seemed odder than ever to Sydney, eyeing these couples, that men and women should be expected to pair off for life. (p.18)

Pairing off for life – the basis of the traditional marriage plot, its denouement, its aim – is defamiliarized by Sydney and by Bowen, 'eyed' uneasily by them both, and is made to seem odd, or is acknowledged in its oddness, not to say in some sense its impossibility.

Marriage and the marriage plot, and therefore even plot itself, is largely interdicted, then, in early Bowen. In *The Hotel*, Sydney agrees, somewhat reluctantly, to marry James Milton, an uninspiring, middle-aged vicar and fellow guest at the hotel, even though, as she explains to Ronald, she thinks of being in love as a 'mistake' (TH, p.143). And then, towards the end of the novel, Sydney decides rather suddenly not to marry him after all. The novel's denouement (its *peripeteia* in the Aristotelian sense, as well as its moment of recognition, *anagnorisis*) and therefore its trajectory as a whole, turns on this second decision. This non-decision is a reversal, not only of marriage, but also of plot, of the narrative itself. Sydney determines, in other words, that nothing will happen. The scene of her decision not to marry involves transport and speed, as well as its opposite, standstill or blockage. A group of hotel guests, including Milton, Tessa (Sydney's older, neurotic cousin and travel companion), and Sydney herself, are returning from an afternoon excursion in a Fiat up a local mountain. The driver, a 'brigandish individual in a check cap' (p.156), drives terrifyingly fast down the hair-pin bends, swerving violently and flinging the passengers from side to side in the car. 'It's not like motoring at all', Tessa comments, 'it's more like dropping' (p.157). While Tessa's response is to 'wish there were not such a long way to go', Sydney by contrast relishes the possibility of a violent death ('"If it could be the next corner", she thought, "we could go over clean – there is that clear drop. Let it be the next corner"'), and she reasons not only that no one would really mind much if she and the others died, but that for Ronald, at least, 'it would be better' (p.157). Just at this moment of thanatological automobile fantasy, the car comes suddenly to a halt and 'stop[s] dead' as it meets a blockage in the road. And it is just then, at a standstill on the road, that Sydney declares to Milton, apparently without thinking, that their marriage is 'quite impossible' (p.159). It is speed itself and the 'shock' of Sydney's consequently awakened sense of 'being alive' (p.160) that has made it clear to her that marriage to Milton cannot be contemplated, and that marriage leads to a dead standstill. So The Hotel turns out to involve a plot or non-plot, an anti-narrative despite its speed, in which several people meet in a hotel and then, some time later, after nothing very much has happened, leave to go their separate ways.[10]

To the North literally and more violently ends in a death drive that also marks the end of an affair, the end of (non-)marriage. Emmeline literally drives her ex-lover Markie and herself to their deaths as she drives, her car 'strung on speed' (TN, p.245), along the Great North Road out of London, where they collide head-on and fatally with an oncoming vehicle. The novel begins with another northward journey, as Markie meets Cecelia (the widow of Emmeline's brother) travelling on a train from Italy back to England. The novel begins and ends in travel, then, just as travel is embedded in its title. In fact, speed constitutes one of the larger thematic concerns of a novel in which the protagonist, Emmeline, is a travel agent: she has 'sent so many clients flying', Bowen remarks ambiguously, 'that her Bloomsbury offices seemed to radiate speed' (TTN, p.144). And the narrative not only thematizes and frames itself through travel, but is driven, in a sense, by the liaisons that are made and broken by, and in, transport, at speed: Bowen emphasizes the importance of travel in the modern world not only through Emmeline's profession and by means of the novel's title, but by placing some of the central scenes aboard trains or planes or in cars.[11] In particular, it is on an aeroplane to Paris that the impossibility of Emmeline marrying Markie is spelled out (literally), when Markie writes out the message (speech being impossible above the noise of the plane's engines) 'if I COULD marry, it would be you', and then, however, 'We could not marry' (p.138). That the couple could not, cannot, marry, is gradually affirmed by the break-up of their relationship, by the non-return of Emmeline's telephone calls to Markie and, violently, in the post-relationship drive to the ex- or non-lovers' deaths at the novel's end. In To the North something does happen, then, and something happens through transport and speed, but that something is only, can only be, death, death as the consequence of a relationship that cannot last, that does not work, of marriage that cannot happen. Violence, death, is the response to the narrative of marriage, and even to narrative itself.

Friends and Relations is different: both of the two young women on whom it focuses do marry, and the novel is structured not through travel and the evocation of speed but through a triangulation of place (Cheltenham, London and Sussex), at which its (non-)events take place. Bowen's third novel, one of her shortest, is also one of her most underrated, and under-read: it is a novel that, according to her biographer Victoria Glendinning, 'even Elizabeth Bowen enthusiasts tend to forget about'.[12] It has been described as Bowen's 'most intransigent and least accessible novel',[13] a book that is characterized by 'narrowness and hesitancy',[14] and an 'evasive text which seems to resist interpretation by over-interpreting itself'.[15] Suggesting that it is 'the weakest of her novels', Maud Ellmann comments that it is 'lifeless' and 'awkwardly schematic', and that it 'exhibit[s] good structure without compelling feeling'.[16] But what critics respond to as the novel's 'lifelessness' may have to do with its interest in the intractability of feeling and of human relationships, of life itself, indeed; what is interpreted as narrative and characterological inertness has to do with an investigation into an existence in which, as Edward thinks, 'life after all' is 'not an affair of passion' (FR, p.99). Edward has 'a dread of love' and a 'more than moral distaste for the cruel inconvenience, the inconvenient cruelty of passion' (p.119). In this sense, the novel is as much an exploration of the resistance to what one character thinks of as the 'axiomatic selfishness of all lovers' (p.145), an exploration of passionlessness and the ethics of a resistance to passion, as it is a study of repressed or conflicted or interdicted passion. It is a love story, in other words, that takes the extraordinary (experimental, even avant-garde) risk of resisting passion and that therefore resists narrative movement, development, plot.

Friends and Relations is unlike The Hotel and To the North in that rather than being about young unmarried women it is about married couples. The novel centres on two sisters, Laurel and Janet Studdart, who marry Edward Tilney and Rodney Meggatt respectively within pages of the start of the novel. This is part of the reason why nothing much happens in *Friends and Relations*: in a sense, nothing much *can* happen. Nobody does much, and the novel is remarkable for a plot that involves a return on itself, a resolution in which the married women go back at the end, while still married, to their family home: the final chapter concerns the way that each daughter regularly visits, 'solitary as a maid' (FR, p.154), their parents' Cheltenham house. And the final sentence, returns, decisively, to the moment before the marriage of Laurel and Edward with which the novel opens, as Colonel Studdart pauses in town with his two daughters outside 'the hotel where Edward had stayed before the wedding' (p.159).

A summary of the novel's plot cannot fully express the extent, or the quiet, disturbing force, of its evocatively 'gnarled' syntax (as Ellmann calls it),[17] or its unsettling and (or even because) underplayed narrative intransigence. But a summary might at least suggest the nature of marital and other difficulties with which Bowen is concerned, as well as the plot's refusal, really, to get anywhere, its resistance to change, speed and story. Like a number of Bowen novels of this period, such as *The Last September* (1929), *The House in Paris* (1935) and *The Death of the Heart* (1938), *Friends and Relations* is in three parts. Set soon after the First World War, with a 'still recent sense of catastrophe' (FR, p.82), Part One opens with the marriage in the early summer of Laurel and Edward. This is followed in the autumn of the same year by the marriage of Laurel's younger sister Janet to Rodney, whom she meets soon after her sister's wedding: 'Though she did not love him', Bowen remarks decisively although seemingly in passing, 'she began to understand desire' (p.18). The complicating factor in this second marriage is that Rodney is the nephew of a once-famous big-game hunter, Considine Meggatt, who happens to have been the co-respondent in the divorce of Edward's parents. Although this difficulty, or embarrassment, is overcome, it never disappears and indeed continues to condition both marriages, which involve delicate and largely unexpressed negotiations regarding the awkward Meggatt uncle and Tilney mother. Part Two is set ten years later, when Janet and Rodney, now with a daughter, Hermione, and living in Uncle Considine's large house, Batts, in Sussex, are host not only to the offspring of Laurel and Edward but also to Edward's mother, Lady Elfrida, as well as to Considine himself (Considine lives abroad but regularly pays extended visits to the house). Elfrida and Considine get on well now, like old friends, despite finally failing to make it as lovers two decades earlier. Edward, permanently traumatized by his parents' divorce, and determined not to let his children visit Batts when both Considine and Elfrida are present, hears that both are visiting, and travels to Sussex in order to retrieve his children. In a fraught conversation in the library, Edward and Janet almost imperceptibly acknowledge what might be described, albeit rather crudely, as their 'desire' for each other; the most explicit declaration being Edward's explanation that he came not only to rescue the children but also because 'I had to see you', before speculating ambiguously: 'If you and I had fallen in love – But I didn't want that' (p.95). Later, once he has left, the romantically hyper-alert Lady Elfrida explains to Janet that 'of course' Edward loves her (p.105). Part Three concerns the span of a crucial twenty-four hours, three weeks after Edward's fatal conversation with Janet at Batts. Janet visits London to see her sister, but misses her and ends up having lunch alone with Edward before meeting him at her hotel in the evening. Without very much being said directly, it emerges that becoming lovers is not a possibility, and rather than sleeping or eloping with Edward, Janet returns to Batts on the night train. Fearing that her sister and her husband *are* sleeping together or eloping – the dawning realization that her husband may be in love with her sister has been a 'catastrophe' for Laurel, 'like the beginning of a war' (p.129) – Laurel spends an insomniac night and early morning worrying about, and then searching in desperation for, her missing husband, who has in fact been sleeping alone at his mother's empty house in another part of London. The novel ends with a final chapter set a year later when both Janet and Laurel visit their parents' Cheltenham home: nothing has changed (both couples are still married; no affair has taken place), and symbolically, if not in reality, the ending returns the two women to a premarital state.

I want to suggest that this non-happening of plot, and the sisters' near-return to a pre-narrative condition, the condition prior to any marriage, is indicative of Bowen's conception of the impossibility of conventional – pre-modernist – narrative. In this sense, it is not too much to say that Bowen's novel deconstructs the very foundation of the marriage plot, not by refusing or resisting marriage, but by encompassing two marriages and demonstrating the intransigence of such an arrangement – as well as the impossibility of any other form of romantic love. Lesbian love, for example, constantly hinted at and sometimes more explicitly articulated in all of Bowen's early novels, ultimately offers no solution, no real alternative, to the narrative *aporia* of patriarchal or heterosexual relations. The change that *Friends and Relations* expresses, then, the Modernist change, is that of changelessness, the 'large nonoccurrence', as Bowen puts it (FR, p.151), that may be said to characterize her early fiction. The 'weakness' that critics perceive in *Friends and Relations* might instead be read, therefore, as Bowen's articulation of a concern with the change that has happened to peoples' lives – to women's lives, in particular – after the war. Subtly 'experimental' in form ('Modernist' in that sense), Bowen's novel asks a lot of its readers – asks indeed for slow, patient reading that is sensitive to almost imperceptible changes in mood and sensibility and to almost indiscernible plot events. It demands something like the 'annoying slowness' with which Janet herself is said 'at all times' to read (FR, p.93) – as opposed to the kind of 'rapid and superficial' reading that Lady Elfrida practices on her son's letter, a letter which she finds, much like a Bowen novel to the hasty reader, 'all qualifications qualified, almost unintelligible' (p.17).

If Bowen is not a 'Modernist' in the high Proustian or Joycean sense – if she does not set out radically to reinvent literary language or the form and purpose of the novel, but instead develops traditional form, pushing it even as she does so to its limits – the early novels certainly respond in remarkable and provocative ways, both thematically and in their very narrative texture, to the profound social, cultural and material changes to which other Modernist writers of the 1920s and early 1930s also reacted. All of Bowen's early novels, and *Friends and Relations* in particular, take on the question of the story of modern women's lives and, while working firmly within the conventions of the traditional marriage plot, quietly undermine, and in so doing help to renew or reinvent, the possibility of narrative itself.

NOTES

1. Bowen's second novel, *The Last September* (1929), is considered elsewhere in the present volume. Quotations from Bowen's novels are from the following editions: *The Hotel* (London: Penguin, 1943), hereafter referred to in the text as TH; *Friends and Relations* (London: Penguin, 1943), cited as FR; *To the North* (London: Penguin, 1945), cited as TTN.

2. Virginia Woolf, 'Character in Fiction' (1924), in *The Essays of Virginia Woolf*, ed. Andrew McNeillie (London: Hogarth, 1988), vol.3, pp.421–2; 'Make It New' is, amongst other things, the title of a 1934 collection of essays by Pound.

3. Elizabeth Bowen, *The Mulberry Tree: Writings of Elizabeth Bowen*, ed. Hermione Lee (London: Virago, 1986), p.287, hereafter referred to in the text as MT.

4. Elizabeth Bowen, *English Novelists* (London: Collins, 1945), p.46. In fact, the First World War goes on being registered in Bowen's fiction at least into the middle of the century: her 1955 novel *A World of Love* centres around the long-dead Guy, who was 'mown down' in the First World War. See Heather Bryant Jordan, *How Will the Heart Endure? Elizabeth Bowen and the Landscape of War* (Ann Arbor, MI: University of Michigan Press, 1992), on the 'pervasive' influence of the First World War on Bowen's early work (p.13 and ch.2 passim). In 'The Bend Back', Bowen declares that 'confidence was broken by 1914' (MT, p.54).

5. See Maud Ellmann, *Elizabeth Bowen: The Shadow Across the Page* (Edinburgh: Edinburgh University Press, 2003), on Bowen's questioning of 'the very possibility of a desiring subject' and the 'impasse of romance' in these novels (pp.71, 70, and ch.3 passim).

6. See ibid., pp.81–2, on the question of the war in *The Hotel*; and compare *The Last September* (London: Penguin, 1942), p.120 (hereafter referred to in the text as LS): Lady Naylor sees herself as having been a 'rebel' as a young woman, but thinks that since the war young people 'had never ceased mouching' (i.e. slouching, skulking, loitering, wandering, rather than rebelling).

7. See Virginia Nicholson, *Singled Out: How Two Million Women Survived Without Men After the First World War* (London: Viking, 2007). The minor characters Miss Fitzgerald and Miss Pym, who together open and close *The Hotel* and whose naming in these opening pages itself defines their spinster status, are two such women: the novel opens with the Misses Fitzgerald and Pym avoiding each other after what looks like a lovers' tiff; its last sentence depicts the couple sitting 'Hand in hand, reunited, in perfect security' remembering that occasion, on which they 'so nearly lost one another' (TH, p.175). In addition to the possible attractiveness of same-sex relationships, there is, of course, another positive dimension to women's changing lives that Bowen registers – the possibility that a career might replace for some young women the putative fulfilment of marriage: Sydney had intended, at least, to be a doctor (she is recovering, though, from a near breakdown after taking too many exams [TH, p.17]); Emmeline in *To the North* runs her own business; and generally, as Lady Naylor remarks in *The Last September*, careers offer 'a future for girls nowadays outside marriage' (LS, p.174).

8. Bowen is coy about the date, stating only that it is '192_' (FR, p.15), but since Part

Two is set ten years later and the final chapter a year after that, and since the novel was first published in 1931, it is clear that the year is 1920.

9. See also Lady Elfrida's remark, in *Friend and Relations*, that social niceties had changed now, 'when everybody was different, everyone else dead' (FR, p.17).

10. The plot of Bowen's second novel, *The Last September*, is not altogether dissimilar: Lois decides to marry a British soldier, Gerald; and then, towards the end of the novel, she decides not to marry him after all (because he has not been able to make her fall in love with him). In this case, though, Gerald is killed by the IRA soon after Lois decides that she cannot marry him.

11. On transport in *To the North*, see Andrew Bennett and Nicholas Royle, *Elizabeth Bowen and the Dissolution of the Novel: Still Lives* (Basingstoke: Macmillan, 1994), ch.2, especially pp.33–41, and Ellmann, *Elizabeth Bowen*, pp.96–112.

12. Victoria Glendinning, *Elizabeth Bowen: Portrait of a Writer* (London: Orion Books, 1993 [1977]), p.81.

13. Bennett and Royle, *Elizabeth Bowen*, p.29.

14. Jordan, *How Will the Heart Endure*, p.63.

15. Hermione Lee, *Elizabeth Bowen: An Estimation*, revised edn. (London: Vintage, 1999), p.64. The same phrase ('evasive text') is used by Renée C. Hoogland in 'Elizabeth Bowen: Unconscious Undertows: Queer Perspectives on *Friends and Relations*', in *Recharting the Thirties*, ed. Patrick J. Quinn (Selinsgrove, PA: Susquehana University Press, 1996), p.85; compare Glendinning, *Elizabeth Bowen*, p.81, who comments that in *Friends and Relations* Bowen 'sits on the fence abominably'.

16. Ellmann, *Elizabeth Bowen*, p.88. Similarly, Hermione Lee sees *Friends and Relations* (like *The Hotel*) as 'about the failure to rise to crisis or tragedy' and suggests that Bowen's later novels are 'more complex and dramatic because the characters are capable of drastic actions' – the result, in *Friends and Relations*, being what Lee calls 'tepid formulations' (pp.65, 66, 70). My suggestion is that we should understand such formulations and such apparent weaknesses in terms of Bowen's 'Modernist' attempt to revise narrative structure itself and, relatedly, in terms of her response to the predicament of women after the war. Glendinning refers to the novel as having 'too many knots in the rope' (*Elizabeth Bowen*, p.82). She is alluding to a comment that Bowen remembers Woolf making to the effect that although she enjoyed it, the novel was 'spoilt' because 'I feel you're like somebody trying to throw a lasso with a knotted rope' (Joan Russell Noble, ed., *Recollections of Virginia Woolf* [London: Peter Owen, 1972], p.48). But it is just this knottedness of narrative and emotional formulation that is so extraordinary and so powerful in, and in some ways unique to, *Friends and Relations*. While John Coates is one of the few critics to argue for a re-evaluation of Bowen's novel, his reading of it in terms of its affirmation of traditional family values (and as against the values of romantic love and erotic fulfilment at any cost) seems to me to be so limited in its exclusive focus on the positive value of married life as to constitute something approaching a misreading of the novel. See John Coates, *Social Discontinuity in the Novels of Elizabeth Bowen: The Conservative Quest* (Lewiston: Edwin Mellen, 1998), ch.2.

17. Ellmann, *Elizabeth Bowen*, p.95.

CHAPTER FOUR

'Not like a person at all': Bowen, the 1920s and 'The Dancing-Mistress'

PATRICIA COUGHLAN

Vigorous critical growth during the 1990s and 2000s in the re-conceiving of anglophone modernisms and in arriving at less monolithic and more varied understandings of the inter-war decades is healthily affecting Bowen studies, as has strong and increasing feminist interest in her work from the 1980s onwards. An equally productive turn by scholars of Irish literature towards less parochial analysis of her writing has also become evident. From another critical direction, the rich and innovative socio-historical work by cultural historians and biographers on the first three decades of the twentieth century, including the development of queer studies of this period, are also gradually providing Bowen criticism with deeper, fuller and more accurate contexts and interpretative perspectives. The appearance since 2000 of the Corcoran and Ellmann monographs, both useful and serious contributions to the field, is a sign of the continuing development both of critical thought concerning Bowen's work and of fuller acknowledgement and appreciation of her extraordinary fictional vision.[1] There remain, however, many avenues in Bowen criticism which have yet to be adequately explored.

Of the two recent full-scale studies, Maud Ellmann's psychoanalytically attuned discussion especially advances the analysis of questions of desire and their role in Bowen's art. Furthermore, it is the most effective, focused and searching analysis to date of Bowen's constantly recurring and intensely felt representations of triangular loves and of the extraordinary difficulty for characters in her fictional universe of achieving relationships *à deux*. I see this seemingly inescapable triangulation as itself an indication of Bowen's pervasive scepticism about the adequacy of given social forms, a scepticism which her work most satisfyingly realizes and most arrestingly expresses in connection with the norms of romantic and sexual love. Her writing always also interests itself in the social construction of femininities: Bowen's delicate, sceptical anatomy of the permissible modes of being feminine, in all its ironies, is emerging in the best recent criticism as one of her most remarkable achievements. Focusing on a single short story from 1928, this chapter considers our current thinking about Bowen's larger treatment of these interrelated questions.

The texts of Bowen's (and the century's) twenties are still a neglected part of her work, though they are of such interest that to attend to them in more depth and detail will be a productive critical strategy. Especially under-discussed are the first three short-story collections: *Encounters* (1923), *Ann Lee's* (1926), and *Joining Charles* (1929). Of the three novels of this period, *The Hotel* (1927) and *Friends and Relations* (1931), both elegant and mordant English novels of manners, have also had a muted reception by comparison with *The Last September* (1929), deservedly treated as a classic exploration of the demise of colonial culture. It is timely for several reasons to give much fuller consideration to the significance of these earlier stories. For one thing, they include powerful and beautifully executed works of narrative art which question and disturb inherited British ideologies in the era of rapid modernization, with its attendant oscillation between feverish excitements and *anomie*. For another, these early stories play an important role as precursors to the great novels and later classic tales, into which they offer important insights. In particular, their explorations of gender are of great interest, interwoven as these often are with explorations of volatile sexual feeling and of the will to power in interpersonal relations. Furthermore, they were being written at formative intersections of modernity, place and period, as is shown by recent research and writing on anglophone culture *circa* 1922–39, a body of criticism which is dismantling previous monolithic models of modernism.

These stories are predominantly set in the south of England, with a very few in Ireland. In them, Bowen conducts a merciless enquiry into contemporary ways of life, principally among the middle and upper-middle classes, in the rapidly altering context of post-First World War modernity. It has often been suggested apropos of the novels that this enquiry, with its curious self-positioning both inside and outside these social worlds, is connected with Bowen's own equivocal placing geographically and culturally. All the evidence shows that her Irish planter history and her deeply felt roots in North Cork persist in emotional importance. They form a constant cultural counter-current to her enthusiastic social and intellectual involvement from the mid-1920s onwards with the elite circle of Oxford academics, critics and other writers whom she encountered mainly, at first, through her husband Alan Cameron. She had initially gained access to publication, however, and therefore to intellectual agency in her own right, via the female network of her old headmistress's acquaintance with Rose Macaulay.[2] The chic and witty smartness of her social life as it developed in this period, during which she gradually attained a writer's reputation, forms a glossy patina of faintly ironic grace over the ultimately dark and disruptive scepticism of her work itself. To demonstrate the riches which still lie half-unregarded in these early writings, I have chosen to consider, partly as an exemplary text, 'The Dancing-Mistress'.[3]

This story offers an especially pointed instance of femininity as display, and simultaneously poises this extravagant masquerade amid both verbal and sexual inversion, ambiguous and unfixed gendering, and startling cruelty. Its central character is a memorable obsessive. Shown as driven both by inner forces and economic necessity, this anti-heroine is named Joyce James. I shall argue that, despite (or perhaps partly because of) its relatively low-life setting among characters clinging to the edges of respectability, the story is important in broaching main themes and patterns of desire, ruthlessness and desperation which the mature novelist explores elsewhere on a larger scale. For the setting of the dancing-class, as Glendinning notes, Bowen probably drew material from her own girlhood in Kent between the ages of 7 and 13, during what were to be her mother's last years.[4] The immediacy of this setting is akin to that of another intensely focused story, written before 1923, 'Coming Home'.[5] Both also concern mothering and motherlessness, quintessential Bowen subjects, and, not coincidentally, both invoke raw anger and aggression.

'The Dancing-Mistress' appeared fourth among eleven stories in the collection *Joining Charles*, published on 11 July 1929, only five months after *The Last September*. As the author by then of two previous short-story collections and a novel, *The Hotel*, Bowen did sometimes get individual stories accepted by periodical editors, but not, it seems, this one.[6] The title story of *Joining Charles*, a pointed critique of domestic patriarchy, had appeared in 1926. It is not surprising that 'The Dancing-Mistress' did not find separate publication in the 1920s, though it was later reprinted twice, opening Bowen's 1946 *Selected Stories* and accompanying many of her most celebrated pieces in *A Day in the Dark*.[7] It is a downbeat, darkly concentrated and rather shocking story with overtones of sadism, largely without humour or even Bowen's characteristic dry irony. It is also, however, a compelling work. In her novels (all but the final two, at any rate) Bowen liked to preserve the surfaces of polite society, however intense the emotional and moral disruptions underlying those surfaces. The narrower compass of the short-story form, as she herself observed, enabled her to breach those surfaces and represent intense and disedifying struggles, on occasion with uncanny overtones, beneath.[8] Also collected in *Joining Charles* is the powerful, uncanny story 'Foothold'.[9] Set in an upper-middle-class Home Counties milieu, this uses a motif of haunting but, as I shall argue, also shows, from a different angle, Bowen's concentrated anatomizing of the array of conventional femininities as these were enjoined upon women in her era.

In the small compass of 'The Dancing-Mistress' Bowen establishes a scene of weariness and drudgery and a set of mainly unspoken tensions. I shall return to the specifics of these strains, and how they are played out, after exploring more fully some central aspects of the story's themes as they are evident more generally in the period and in Bowen's thought. As I have said, the brevity of the genre enforces compression, which can work as an enabling factor rather than a constriction. Here it enables her to look askance at the processes of gender construction and performance and at how these processes are interwoven by the bourgeoisie as a vital part of its own self-reproduction. The story flagrantly connects these processes with cruelty and manipulation; it also hints at the operations, within harsh containment, of irregular sexualities, including what sexological discourse then called 'inversion'. In the months before its first appearance in print, this, as we shall see, was a prominent and contentious topic. Radclyffe Hall's *Well of Loneliness* had caused a furore from its publication in August 1928 through and after the subsequent obscenity trial, which opened in November 1928, eight months before 'The Dancing-Mistress' was published.[10]

The story exemplifies that powerful focus on the morally and psychologically disturbing which is often evident in Bowen's writing. Set in a south-eastern seaside resort, its action is completed in the space of a single foggy November afternoon and evening. The narration is mainly omniscient, with an austere and slightly eerie use of zero focalization: this gives the story a distinctive feel of almost-nowhere-ness. Bowen focalizes her narration only intermittently when she does it through the three main female characters: the dancing-mistress Joyce James, Joyce's pianist Miss Peel, and the child Margery Mannering, a pupil in the weekly class. Lulu the 'hotel secretary', a young Swiss whose viewpoint we are not given, completes the cast of significant adult characters. Despite the normally feminine name, Lulu is male. The swooping, almost predatory, handling of viewpoint produces a pulsing rhythm of competing interiorities, interspersed with a chill detachment on the narrator's part. This spare deployment of focalization leaves the reader with only glimpses of the characters' inner perceptions and motivation, glimpses which are themselves mainly dark and chill like the fog with which the story opens and which deforms the streetscape, making everything appear unreal and impermanent, 'like a painting on blotting-paper': a vintage Bowen effect of insubstantiality, fading and unreliability of perception (CS, p.253).

The adult principals are a strange trio. There is the 21-year-old, yet permanently exhausted, Joyce James (an inversion, seven years after the scandals of *Ulysses*, with its literary significance hidden in plain view), her accompanist who lacks a given name as if to underline her purely performative role, and Lulu. He and Miss Peel ('Peelie' to the others) share an intense emotional involvement with Joyce, accompanying, looking after and longing for her. The pianist is swiftly invented in one tiny but telling narrative notation at the outset: she 'moistened the tops of her fingers to flatten her hair back; it was polished against her skull like a man's' (CS, p.253; my emphasis); she also wears 'a slave-bangle' on each arm. Connected – or rather yoked – to Miss Peel by their common attachment to Joyce is Lulu, described as 'distressingly beautiful' and (femininely) 'fervent and graceful', with his girlish name, who nevertheless pines for her and once gives her a 'straight level look of desire' (p.257). During the dance lesson he covertly coaxes Peelie, 'brushing her back as she played', to bring Joyce to supper *à trois*: his 'I want her tonight' contrives to sound both pettish and passionate (p.258). They are in competition for her attention, yet also paradoxically in league. Furthermore, they seem interchangeable in role. In the final scene Peel literally swaps places with Lulu when she gently withdraws her supporting arm from under the sleeping girl's head, allowing Lulu to substitute his, in the taxi to the station.

The story's sexualities are plainly non-phallic. Miss Peel is equivocally masculinized, Lulu equally equivocally feminized, and neither can consummate her or his desire. This is partly because its object, Joyce, is desexed, in all but very fleeting moments of affect, by her absolute preoccupation with dance, which the story shows as something between an artist's vocation and punishing hard labour. Furthermore, marrying, pairing off correctly according to the social rubrics, is not envisaged in this off-beat, almost under-world. The reasons for this inability are overdetermined: there are economic factors, in that all three struggle hard for their living and must be seen to maintain respectability, but emotional dysfunction also figures, and it seems to be this which most interests Bowen. 'Distressingly beautiful', Lulu lacks what Donne called 'masculine persuasive force'.[11] This feminized man, then, shares the position of unsatisfied desire with the masculinized woman Peelie (to the fact, already noted, that we know only her *surname*, we might add that we have only his *given* name, which itself inverts the social custom of calling women by their first names and men by their last). If we put this purely in the classic patriarchal (or Lacanian) terms of the inescapable family predicated on heterosexuality (with Peelie and Joyce in a mother–infant dyad), this male figure has not the capacity to break the three-handed relationship in order both to possess the desired woman and to establish the safe future-oriented patriarchal order. I shall return at the end to this curious echoing of the family in the Lulu–Joyce–Peelie threesome.

This triangular relation shares the story with another principal idea and is interwoven with it: the teacher's victimization, amounting to cruelty, of the ungainly and 'overdressed' little girl Margery Mannering. Poor Margery has 'red sausage-curls tied up with lop-eared white bows and spectacles that misted over, blinding her, when she got hot' (CS, p.255). She cannot dance, belongs only to 'a grandmother' (p.55), and

45

is accompanied by a servant where the other little girls have mothers or governesses. Still, she cannot escape the femininity whose painstaking – and painful – construction the story is anatomizing: she also has 'pretty-child affectations that sat forlornly upon her. Now she flung back her hard curls; they bounced on her back' (p.256). The small dancers are being schooled precisely in a repertory of bourgeois womanly graces; the class's handful of little boys are specifically excluded from the 'springing exercises, so graceful' (p.256): a flash of Bowen irony, all the more striking for the general absence of such effects from this text. Bowen's account of that bodily schooling pinpoints the contradiction between these graceful surfaces and the discipline and regimentation of the work necessary to bring about the almost military precision the 'rows of little girls' are required to achieve (pp.253, 256). The story is clear-sighted about the punishing technologies of perfection underlying these feminine forms: compare the child Adele's being recurrently beaten over the knuckles by her piano teacher in Beckett's radio play Embers (1955), another scene where the brutal inculcation of feminine graces in the middle-class child is sceptically rehearsed by an equivocally placed Irish writer. This force and effort is displaced into the musical accompaniment, where it is eloquently mimed in the pianist's mute aggression: 'Miss Peel spanked out the Marche Militaire' and 'the chords clanged vindictively, like choppers falling' (pp.255, 256). Margery's last name suggests the 'manner[ing]' of the girls as future ladies, the ways in which they must become mannered.

'The Dancing-Mistress' is of especial interest because of its oppressive staging of a process evidently important to Elizabeth Bowen's own self-presentation, both in actual social life and, arguably, in the contained, distanced elegance of her work. Looking at the photographic studio portraits of Bowen (as distinct from and indeed in contrast to the paint-ings), the glossy surface patina is striking: within the gleaming hair, dark lipstick and heavy glittering jewellery, what we see is a woman stilled, pre-sented formally in an almost hieratic pose, artfully arranged and offering a smooth, seemingly varnished object to the eye (the 1950 Angus McBean portrait reproduced in Glendinning and Lee is the best exam-ple).[12] Whatever may be within withholds itself severely and formidably: the strong bony face suggests not only Anglo-Irish good breeding (the quality Virginia Woolf in her diary unkindly labelled 'horse-faced'), but also, with mild incongruity, a carapace of urbane social performance.[13] The emphatic femininity announced by such images is simultaneously and piquantly countered by this strength of Bowen's facial features, much more handsome than pretty and easy to re-imagine as capable of a rather different, masculine presentation. Indeed her friend John Lehmann, visiting Bowen in Ireland in 1953, discerned 'a stylish, rather masculine carriage, as if about to settle on a shooting stick and lift binoculars'.[14] Five decades later, gender self-presentation is, of course, often conceived of by theorists as indeed a performance (or a sequence of them). We might, then, read Bowen's portrait images as what Judith Butler calls a set of 'citations' from among certain femininities of the early to mid-twentieth-century period: decorative, highly polished and maybe engaged in containing masked anxieties about inner otherness.[15] The evidence for such anxiety of feminine perfection in Bowen's actual social life has been previously discussed and is not my principal concern here.[16] But this outward image of a high-gloss femininity, with its curious effect of occluding or even blotting out the interior self, is also closely concerned in one of the principal interlocking themes of 'The Dancing-Mistress' as I read it, namely the constraints upon selves of the array of mandatory feminine subject positions. The story, of course, already focuses outwardly on performance in more conventional senses, since it recounts a dance class, including graceful exemplary solo work by the expert teacher.

To help us understand Bowen's working out of these themes, the contemporary socially gendered and sexed contexts of 'The Dancing-Mistress' are worth considering. Recent feminist cultural-historical and biographical, as well as literary, studies of the 1920s and the 1930s have greatly increased our knowledge of this period.[17] As against the constraints upon women to maintain a sanctioned femininity within the rules, we are gaining more detailed and nuanced views of energetic challenges posed by an articulate minority of – mainly upper-middle or upper class – women to the dominant ideology of gender. Such challenges were conducted via dress and coiffure, writing and various other arts, by engaging in concrete physical adventure, and by seizing upon the provisional freedoms women gained by default during the emergency conditions of the First World War. The work of Laura Doan and other scholars from the 1990s on has greatly advanced the study of social and cultural gendering in these two decades.[18] Where sexual forms and expressions are concerned, research and discussion has illuminated the definitional work of sexology, the new field crucial to modern understandings of the self. This was jointly constituted, from the mid-1880s onwards, by the invention of psychoanalysis and by attempts under the sign of positivism (sometimes prior to, sometimes concomitant with, the psychoanalytic) to classify and explain human sexuality and gendering.[19] On a point specifically relevant to Bowen's story, Doan carefully explores both the distinctions and the connections between a widespread 1920s fashion for masculine dress and coiffure, on the one hand, and the leading of lesbian or female-masculine lives on the other.[20] Those pervasive, widely adopted boyish fashions, whatever their varying relation to women's exploration and expression of variant sexualities, however, met an abrupt disavowal when the *Well of Loneliness* affair erupted late in 1928. Only then, Doan shows, did they become inextricably and narrowly associated with the scandal of female 'inversion'. This, as I have noted, was the exact moment of 'The Dancing-Mistress' , with its silk-clad but mannishly coiffed Miss Peel: the multiple inversions in the story as a whole underline this figure's real emotional investment in alternative sexual object-choice, however gracelessly it coexists with her compulsory femininity. It seems clear that the story is invoking such alternative configurations and linking them with the central importance of performance(s).

What is the role of such non-normative or variant sexualities and gender appurtenances in Bowen's vision? The various challenges to normative femininity by women in the period held considerable potential to disturb conventional gender roles and relations, and the self-understanding of thinking individuals, even if in their own lives the norms were ostensibly observed. (At the heart of Bowen's and her husband's personal lives was an example of variance in sexual behaviour, the non-consummation of their marriage, as recorded by her 1930s lover Humphry House.[21]) Contemporary criticism is coming to realize how non-standard sexual arrangements of various kinds are registered, far more widely than has always been granted, in Bowen's earlier work as well as in her last two novels. Often this registering appears mocking, and sometimes also apotropaic, for example in gestures of self-distancing from non-normative sexuality made here and there by characters within the texts: but the issue is complex, and Bowen's own position rigorously masked.

Readers will recall many such moments of *frisson* and disturbance: I mention only two examples. In *To the North* (published three years after 'The Dancing-Mistress') the young widow Cecilia, the cannier and more conventional of the book's two heroines, warns the other protagonist Emmeline of the undesirability of close association with their acquaintance the lesbian Connie Pleach, whose friendship Cecilia clearly judges to have predatory overtones which risk the social devaluation of Emmeline ('anyone can see her affection for you is unholy').[22] But a significant irony surrounds this reproving moment, undermining Cecilia's exact sense of the socially imprudent. Instead of lesbian Connie with her 'unholy' desires polluting the angelic Emmeline, the latter is in fact using Connie and her convenient possession of a country cottage as a blind for her own non-marital but heterosexual relationship with the cad Markie. This undercutting neatly instances the ambiguous, wavering quality which often marks Bowen's references to lesbian characters and attachments, with distaste voiced by characters not themselves always capable of reliable judgement. In another instance of this, also in *To the North*, the egregiously controlling Lady Waters plays hostess to temperamental composer Marcelle Veness, who has just lost her girl-friend. Bowen represents Veness's tempestuous chain-smoking unhappiness rather less negatively than she does Lady Waters' domination of whomever she can overpower. And Miss Tripp, the bluestocking secretary who falls in love with the abstracted Emmeline, wrapped up in her own emotions, is a semi-comic and pathetic, but morally far from negligible, characterization: her rebellious outburst serves to show up Emmeline's heedlessness of others, symbolized physically by her extreme myopia, a trait of Bowen's own (*To the North*, pp.124–6).

'The Dancing-Mistress', however, is disturbingly different from these instances of a nice balance of negative and positive judgements of lesbian desires. Its representation of Peelie is darkened towards the end by her unpleasant emergence as a quasi-pander figure who enjoys half-pimping Joyce to Lulu, half-withholding her. At first the two 'girls' [*sic*] (*CS*, p.259) appear as companions wearily sharing their day's work, 'holding the mirror for one another', with one, Peelie, doing more of the empathetic caring than the other – 'I say *sure* you don't feel too rotten?'

(p.253). But this affectionate solicitude of the plainer, supportive friend comes to be bound up by the end with manipulation and voyeuristic affect. During the class Peelie repeatedly draws Joyce's attention to Lulu's hovering, watching presence, and when he touches Joyce, even if only to guide her to the dining-table, Peelie's 'hard unabashed eyes contemplated them curiously' (p.262; my emphasis). Later, as they walk by the harbour, in a voice 'tinged with contempt' she underlines her own indispensability in this shared performance of desire, asking 'I wonder what you two would do next if I fell in and never bobbed up again' (p.261). The scene is rendered with all Bowen's economy of figuration to suggest balked sexual appetite and to render it repulsive and predatory (despite the 'slave-bangles' she wears). The extent of Lulu's fulfilment, for his part, is a snatched kiss in the darkness between lamps, beside where 'the dark, polished water sucked hard-lipped at the embankment' (p.261; my emphasis). I have noted Doan's account of the move to repudiate any hint of lesbian sexuality from the moment when the Well of Loneliness scandal broke: can Bowen's characterization of Peelie be considered an instance of such disavowal? The narrator does little to render sympathetic either Peelie's masculine self-presentation, or her unrequited adoration of Joyce. Altogether this seems a quasi-homophobic representation of lesbian desire and a deliberate recoil from Peelie's part-rejection of prescribed femininity, as from a thing almost grotesque (the man's hairstyle and the silk dress).

I shall return to the specifically psychological struggles of power and desire at the centre of 'The Dancing-Mistress'. But another of its points of especial interest is the important role played in it by the question of class, not a consideration much attended to in Bowen. The dancing-mistress is completely drained by her work, rising early to perfect her dancing at 'Madam Majowski's' studio, then travelling out of London daily to teach. This sharply differentiates her from most of Bowen's heroines: she is respectable but is not a gentlewoman. Such a class perspective, among the underlings of the bourgeoisie – a class still sedulously reproducing itself in the 1920s despite the cataclysms of war and the accompanying and subsequent revolutions and radical shifts – is unusual in Bowen. 'The Dancing-Mistress', which with its opening fog scene echoes Bleak House, is nevertheless exceptionally convincing compared to Bowen's other – often quite strained – representations of lower- or lower-middle class characters, even in some of her finest novels. Besides her eight dancing dresses 'like clouds, in gradations of beauty', a fur coat to cover them and a practice tunic, Joyce possesses only 'a cloth coat-and-skirt that looked wrong in the country and shabby in town' (p.254). Joyce, Peelie and Lulu are, indeed, all credibly rendered as economically subaltern figures under the constraints of an iron respectability. Joyce and Lulu may not be seen to dine *à deux* in the town because he 'showed ladies into their bedrooms' and she 'spent hours in clumsy men's arms', hence it 'did not do' for them to be 'patently man and woman' (p.259). Among the scanty critical mentions of 'The Dancing-Mistress', Mitchell discusses it primarily as an example of Bowen's interest in the inauthenticity of 'being forced to play a role' and considers that 'the essence' of the story is what he calls 'perversion', which he characterizes as a reversal of ' natural and artificial'.[23] He neither addresses the question of specifically economic constraints upon Joyce and Lulu, nor considers Joyce's performance as a gendered one. He therefore passes over the centrality to the story of constructions of femininity, as do most other earlier critics, despite the overwhelming majority of female protagonists in Bowen's work, this story included.

Joyce has aspirations to rise above her chagrin-inducing class position with its oppressive regulation and physically gruelling work. Her art, including her dawn labour, is co-extensive with this ceaseless painful discipline, even punishment, of her own suffering body. This in itself, the intense and vivid realization of Joyce's work *as* work, makes the story stand out amid Bowen's writing, which elsewhere is not especially a writing of the body, still less one which attends to ordinary, harsh working lives as French and English Naturalists such as Zola, Hardy and Gissing had done in pre-First World War novels. Here, however, she does give an arresting, if small-scale, representation of the constraints upon an equivocally classed middle group who served the aesthetic, sensuous and ideological needs of the English middle classes, in whose consciousness they did not figure as existential individuals. The fact that Peelie and Joyce are paid working women, and this in itself no longer compromises their respectability, interestingly acknowledges the twentieth-century widening, however, gradual and grudging, of women's possible roles in non-domestic spheres and in the economy, a widening especially occurring in the 1920s. (If 'The Dancing-Mistress' is indeed, as Glendinning suggests, autobiographical, then it draws its material from the pre-Great War period, but Bowen does not project the action into that lost pre-1914 world: Peelie's coiffure, to choose only one telling detail, definitely belongs to the 1920s.)

Both women cling to respectable status, but they are paid (however poorly) to serve the partly forcible, even physical, shaping of little girls towards bourgeois womanliness, which is also much more literally examined than is usual for Bowen's work. In her early fiction she more often stages the assumption of femininity as a conscious act, and its mandatory character is less blatantly evident to the protagonists of the gestures making up this act. This is particularly clearly a matter of performance when the character assuming – or, in Butler's term, citing – it is adolescent or a very young woman (the very funny 1926 story 'Charity' offers a vivid example of the channelling and fixing of desire in correctly opposing genitalities, and the corralling of young girls' frank bodily vigour). Theodora, the tall, awkward and clever teenager in *Friends and Relations*, constructs the hilarious telephone persona of Lady Hunter Jervois, nonchalant female aristocrat, as an ironic performance. In various works Bowen adopts a dryly sceptical stance towards almost all the possible modes of femininity. Her fictional vision, taken as a whole, sees – and sees beyond – the channelling and fixing of girls' energies; yet the body of Bowen criticism (with significant exceptions, such as Lee) has managed not to acknowledge the subversiveness of this. 'The Dancing-Mistress' offers a peculiar angle on this complex theme, when in the character of Peelie it shows both equivocal gendering and desire finding its object without discrimination as to gender, indeed in implicit though concealed defiance of conventional social regulation (though as we have seen this is not represented as any kind of moral or emotional ideal).

At the centre of the story, however, the figure of Joyce most clearly shows how female (and indeed Lulu's male) *desire* does not coincide with the living of *femininity*. A central and abiding concern in Bowen's work as a whole is how, even perhaps whether, normative womanhood can be negotiated and lived, and what the living of it might do to the self (as for instance to Lois, Karen, Stella, in three of her major novels). An important strand of my argument in this chapter is that in 'The Dancing-Mistress' Bowen is experimenting with a limit-case of extreme femininity: the dancer who must subdue and distort her whole bodily and emotional being to the performance of a quintessence or apotheosis of feminine beauty and grace, and as a result becomes 'not like a person at all', as one of her pupils thinks (CS, p.256). This late 1920s experiment, with its lower-class register, is part of Bowen's framing of the whole question of feminine being, in the self and in the world, before the majority of her most celebrated work was produced and in an era of fashionable and partly permitted transgression.

Another of her 1920s stories, 'Foothold' (1926), offers a contrasting exploration of different femininities, in the highly regulated milieu of the upper-middle classes (Bowen's more usual territory). Like 'The Dancing-Mistress', it sets up a triangle of attachments, though this is much more Jamesian and less rawly sensational in tone, and the central figure ultimately splits, under the strain of conforming to femininity, into a self and an uncanny double. Janet is married, apparently happily, to the conventional Gerard, and they have moved to a smallish country house at commuting distance from London. Thomas, an unmarried intellectual and old friend, has come to stay. Intensely aesthetic, he admires the perfection of Janet's beauty and is happy to be rid of Gerard during the days so as to wander the house and garden in her company. It is clear that Thomas meets emotional and intellectual needs of Janet's which Gerard does not, but equally evident that his fanatical detestation of children (he will visit only after hers have been packed off to boarding-school) and his arid, fastidious self-importance are markedly negative aspects of his characterization. (They very clearly anticipate Bowen's hostile rendering of Eva Trout's homosexual stepfather and his partner.) He appreciates Janet as aesthetes admire fine things: the narrator labels this admiration 'academic'. Thomas is writing a book about monasteries and is also an expert on gardens, with aspirations to be a Great Writer figure. 'Foothold' alludes to Meredith and Proust (to whose stature Thomas, laughably, aspires), and also, via a teasing remark of Janet's, to the polar opposites of Victorian Catholic devotional author Francis Thompson and the aggressively secular, rational and modern H.G. Wells. The real business of the story, masked by English restraint and phlegm, only slowly emerges: Janet is being haunted by a figure she calls Clara, a previous occupant of the house. The Wellsian rational modernity which Thomas thinks he espouses is disturbed as the story unfolds by psychic phenomena which have not, after all, been suppressed by the practical rationality of the mid-1920s. Playing mockingly with Wells's name, the narrator gives Thomas 'an intuition of some well he had half-divined in her having been tapped' (CS, p.305; my emphasis). The ghost Clara is an obvious *doppelgänger* of Janet's, and Thomas himself, despite his sceptical stance, eventually sees her walking on the upper landing, at first mistaking her for Janet herself. It gradually emerges that Janet is in the process of mental disintegration, despite her own vehement denials of any trouble.

'Foothold' makes clear that it is indeed the upper-middle-class lady's life, the state of being genteelly *désoeuvrée*, which is psychologically destroying Janet. This scenario, while unfolding in quite a different setting from 'The Dancing-Mistress', has in common with it the positing of a woman's fundamentally unachieved personhood. Thomas, who fancies himself as an interpreter of culture and society, despises the maternal and sensual sides of Janet's being and tries to turn her into an *objet d'art*. Meanwhile, immured with her dogs and her herbaceous borders, in desperation she conjures from within herself the dead woman, who seems, unsettlingly, partly *alter ego* and partly lover. 'Foothold' is full-blown Gothic, playing out the split-personality motif with a ghost, while 'The Dancing-Mistress' might be called merely sensational. Both, however, work from their different angles and class positions to trouble the category of the feminine and to interrogate feminine social roles. Janet's splitting and Joyce's inner emptiness (and, as we shall see, her sadistic affect) are parallel horrors which both manifest the oppression of required feminine roles. Compare the passage in The Heat of the Day recalling the near madness of Stella's female Mount Morris ancestors: 'Ladies had gone not quite mad, not even that, from in vain listening for meaning in the loudening ticking of the clock'.[24]

The earlier story 'Ann Lee's' (1924)[25] experiments, by contrast, with feminine agency, as opposed to the hardening or splitting enacted respectively in the constraints upon Joyce and Janet. 'Ann Lee's' is, like 'The Dancing-Mistress', among the few explorations in early Bowen of subaltern lives (a less assured example is 'The Return', whose protagonist is a lady's paid companion who chafes at her subordinate position[26]). 'Ann Lee's', a much more striking parallel with 'The Dancing-Mistress', focuses on a mysterious, priestess-like hat-maker; this brings out another aspect of the 'The Dancing-Mistress' theme, namely the woman-as-artist. Ann Lee works with her hands and, like Joyce, provides a service to ladies of means, but it is clear that in her own eyes she is an artist, not an artisan. Bowen uses a different narrative technique in this story, never once showing us Ann Lee's inner thoughts and as narrator confining herself to the joint viewpoints of the two vapid young wives who slum it (in the meaner streets of early 1920s Chelsea) in search of elegance. Mysterious and almost silent, by talent and sheer personal force Ann Lee achieves ascendancy over these silly women who come prepared to patronize her but leave overawed (and having spent their husbands' money heavily).

Both Ann's transcendent skill, exercised in a faintly minatory quietness, and Joyce's speechless grace when she is dancing, might be seen as figures of the artist's performance, and therefore as early symbolic explorations by Elizabeth Bowen, angular (and 'farouche') Anglo-Irishwoman relocated to smart London and Oxford, of her own possible creative powers. The hint of malice in Ann, Joyce's far harsher vindictiveness, and the sharp ironic sensibility and occasional capacity for ruthlessness of Bowen their creator, are revealingly linked. Both Joyce and Ann use their art to serve in the construction and adequate maintenance of femininity. Ann also differs from Joyce, however, in two ways. One is the possibility of her self-empowerment, against the odds and all the rules of polite, that is still rigidly hierarchical, society (despite the advent of modernity in some spheres). The other is the fact that Ann Lee uses materials apart from her own flesh, while in her creative enterprise Joyce creates her art in her own body. Bowen represents Ann as capable of seizing and exercising a kind of power over her customers, which reverses the relation of dependence in which, they feel with a certain impotent indignation, she ought to be kept. In this connection it is especially intriguing that Bowen herself had felt attracted by the idea of becoming a maker of hats, handbags and jewellery before her writer's vocation had firmly established itself.[27]

Joyce exercises complete hegemony for the duration of the dance-class, and in this respect resembles Ann Lee. In another sense, though, she is scarcely there at all, being arrestingly characterized as only an appearance. In a phrase suggesting depths of ontological awareness below the story's vivid and carefully delineated scenes, late at night she 'stopped *"seeming"* too tired to "be"; too tired to eat or speak' (*CS*, p.254; emphasis and quotation marks in original). As the little girls lovingly watch the grace of her curtseying, 'melt[ing] into the floor' and 'flowing', they think: 'If I had a dress like that ...' but also, as we have seen, 'She's not like a person at all' (p.256). 'All day long', says the narrator, Joyce is 'just an appearance, a rhythm'. Dancing, she spreads out into 'delicate shapes like a Japanese "mystery" flower dropped into water' (p.254). Yet, constituted in and by the adoring gaze of so many watchers including Peelie and Lulu, within herself Joyce experiences only emptiness, looking out over her 'delicate cheekbones' with 'dreamy and cold eyes in which personality never awakened' (p.254). Her beauty is a sign with only an aesthetic, not a human, referent or signification: the willed bewitchment of the feminine masquerade in which she has schooled herself has supplanted, or prevented the development of, the potential person.

While Glendinning's vivid biography is still indispensable, we need a much more detailed knowledge of Bowen's social life and connections in England, perhaps especially during her (and during the) twenties, so as to be able to situate her more fully among the various intellectual and other formations of the period. It is possible to gain insights about this from the writings themselves, however: sometimes, as I have suggested, from gestures of disavowal made by characters within them. Where psychoanalysis – in the 1920s a prominent discourse among intellectuals – is concerned, her narrators overtly adopt an amused distance from its aspirations to explain the psyche, including such (then still shocking) notions of the unconscious as a realm inaccessible to everyday rationality, and of the polymorphously perverse character of infancy. Nevertheless her writing shows evidence of its subliminal presence and strikes resonant chords with certain major psychoanalytic writings of the same decade. I shall argue that this is particularly true of 'The Dancing-Mistress'.

Bowen came a generation too late to be part of the early, radical excitement of psychoanalytic invention or discovery, and probably to encounter directly the energetic intellectual women who played such a major role in creating its English traditions: powerfully creative and disruptive at once, such women belonged to the First World War and immediate post-war era. Nevertheless, when in the early 1920s she began as a young adult to write and publish stories, the institutions of psychoanalysis in London were well established and prominent among upper-middle-class intellectuals, complete with the internal variations and competing practices and understandings of those institutions (Appignanesi and Forrester give an excellent account of this flourishing period of psychoanalysis, including its English manifestations).[28]

Topographically, the psychoanalysts were located principally in Bloomsbury, a district of the mind as much as of the London postal system. In *To the North* Julian Tower, one of Bowen's English gentlemen *par excellence* and a non- or anti-intellectual, evidently sees it as eccentric and slightly threatening, perhaps even desexing to a lady. He asks Emmeline if *all* the clients of her travel bureau are from there, implicitly deprecating its location in that district where so many young women, even well-bred ones, were engaged in paid work by the 1920s. Bowen first met Woolf (herself, of course, both well aware of psychoanalysis and sceptical of it) in Gower Street, Bloomsbury.[29] Certainly it is Lady Waters, not a discerning judge, who, we see in *To the North* bustling off to a lecture by Adler (who conceived the 'masculine protest'). But it is a fair assumption that either the figures themselves of Melanie Klein and Joan Riviere, theorist of femininity as masquerade, or at least talk of their startling work, were not entirely absent from Bowen's intellectual horizons, or at least that their ideas might have indirectly informed her own contemporaneous realizations in fiction of the workings of desire, power and inner compulsion. Riviere was at work in London from the start of the 1920s, and Klein from 1926.

Whether or not Bowen was aware of their writings, the theories of both Riviere and Klein, with their differences from classic Freudian male-centred Oedipal narrative, can be brought into illuminating relation with her work. 'The Dancing-Mistress' might even be read as, in its way, a kind of case-study, exactly contemporary with the work of this second generation of psychoanalysts. Bowen's intense interest in childhood and its formation of the adult self is one of the most characteristic aspects of her vision, and potentially aligns her with Klein's pioneering work in child analysis. Nor are Bowen's child-figures at all sentimentally imagined: the celebrated remark of *The House in Paris*'s narrator about cruelty between children is only the most explicit indicator of this. Furthermore, despite her overt suspicion of psychoanalysis considered as a universal explanatory model, a suspicion shared with Woolf, Bowen's fiction is nevertheless deeply akin and congenial to psychoanalytic theory, not least in the brilliance and modernity of its insight into the significance of childhood experience. But more specifically, I see 'The Dancing-Mistress' as resonating both with aspects of Klein's 1920s writings, and with Riviere's classic essay on womanliness as masquerade, where Riviere cites passages from Klein which are startlingly relevant to 'The Dancing-Mistress'.[30] Klein's highly original work with children was then foreshadowing the challenge which object-relations theory would eventually offer to Freudian masculine biases: the key essay, 'Early Stages of the Oedipus Conflict', on which Riviere draws, appeared in 1928.[31]

Detailing what she calls the criteria of 'complete feminine development' (an unsurprising list focused on wife and mother roles, on domesticity in general, and on 'maintain[ing] social life' and 'assist[ing] culture'), Riviere observes a certain hollowness and perhaps a secret resistance about some women's fulfilment of these functions, and conceives the sum of such feminine characteristics as a masquerade, that is, a mere guise which is assumed more or less pragmatically but devoid of inner assent. Riviere locates such performances in the carefully managed lives of professional women she had encountered as patients. But her notion of femininity *itself* as a performance and not nature or essence carries a charge of significance far beyond the specifics of case-histories, as its wide influence on feminist film theory shows.[32] Bowen's persistent and sceptical investigation of modes of femininity, and of desire and power, is illuminated by being brought into relation with Klein's and Riviere's thought. The delineation of Joyce and her life may indeed be read as the representation of a masquerade, but one in which the performance has so possessed the woman, in almost a Gothic-demonic sense, that it has supplanted her selfhood. Hence the emptiness, or paradoxical absence, discerned in her presence by the watching girl-pupils; it attracts their admiration as something so perfectly done that it has obliterated her personality, but elicits horror from the reader. It is as if Bowen inverts Riviere's observations, creating a limit case of absolute feminine performance which, to change the metaphor, has supplanted whatever selfhood might have lain behind it.

Furthermore, in the course of her 'Masquerade' essay Riviere cites a

1927 lecture by Klein (who had once succeeded Freud as Riviere's own analyst), on a point which resonates startlingly with 'The Dancing-Mistress'.[33] Klein reported intensely sadistic fantasies by her child-patients, including desires to bite off the mother's nipple and destroy, penetrate and disembowel her ('in consequence of disappointment or frustration during sucking or weaning'), and to castrate the father by biting off his penis. Klein interprets these wishes as responses to a prior fear that the mother will 'destroy the girl's body, her beauty, her children, her capacity for having children, mutilate her, devour her, torture her and kill her'.[34]

If we provisionally sever this intense *affect* – the violent fantasies of causing physical pain – from its fantasized *objects* in Klein's account (i.e. the child's parents), a striking parallel with Joyce comes into view. Recent critics have observed that Bowen herself frequently performs such moves, so dividing affects from their apparent and motivating contexts: Corcoran, for instance, eloquently describes Bowen's 'hollow-ing-out of subjectivity, as characters... becom[e] sites traversed by the endless mobilities of desire'.[35] In this case Bowen seems to reverse the direction of the violent impulse in Klein's version: Joyce wishes harm, not to a mother- but to a daughter-figure. To Margery (who is mother-less at the dancing class) she is a perverse mother, like a nightmare ful-filment of those prior fears of the all-powerful mother by Klein's child-patients. Under its surface, 'The Dancing-Mistress' is among other things a text about mothering, bad and good: I revisit this topic at the end of this chapter.

A realist reading might motivate Joyce's malevolence towards Margery as a displaced resentment of her own harsh life, which earns her so little, apart from the admiration of the miniature world of the dancing class (Gauthier perceptively observes how '*épuisée par son métier*', Joyce is revived only by her own murderous impulses).[36] But the phenomenon is in excess of this: Bowen is elaborating a predatory female characterization which clearly interests her psychologically and which is bound into her several other, mainly later, representations of menacing female authority. These range from the silky and manipulative (Mrs Kerr in *The Hotel*, Mme Fisher in *The House in Paris*), to controlling mothers or aunts (Mrs Michaelis in *The House in Paris*, Lois Farquar's Aunt Myra in *The Last September*) who rigidly preserve the social order, dampen down the transgressive impulses of the young, or play them puppet-like (Lady Waters in To the North). Joyce's cruelty is disturbing in itself, but much more so is its effect on her: she experiences sexual arousal only when actually tormenting Margery or when recalling this. Utterly disengaged emotionally despite the devoted service of others (including the glimpsed sister at home who gives her Bovril and puts her to bed), she mocks the dark-eyed and long-lashed Lulu, who to her is merely instrumental (CS, p.260: 'he won't melt any glaciers'), as is the equally devoted Peelie. Though she does not stop him kissing her on the quay between lamp-posts, it is impossible to conceive of Joyce engaging with Lulu – or indeed Peelie – in genital sex.

If we adopt the psychoanalytic focus on the family as matrix and crucible of all subsequent experience, the adult threesome re-emerges as a grotesquely parodic family. This trio is configured with Peelie and Lulu playing the female and male parents who nurture the infantile Joyce between them, competing for her regard and in the concluding scene passing her tenderly from her to his embrace as she sleeps, as parents might a tired child. Lulu's insufficiently forceful masculinity – his querulous pleading and moody hovering – is, however, as I have suggested, quite devoid of the force to enact Lacan's stipulated programme of breaking up the mother–child dyad and thereby establish the normative Oedipally structured domestic unit as conceived in classical psychoanalysis. This impossible family, then, remains inchoate: a situation with strong resonances throughout Bowen's fictional worlds, with their many triangular configurations of characters (Naomi, Karen, Max in The House in Paris; Anna, Eddie, Portia in The Death of the Heart, and perhaps Eva, Jeremy and Henry in Eva Trout).

Within this parodic family structure, Joyce herself is a monster-infant, overwhelmingly bodily and apparently devoid of empathetic emotional or moral interiority. In her fantasy of plunging a knife into Margery's eyes, she also shows a horrifying aggression reminiscent of Klein's child fantasies. As Margery's teacher Joyce owes her the duty of enlightened kindness, a version of good-parent obligation. Instead, however, Joyce offers frank hatred and oppression. As well as being plain, physically graceless and herself sullen and resentful, Margery is isolated and needy, and the sight of that need offends Joyce by making an implicit claim on her: it risks displacing her own centrality to herself, hollowed out as she is, and she reacts by striking out repeatedly: 'Did you see me killing that child?', she repeatedly asks Peelie, in excitement; and 'I made her waltz till she cried' (CS, p.260). Joyce has retained the naked desire of childhood to lash out blindly, without either the inhibition of social regulation or the emotional empathy which is expected to supervene before adolescence.

In this dark world, there is one luminous interval. About midway, 'The Dancing-Mistress' contains a vignette which strikes a classic Bowen note. There is another little girl, Margery's opposite: Cynthia, pretty and talented. She not only is 'Spain itself in the Spanish dance', but holds hands with her mother while they delightedly discuss the castanets she has been invited to bring to the next class (CS, p.257).[37] We recognize that intimacy of the mother-and-daughter pair which is Bowen's signature of happy attachment: compare Portia's intensely evocative memories of her and her mother's stay in the Swiss hotels in The Death of the Heart. This figure of the pair rapt in reciprocal love is deployed here, however, to do specific work in Bowen's fictional design. It sharply contrasts with the unfulfilled desires of Peelie and Lulu, with the solitary shame of Margery, pilloried for literally putting a foot wrong, and with Joyce's own utterly alienating elevation as ego-ideal and beautiful, but exhausted, object.

Bowen places this mother–daughter scene of happy love at the edge of the story's main action, where it structurally resembles those – normally marginal – figures in medieval or Renaissance pictures, who are blessed in being allowed to lead ordinary lives at the peripheries of great and terrible events. The peasants continue drinking, the woman comes from the well, going about their business, tiny in the corners while Sebastian or Marsyas is pierced or flayed in large scale and centre field. Auden's poem 'Musée des Beaux Arts', about Breughel's 'Fall of Icarus' (beginning 'About suffering they were never wrong, the Old Masters') makes a similar point about the painter's contrast between the spectacle of important suffering and the continuance of everyday life, though Breughel reverses Bowen's disposition of the contrasting events and figures: in his picture the 'boy falling out of the sky' is placed in the distance, scarcely noticeable compared to the normal quotidian ploughman with his horse on the side of a hill in the foreground. In 'The Dancing-Mistress' the small vignette of Cynthia and her mother's enchanted mutual love throws into a sharper, contrasting light Joyce's evil-mother hurting of Margery, who sees all too clearly that 'Cynthia never seemed bare of being loved, it was round her at school, everywhere, like a sheath' (CS, p.257). By contrast we see Joyce as almost a Snow Queen or monstrous child-eating step-mother from a fairy-tale. It is tempting to suggest that in this aspect of the story (as indeed in the 1923 'Coming Home') Bowen was perhaps transacting emotional work of her own, staging in the one fictional moment what in her own experience were successive states: secure pos-session of the beloved mother, followed by the completely unannounced loss and absolute bereavement which followed and exposed the child to the colder, comparatively indifferent world. The luminous loving union of Cynthia and her real, kind mother suggests a promise beyond its wicked echo in the oppressive dark pairing of Margery and Joyce, and also beyond Lulu's and Peelie's mimicked parental care and their unsatis-fied longings. But the predominating moral-emotional world of the story which remains in our minds is one of cruel command perform-ances, where the warm reality of fulfilled love is almost inconceivable.

NOTES

1. Neil Corcoran, Elizabeth Bowen: The Enforced Return (Oxford: Oxford University Press, 2004); Maud Ellmann, Elizabeth Bowen: The Shadow Across the Page (Edinburgh: Edinburgh University Press, 2003).

2. Victoria Glendinning, Elizabeth Bowen: Portrait of a Writer (London: Weidenfeld and Nicolson, 1977), p.44.

3. Elizabeth Bowen, 'The Dancing Mistress' (1929) in Collected Stories (Harmondsworth: Penguin, 1980), pp.255–62, hereafter referred to in the text as CS.

4. Glendinning, Elizabeth Bowen, p.68.

5. Elizabeth Bowen, 'Coming Home', in Collected Stories, pp.95–100.

6. J'nan M. Sellery and William O. Harris, Elizabeth Bowen: A Bibliography (Austin, TX: Humanities Research Center, 1981).

7. Elizabeth Bowen, A Day in the Dark and Other Stories (London: Jonathan Cape, 1965). Sellery and Harris, Elizabeth Bowen, pp.29, 63, 91, 129.

8. See Bowen 1959, quoted in Mary Jarrett, 'Ambiguous Ghosts: The Short Stories of Elizabeth Bowen', Journal of the Short Story in English, 8 (Spring 1987), pp.71–9 (pp.72–3).

9. Elizabeth Bowen, 'Foothold', in Collected Stories, pp.297–313.

10. See Sally Cline, Radclyffe Hall: A Woman Called John (London: John Murray, 1997), pp.242ff.; Laura Doan, Fashioning Sapphism: The Origins of a Modern English Lesbian Culture (New York: Columbia University Press, 2001), pp.95–125 (p.197, n.17).

11. See John Donne, 'Elegy 16', in *The Complete English Poems*, ed. A.J. Smith (Harmondsworth: Penguin, 1971), p.118, l. 4.

12. See Glendinning, *Elizabeth Bowen*, front cover, and Hermione Lee, *Elizabeth Bowen*, revised edn. (London: Vintage, 1991).

13. Quoted in Deirdre Toomey, 'Bowen, Elizabeth Dorothea Cole (1899–1973)', in *Oxford Dictionary of National Biography* (Oxford: Oxford University Press, 2004). http://0-www.oxforddnb.com.innopac.ucc.ie:80/view/article/30839.

14. Quoted in Glendinning, *Elizabeth Bowen*, p.187.

15. See Judith Butler, 'Performative Acts and Gender Constitution: An Essay in Phenomenology and Feminist Theory', in *Writing on the Body: Female Embodiment and Feminist Theory*, ed. Katie Conboy *et al.* (New York: Columbia University Press, 1997), pp.401–17.

16. See Glendinning, *Elizabeth Bowen*; also Patricia Coughlan, 'Women and Desire in the Work of Elizabeth Bowen', in *Sex, Nation and Dissent*, ed. Eibhear Walshe (Cork: Cork University Press, 1995), pp.103–34.

17. See Janet Montefiore, *Men and Women Writers of the 1930s: the Dangerous Flood of History* (London: Routledge, 1996); Jane Dowson (ed.), *Women's Poetry of the 1930s: A Critical Anthology* (London: Routledge, 1996); Jane Dowson, *Women, Modernism and British Poetry 1910–1939: Resisting Femininity* (Aldershot: Ashgate, 2002); Cline, *Radclyffe Hall*; Diana Souhami, *The Trials of Radclyffe Hall* (London: Weidenfeld and Nicolson, 1998); and Doan, *Fashioning Sapphism*. Valentine Cunningham, *British Writers of the Thirties* (Oxford: Oxford Unversity Press, 1988) on 1930s literary culture remains indispensable.

18. See Doan, *Fashioning Sapphism*; Laura Doan and Jane Garrity (eds), *Sapphic Modernities: Sexuality, Women and English Culture* (Houndmills: Palgrave, 2006).

19. Lucy Bland and Laura Doan (eds), *Sexology in Culture: Labelling Bodies and Desires* (Cambridge: Polity, 1998).

20. See Doan, *Fashioning Sapphism*, pp.95–125.

21. Letter quoted in Toomey, 'Bowen, Elizabeth Dorothea Cole (1899–1973)'.

22. Elizabeth Bowen, *To the North* (Harmondsworth: Penguin, 1984), p.95.

23. Edward Mitchell, 'Themes in Elizabeth Bowen's Short Stories' (1966), reprinted in *Elizabeth Bowen: Modern Critical Views*, ed. Harold Bloom (New York: Chelsea House, 1987), pp.39–50 (pp.41–2).

24. Elizabeth Bowen, *The Heat of the Day* (Harmondsworth: Penguin, 1979), p.174.

25. Elizabeth Bowen, 'Ann Lee's', in *Collected Stories*, pp.103–11.

26. Elizabeth Bowen, 'The Return', in *Collected Stories*, pp.28–34.

27. Glendinning, *Elizabeth Bowen*, p.41.

28. Lisa Appignanesi and John Forrester, *Freud's Women* (London: Weidenfeld and Nicolson, 1993).

29. Glendinning, *Elizabeth Bowen*, p.99.

30. Joan Riviere, 'Womanliness as a Masquerade', *International Journal of Psychoanalysis*, 10 (1929), pp.303–13.

31. Melanie Klein, 'Early Stages of the Oedipus Conflict', *International Journal of Psychoanalysis*, 9 (1928), pp.167–80, quoted in Riviere, http://www.ncf.edu/hassold/Women Artists/riviere_womanliness_as_masquerade.htm.

32. See, for example, Mary Ann Doane, 'Film and the Masquerade: Theorizing the Female Spectator' (1982), in *Feminist Film Theory: A Reader*, ed. Sue Thornham (New York: New York University Press, 1999), pp.131–45.

33. Klein, 'Early Stages of the Oedipus Conflict'.

34. Quoted in Riviere, http://www.ncf.edu/hassold/Women Artists/riviere_womanliness_as_masquerade.htm.

35. Corcoran, *Elizabeth Bowen*, p.128.

36. Dominique Gauthier, *L'Image du réel dans les romans d'Elizabeth Bowen* (Paris: Didier Erudition, 1985 [Etudes Anglaises 91]), p.325.

37. See Glendinning, *Elizabeth Bowen*, p.38, on Bowen's own talent at dancing.

CHAPTER FIVE

Ghosts from our Future: Bowen and the Unfinished Business of Living

DEREK HAND

In considering the nature of her own writing Elizabeth Bowen rhetorically asked herself, 'Am I not manifestly a writer for whom places loom large?'[1] Certainly her link to Ireland is usually read in terms of her representations of the Big House. At times it seems that 'bricks and mortar' are of as much importance to her Irish world as the people who inhabit them. Her Big House writing, then, is usually read as an anachronistic elegy to the Anglo-Irish: their marginalized position politically in post-1922 Ireland being compensated for with this vision of aesthetic permanence and stylistic relevance. But in another statement on place she declared that 'Nothing can happen nowhere'.[2] In her curiously idiosyncratic way, this anxious negative assertion suggests that while place is central, the relationship of the person to place is actually more important. In all of her fiction, characters – for whatever reason – are out of place, cut off and cut loose from the safety that a final home might offer, never ultimately belonging anywhere or with anyone.

Such uneasiness between place and personality is perfectly encapsulated in her writing concerning ghosts and haunting. So many of Bowen's concerns come together in this image, her spectral preoccupations centring round characters under pressure in terms of their link to particular places: particular homes and houses. Ghosts being either real or the eruptions of the human mind, the concerns are the same: the desire for presence rather than absence, the need for actuality and 'thereness' as opposed to disconnection and non-existence. Importantly, too, presence is linked to power or the lack of it, in haunting. Ghosts suggest that the rationalized boundary between past and present is permeable, as characters are forced to confront their own stark condition and predicament in the present moment. The presence of haunting in Bowen's Irish writing, particularly, upsets the elegiac reading of the Big House, disrupting profoundly any notion of easy sentiment or nostalgic attachment to the past and tradition. Hauntings are not necessarily orientated toward the past, which fits snugly with the mournful backward look usually associated with Bowen, but can also be read as future-orientated: haunting suggesting that something is incomplete, that there is something yet to be done. In other words, there might be a future moment or time when that life which has been cut off can fulfil itself.

The usual reading of Bowen suggests that whatever ghosts appear in her Irish writing – as the ghosts of Lois Farquar's forebears in The Last September appear in the form of portraits that grace the walls of Danielstown – do so as powerful reminders of the past and the pull of tradition and continuity. But another way of reading haunting and ghostly presence in her work is as a product of the trauma of both the First World War and the gaining of Irish Independence. Ireland and Irishness throw into sharp relief that permeating impression of disconnection and existential foreboding that characterizes much modernist literature of the twentieth century. After the national revolution within Ireland and the nationalistic and imperialistic European war, there is a move inwards with a desire to map interiority and the psyche. For Lois, the Naylors and others, it is a question of continued cultural and political relevance that underpins their anxieties, and haunting is both an opposition to that issue and also a symptom of that condition.

In this chapter I want to trace the developing motif of haunting in Bowen's Irish writing – in some of her Irish short stories and in her novel The Last September – arguing that for her the Irish scene demands a particular kind of artistic imagination, at once open to and challenged by the disrupting 'otherness' that ghosts and haunting might signify. Indeed, haunting becomes a means to consider self-reflexively her own acts of writing as she attempts to make present what is absent, to imaginatively mediate between the past, the present and the future.

The first of her short stories I want to consider is entitled 'The Back Drawing-Room'. This was first published in Bowen's 1926 volume of short stories, Ann Lee's. It does not feature in the Victoria Glendinning collection, *Elizabeth Bowen's Irish Stories*,[3] which is surprising because of its clearly identified Irish setting. Having been written in the mid-1920s before *The Last September*, it must be considered the first piece of published writing by Bowen that may be called 'Irish'. Indeed, reading it can alter radically our approach to the better-known *The Last September*.

The scene of the story is, as Robert Tracy so aptly puts it, an 'intellectu-ally pretentious party'.[4] A little unnamed man, not a part of the main group, interjects when the talk turns to ghosts and ghost stories. He tells of being in Ireland visiting a cousin. Though the time is not exactly specified, it is clear his visit is set about two years after what is euphemistically labelled the 'civic disturbances';[5] that is, after the war of independence and the civil war in Ireland. The little man tells of being out cycling one afternoon, of getting a puncture, and looking for some assistance in a nearby Big House. As no one answers his knock on the door, he lets himself in and eventu-ally finds himself in the back drawing-room: 'Here was I, unintroduced, in a back drawing-room, really quite an intimate room, where I believe only favoured visitors are usually admitted, with a lady sobbing on the sofa' (CS, p.208). It is an uncomfortable and disturbing experience, and he quickly leaves the place. Later, at his cousin's, he is told that he could not have visited that house nor could he have met anybody there: 'There was a place, you see, until two years ago – very fine it was; then they came one night and burnt it, the winter before last' (p.209). The end of the story provides the customary 'shock'. The story-teller relates how his cousin's wife talks of the those who had lived at Kilbarran 'as though they were dead', only to be disabused of this notion when the wife confirms that they live 'in Dublin, I think, or England'. He questions her supposed 'lack of interest' in her old friends, and she answers: 'Well, how can one feel they're alive? How can they be, any more than plants one's pulled up? They've nothing to grow in, or hold on to' (p.210). The significance of the tale is, here, unequivocal: the loss of the Big House leads to a kind of living death for those who dwelt there. And, not unlike ghosts, they are doomed to wander the earth as shadowy figures, rootless and dislocated.

In the story, there are numerous literary references – to Edgar Allan Poe and Walter De La Mare, for instance.[6] These intertextual references reflect the tendency of the other guests to interrupt the little man who tells his 'ghost story', comparing it against other stories they have read. In essence, the guests fill in the narrative lacunae in the man's story: 'Something was over taking you … Something was coming up from the earth, down from the skies, in from the mountains, that was stranger than the gathered rain. Deep from out of depths of those dark windows, something beckoned' (p.205). A while later we are offered an illustration of the pattern a ghost story should follow when a man called Mennister complains: 'My dear fellow, you're an expert in the finer forms of torture … [A]ll ghost stories have one of three possible climaxes, A, B, or C, and every climax has its complementary explanation. Get on to the climax, and I'll guarantee you the explanation' (p.207). It is clear from these many interruptions, that the little man's story does not fit the expected trajectory of the literary Gothic tale or poem. It does not conform to what is thought of as conventional. They cannot appreciate the man's tale because it is beyond them; they do not have access to the codes in order to decipher it.

Moving the focus out from the story itself to include Bowen as a writer and author, this self-reflexiveness can be read as Bowen establishing her own apartness from this English gathering. Throughout the story, Ireland is seen as a place where 'unconventionality' persists, as the little man points out on two occasions (cf. pp.205 and 206). Perhaps Bowen is commenting on her own situation as an Anglo-Irish writer, or teller of stories, in an English marketplace. Her stories will necessarily be different to the norm and the conventional. Certainly Ireland's otherness is emphasized in the story. At one point Mrs Henneker offers the 'literary' or 'writerly' commentary that the little man fails to include: 'One lives in a dream there, a dream oppressed and shifting, such as one dreams in a house with trees about it, on a sultry night' (p.203). Ireland and Irish stories are, therefore, nonconformist and, ultimately, challenging.

On another level, Bowen's knowing references to the Gothic literary tradition focus the reader's attention on to the role of the writer/author in mediating between the living and the dead; or, to put it differently, between the past and the present. What becomes important – as it does for the listeners in 'The Back Drawing-Room' – is how the story is told rather than what it is about.

By the end of the story there is an indication that the little man is something of a ghost-like figure himself. He is not given a name and, as the story closes, his leaving is described thus: 'Some one collected the little man and took him away quietly … the broken semi-circle drew closer together, intimately. They asked each other with raised eyebrows,

"Whose importation?" And this remained unanswered; no one knew' (p.210). As with the powerful and disturbing close of W.B. Yeats's play *The Words Upon the Window-Pane* when the voice of Jonathan Swift appears to speak to the audience 'unmediated', or the disconcerting close of Tom Murphy's *The Gigli Concert*, the reader of this story may be left with the question of whether the little man has just been telling a 'story' or, in some way, has actually been haunting the gathering.[7] There is a verbal indication of this in the image of the 'broken semi-circle' that can be interpreted as a faint echo, perhaps, of a seance. While this ending lacks the powerfully unsettling and disturbing force that both the close of W.B. Yeats and Tom Murphy's plays possess, it nonetheless registers a breaking of boundaries and a transcending of conventional expectations. Rather than offering a neat conclusion where all the loose ends are tied up or a finish that, in the character Mennister's opinion, can be explained, Bowen presents an ending which evades closure.

Of significance is Bowen's introduction of the idea of 'haunting'. Though in this story she appears to be preoccupied with ruins and the prospect of ruins being haunted, she does not return to this image of the destroyed Big House in any of her writings. Instead, what the reader is offered is an image of the Big House continuing, but of its also being haunted. There is a shift in emphasis away from merely representing Anglo-Irish loss tangibly, toward an investigation of the relationship between the past and the present and how the past haunts the present.

Thus, the moral of the little man's story is quite complex. The Anglo-Irish cannot live without a palpable connection to home: like flowers they die when they are uprooted from the soil. A compensation for this could be the continued existence of the Big House in a textual or written form. Yet this too has its difficulties, not least of which is the possibility that one's readers will fail to grasp the significance of the narrative that is being presented to them. In other words, the Anglo-Irish conception of home cannot be adequately expressed or explained, forever remaining meaningless to others.

In terms of Elizabeth Bowen's engagement with the idea of home in an Irish context, this early story presents the double-edged sword of her Anglo-Irishness. It is ironic that for Bowen home only comes into sharp focus when it is under threat or absent. In a circuitous way, then, home-lessness leads to home. Thus, her use of visits, visitors and visitations throughout her writing underlines how the journey away may hopefully lead to an eventual return home. Bowen stated that it was possibly 'England made me a novelist',[8] yet always pronounced upon the centrality of Irish terrain to her work. Perhaps, it is precisely this conflict and tension of loyalties that makes her a writer. It is only when she breaks away from home and begins to visit and make visitations, that she is able to be an artist, who, like the little man in 'the Back Drawing Room', will tell stories that confront and confound metropolitan expectations and metropolitan conventions.

Bringing this idea of haunting to bear on Elizabeth Bowen's *The Last September* forces the reader to reconsider the novel as a simple threnody for Anglo-Ireland, detailing the last rites of the Anglo-Irish before the emergence of the new Irish state. Not unlike the little man from 'The Back Drawing-Room' the main character of this novel, Lois Farquar, is something of an artist figure. The one piece of art that we see in *The Last September* is a stanza of Robert Browning's poem, 'Pippa Passes', transcribed by Lois on a cover page of her drawings and art:

> I am a painter who cannot paint;
> In my life, a devil rather than a saint;
> In my brain, as poor a creature too:
> No end to all that I cannot do!
> But do one thing at least I can –
> Love a man or hate a man
> Supremely – [9]

Lois cannot 'write' herself, cannot speak her predicament as it were, and uses the shelter of somebody else's words to express her dilemma at the crossroads between childhood and adulthood. This, in itself, demonstrates her difficulty: her inability to articulate her problems in her own words, signalling a fundamental lack in her character. It could be argued, too, that this short stanza impels Lois along a certain path of action. With no idea herself of what she wants to do with her life, and certainly no idea of the means by which she can begin to even think about her future, she happily accepts this literary voice as an imperative: she internalizes these assumptions. Consequently, she can either love or hate a man; as a woman there are no other options open to her, except for loving Marda, perhaps?

In conversation with her cousin Laurence she asks plaintively: 'what do you think I am for?' (LS, p.161) She is not content, as the other women are, to submit to the vagaries of the marriage market. Perhaps unconsciously she is aware of the ultimate emptiness of such pursuits and how the outcome of marriage only upholds the old order. Vera Kreilkamp argues that a staple ingredient of the Big House novel is 'women whose lives are reduced to fulfilling the empty forms of power when real power is gone'.[10] Bowen is undercutting the nineteenth-century literary convention of focusing on women's sphere of power and influence in the marriage market because she realizes how in the modern world such action is no substitute for authentic living.

Lois takes on various roles: she thinks she loves Hugo Montmorency, who had had a relationship with her mother, and then she seems to strike out on her own and believes she loves Gerald Lesworth, an English soldier. Lois is constantly prepared to lose herself in someone else's life and would happily be anyone else rather than herself: as she declares as she tries on Marda Norton's coat, 'Oh, the *escape* in other people's clothes!' (LS, p.76) Lois's predicament, then, is one of trying to make an intervention into reality, of making a mark in the world of action. In other words, her existence, and that of the Anglo-Irish society she is representative of, is a ghostly one, predicated on washed-out rituals centred round the Big House of Danielstown.

Throughout the novel this ghostliness is emphasized by the way in which Bowen marks out the Big House territory. Early on, a 'furtive lorry' disrupts the silence of the evening at Danielstown as it crawls 'with such a menace along the boundary, marking the scope of peace of this silly island, undermining solitude' (LS, p.31). The limits of the demesne are identified: there is a clear and unambiguous sense of what is 'inside' and what is 'outside' this space. Increasingly, however, this boundary is breached. Directly after this moment, Lois comes across an Irish soldier making his way through the estate: 'there passed within reach of her hand … a resolute profile, powerful as a thought. In grati-tude for its fleshiness, she felt prompted to make some contact' (p.34). Usually read from Lois's perspective, this non-encounter is evidence of her inability to partake in the world of action. From the IRA man's per-spective, though, what we witness is his utter lack of awareness of Lois's presence. But he too becomes ghost-like as the trees and the bushes of the demesne swallow him up as he moves on. And encroachments are made by the English as well. Gerald drops in to lunch unannounced and un-invited; Mrs Vermont and Mrs Rolfe arrive one morning to a comically frosty reception from the entire household. The Naylors are unable to keep these unwanted visitors at bay. But it is not simply the worlds of action and paralysis being juxtaposed: all the characters are touched by ghostliness. The English soldiers, especially those that have been in the trenches of the First World War, are haunted and haunting characters, tenuously holding on to the world of the living.

Ghostly manifestation depends on which side of the supernatural divide one is on – can the living see ghosts, or can ghosts see the living? – and such is the case here. What is being hinted at is the different epistemological and ontological worlds being inhabited by the English, Irish and the Anglo-Irish, and how at a certain level while there is the outward appearance of interaction, there is, in reality, none.

The events at the mill mark the turning point for Lois. She is transformed by the experience: her and Marda's encounter with the Irish soldier, Marda's being shot at and slightly grazed, is something both frighteningly 'real' but also thoroughly liberating. Suddenly the unknown potential and possibility of the future challenges Lois: she has no need now for the escape of other people's clothes. She is mistress of her own destiny because of the very fact that she does not exactly know what that destiny might be. She is, in other words, free now to choose her own role to play – imagine her own future, no matter how uncertain it may be – instead of having other roles thrust upon her.

The truly disrupting moment comes near the close of the novel. Lois escapes the final immolation of Danielstown. Her departure from the novel, however, is merely told to us and not dramatized within the plot itself. For a character that has been the main focus throughout the novel, her absence at the close – and the manner of her exit – must be considered significant. It leaves open the possibility that Lois can indeed escape to life, away from the deadening and ghostly ceremonies of Anglo-Irish existence. But, like the little man from 'The Back Drawing-Room', Lois's leaving is suggestive of her future as dislocated and disembodied: as a homeless ghost doomed to wander rather than be rooted to a single place.

At the very beginning of the novel the arrival of Hugo and Francie Montmorency is described as a 'moment of happiness, of perfection'.

Lois wishes 'she could freeze the moment and keep it always. But as the car approached as it stopped, she stooped down and patted one of the dogs' (LS, p.7) At work throughout The Last September is a discourse of time-lessness – this being but one example of it. It is linked to an attachment to unquestioning tradition. To exist in an eternal now and embrace eternal recurrence means that one can remain steadfastly apolitical and ignore the realities of the present conflict and the choices that might be made.

But the moment of happiness and perfection is lost. This early observation concerning transience shows that the beginning bespeaks the ending, for this is what Bowen comes to understand – the transient nature of all human things that were once thought permanent. Thus, the discourse of timelessness is also a tacit acknowledgement of universal currents of change and transformation: all things come and go and all things rise and fall. It is interesting to note that much of W.B. Yeats's poetry after Irish independence also makes efforts to transcend the here and now and exist on a universal plane where universal tides hold sway. For Bowen, as for Lois, it is that shock of recognition that means she can break free into the business of living.

But, of course, such images of ghosts continue to haunt her Irish writing through the 1930s, 1940s and 1950s. It is as if the trauma of that moment of transition, that rupture between the old world and the new, must be returned to again and again in order that it can perhaps be finally understood and then, appropriately enough, exorcised.

'Her Table Spread', written in 1930, presents another kind of haunt-ing.[11] At first glance, it seems to be very much like The Last September in that Valeria appears, like Lois, to be on the cusp of adulthood and needs to make choices as to what she will do with her life. Unlike Lois, however, she is tied to her Big House and cannot easily escape it and its respon-sibilities. Her options are limited. The English Destroyer that Valeria sees seems to be a 'ghost ship', as this is post-independent Ireland. However, as is explained in the story itself, 'By a term of the Treaty, English ships were permitted to anchor in these waters' (CS, p.419). Nonetheless, their presence is something of an anachronism, as is Valeria's interest in the ship and the men on board it. So, for all intents and purposes, the Destroyer does haunt the scene as described in this story, in that it represents the past and the burden of the past. Valeria herself becomes something of a ghost-figure haunting the castle, as she rushes about on a hilltop waving her lantern in a demented fashion.

Bowen shifts attention in other stories and biographical writing away from people and personality and toward the Big House itself. In *Bowen's Court* (1942), her magnificent family history, the opening pages are taken up with a lovingly detailed description of her family home in County Cork.[12] That this piece of writing about home is very much influenced by the experience, destruction and threat of the Second World War, means that such a stable celebratory vision is a necessary one of peace in a time of war.

There is a dreamlike quality to Bowen's descriptions of the house in the opening pages: 'Bowen's Court shows almost living changes of colour. In the fine weather the limestone takes on a warm whitish powdery bloom ... In cold or warm dusks it goes either steel or lavender, in full moonlight it glitters like silvered chalk' (BC, p.22). This light not only plays upon the outside of the house, it also enters the house through the big windows which 'not only reflect the changes of weather but seem to contain the weather itself' (p.22). Consequently,

> When rain moves in vague grey curtains across the country, or stands in a sounding pillar over the roof and trees, grey quivers steadily on the indoor air, giving the rooms ... the resigned look of being exposed to rain. The metal of autumn sharpens and burnishes everything in the house. And summer's drone and spring's yellow-green rustle penetrate everywhere. (pp.22–3)

One is reminded of the time-lapse technique made use of primarily in wildlife and nature documentaries. This allows a camera to record events over a long period of time. When replayed, changes that to the naked eye in 'real time' would be almost imperceptible are clearly observable. Thus, cloud formations can be seen to develop and disperse, flowers grow, bloom and die. What is reminiscent of this in Bowen's Court is that the backdrop against which these changes/developments/alterations occur always remains constant. In the midst of all this surface movement, there is an underlying and innate stillness: the countryside, the demesne and the house are the calm points around which these changes happen.

Also, it is a description devoid of human presence or activity: that absence intimating a possible rupture between place and person. Thus the Big House becomes an empty shell faintly echoing the lives that have been lived there. Interestingly, this still-life portrait captures the language of travelogue, as if Bowen is anticipating the fate of numerous ancestral homes in Ireland, as they will be transformed into hotels and guest-houses for the new power brokers in a new Ireland. A short story from 1946 never reprinted in any of her collected editions, 'The Good Earl', deals with this possible outcome, as the Good Earl makes efforts to bring prosperity to his community by constructing a hotel on the shores of a lough.[13] And again in her history of the famous Dublin hotel, *The Shelbourne*, published in 1951, Bowen focuses on the space that allows the ghost of style from a distant past to continue on in the present moment.

'The Bend Back', an essay from 1950, concerns itself with what Bowen feels is the phenomenon of 'Nostalgia' in the literary productions of her contemporary moment. Writers, in their backward look, are retreating from the present moment. She says of her own background: 'As a child of the period may remember – it was considered glory to be alive. "The better days", if one needed them, were the future.'[14] At that time the future was the focus: possibilities were, perhaps, infinite. And, as has been demonstrated, that future was exploded and taken away and what remained was a ghostly relationship with the past that was ultimately debilitating, arresting the development of those characters in its thrall. It would take Jane Danby in Bowen's final novel set in Ireland, *A World of Love* (1955), to confront at last these ghosts and hauntings, to come into a proper and sustaining connection with the Anglo-Irish past so that she can get on with the essential business of living in the present and on into the future.

Walter Benjamin said, 'Each epoch not only dreams the next, but also, in dreaming, strives toward that moment of waking'.[15] Elizabeth Bowen's spectral Irish writing engages with that process of active dreaming, her writing bearing witness to the gains and the losses in that movement toward what is yet to come. Her haunted Irish scene, then, is a place of almost unbearable anticipation, the ghosts and the various hauntings pointing toward possible futures as well as already lived pasts. The stress on visits and visitors, the constant focus on characters that literally do nothing, combine to generate this atmosphere of leisurely waiting. Certainly the apprehensiveness surrounding her Anglo-Irishness in the politically altered reality of post-independent Ireland forces her, as it does other Irish writers of her generation, to question her position and her connection to thoughts of home and home-place, to question attitudes to tradition and modernity, past and future. Irish independence, though, does not create the issue for Bowen or her class, who always had to be creative in relation to making lasting imaginative links to Ireland. Elizabeth Bowen's Irish novels and short stories acknowledge that past, but also look forward to a radically different future. Her ghosts, therefore, and the haunted places they inhabit, link that past to the present, but more importantly anticipate the unknown and the mysteries of what is yet to come.

NOTES

1. Elizabeth Bowen, 'Pictures and Conversations', in Bowen, The Mulberry Tree: Writings of Elizabeth Bowen, ed. Hermione Lee (London: Virago, 1986), p.282.
2. Elizabeth Bowen, 'Notes on Writing a Novel', in The Mulberry Tree, p.39.
3. Cf. Elizabeth Bowen, Elizabeth Bowen's Irish Stories, with introduction by Victoria Glendinning (Dublin: Poolbeg, 1978/1986).
4. Robert Tracy, The Unappeasable Host: Studies in Irish Identities (Dublin: University College Dublin Press, 1998), p.225.
5. Elizabeth Bowen, Collected Stories, introduced by Angus Wilson (Harmondsworth: Penguin, 1983), p.203, hereafter referred to in the text as CS.
6. Edgar Allan Poe, 'The Fall of the House of Usher'; Walter De La Mare, 'The Ghost'.
7. Cf. Derek Hand, 'Breaking Boundaries, Creating Spaces: W.B Yeats's The Words Upon the Window-Pane as a Post-Colonial Text', in W.B. Yeats and Post-Colonialism, ed. Deborah Fleming (Connecticut: Locust Hill Press, 2001), pp.187–204; Derek Hand, 'The Gigli Concert: The Necessity of the Imagination', in The Irish Reader: Essays for John Devitt, ed. Michael Hinds, Peter Denman and Margaret Kelleher (Dublin: Otior Press, 2007), pp.31–7; and Derek Hand, 'The Ontological Imperative in Irish Writing', Brazilian Journal of Irish Studies (ABEI Journal), 5 (June 2003), pp.312–20.
8. Elizabeth Bowen, 'Pictures and Conversations', p.276.
9. Elizabeth Bowen, The Last September (London: Penguin, 1987), p.97, hereafter referred to in the text as LS.
10. Vera Kreilkamp, The Anglo-Irish Novel and the Big House (Syracuse, NY: Syracuse University Press, 1998), p.154.
11. Elizabeth Bowen, 'Her Table Spread', in Collected Stories, pp.418–24.
12. Elizabeth Bowen, Bowen's Court (London: Longmans, Green & Co., 1942), hereafter referred to in the text as BC.
13. Elizabeth Bowen, 'The Good Earl', in Diversion, ed. Hester W. Chapman and Princess Romanovsky Pavlovsky (London: Collins, 1946), pp.133–47.
14. Bowen in The Mulberry Tree, p.54.
15. Walter Benjamin, Reflections: Essays, Aphorisms, Autobiographical Writings, trans. Edmund Jephcott (New York: Schocken Books, 1978), p.162

CHAPTER SIX

Bowen and the Modern Ghost

SINÉAD MOONEY

Bowen begins her 1952 prefatory essay to *The Second Ghost Book* with the claim that the collection, containing stories by Rose Macaulay, L.P. Hartley and V.S. Pritchett, as well as her own 'Hand in Glove', would 'treat of the modern ghost':

> On the whole, it would seem they adapt themselves well, perhaps better than we do, to changing world conditions – they enlarge their domain, shift their hold on our nerves and, dispossessed of one habitat, set up house in another … They know how to curdle electric light, chill off heating, or de-condition air. Long ago they captured railway trains and installed themselves in liners' luxury cabins; now telephones, motors, planes and radio wavelengths offer them self-expression. The advance of psychology has gone their way; the guilt complex is their especial friend. Ghosts have grown up.[1]

Bowen, while on the one hand discussing ghost-story-writing as a long-time practitioner, is also engaged in an attempt to define a specifically modern susceptibility to the supernatural in its protean forms. She also is thinking about the ways in which the supernatural signifies differently at different historical moments. Julia Briggs, in her study of the English ghost story, includes Bowen, wrongly, in my opinion, among those post-First World War writers who struggled with the integration of a realistically depicted contemporary scene with the supernatural. Briggs argues that 'the constant proximity of other people, the continuous, reassuring hum of cars, machinery or canned music are not very conducive to the fear of the unknown'.[2] However, this is to fail to recognize the strong associations in Bowen between the modern and the ghost, and how ghostliness is insistently correlated by her with the intricacies of modernity. Her ghost stories force her reader to accommodate a fictional universe entirely *au fait* with the innovations of modernity – what 'Look at All Those Roses' sums up as 'the typewriter, the cocktail shaker, the telephone … the car' – and which is also ironically conscious of the 'advance of psychology', but which is a world where ghosts, nonetheless, walk.[3]

Bowen's work is obsessed, on the one hand, with the minutiae of manners and decorum, with the genteel artificiality of social convention upon which her disengaged women and questing girls ground their being for lack of any other substantive basis for identity. However it is also marked, on the other hand, by the irruption of a phantom in the drawing-room. Her ghost stories are peopled with spectres, *doppelgängers* and revenants, instances of the *unheimlich*, occult communication and ecstatically or terrifyingly permeable selves, which are, as she notes in her *Second Ghost Book* preface, 'partly personal, partly those of our time' (p.104), personifications of both personal and the larger cultural or historical traumas. Bowen's hauntings are nothing if not various. Many concern haunted houses, but these are more likely to be newly built villas, bourgeois weekend retreats, or bomb-threatened London terraces than the solitary castles of traditional Gothic. Bowen does not subscribe to the variety of modernism which deplores a modernity seen as reifying. Her phantoms thrive on, and colonize, a modern world perceived as fractured, dislocated, precarious.

The collection which contains most ghost stories is her *The Demon Lover and Other Stories*, written out of the dislocation and mass destruction of the war, during which, surreptitiously inhabiting her bomb-damaged house in an empty Regent's Park terrace, she wrote of existing 'illicitly, leading the existence of ghosts'.[4] Trafficking in the ephemeral outlines of the twentieth-century ghost story, the process becomes a vehicle for evoking what was most genuinely frightening in private and public life – what could not be hidden in the comforts of a domsetic heart itself is now revealed as ephemeral, liable to annihilation.

'Persons are as hauntable as places', writes Bowen in 1952, 'perhaps more so' (*AFT*, p.103). This has particular relevance to Bowen herself, who lived ambivalently between literary London and Oxford, and a post-independence Anglo-Irish remnant with its history of expropriation, mingled pride and guilt. Her life and work bring up questions of allegiance and doubleness. Her Anglo-Irishness expresses itself in her autobiographical writing as a matter of continual transit back and forth across the Irish Sea, a quasi-spectral form of bilocation between lives. For R.F. Foster, writing on Irish Protestants' attraction to the occult, her ghost stories, likewise, follow those of Maturin, Le Fanu, Stoker and Yeats in mirroring 'a sense of displacement, a loss of social and psychological integration'.[5] Yet this heritage of Irish Gothic is scarcely present in her ghost stories, as I will discuss in more detail below – I want here merely to point to Bowen's pervasive interest in the dark places of psychology, and its frequent troping as spectral in her ghost stories. Psychoanalysis is a form of science of the forbidden or unacceptable. Self-evidently, the concept of the unconscious dismantles personal autonomy and replaces it with a spectral series of drives, dreams and desires. In one of the most frequently quoted passages of her fiction, Bowen writes that 'each of us keeps, battened down inside himself, a sort of lunatic giant – impossible socially, but full-scale – and that it's the knockings and batterings we sometimes hear in each other that keeps our intercourse from utter banality'.[6] This 'lunatic giant' who crashes through social convention, is both a figure of the resurgence of the infantile impulses of the unconscious, and of all the 'farouche' qualities that threaten to dismantle the drawing-room in her work. It is also, in its 'knockings and batterings', a disruptive ghost making its presence felt, a trope for the blurred threshold where, in her fiction, psychology meets the apparently inexplicable agency of the supernatural. As she notes in her preface to the *Second Ghost Book*, 'our irrational, darker selves demand familiars' (*AFT*, p.102).

While considering the relevance of Irish Gothic to Bowen's supernatural, this chapter argues that Bowen's writing makes eerie capital of a set of real and fantasized contemporary connections in the earlier part of the twentieth century between the supernatural, innovative technologies of communication and the shared roots of psychology and the occult in these forms of 'communication' or 'proximity' between minds. Now the critics have begun to explore Bowen's modernism it is no longer such a surprise to register the fit between, on the one hand, the precise nature of Bowen's highly diverse and career-long interest in the supernatural as subject of fictional enquiry and, on the other, typically modernist concerns with the spectres of modernity. As Pamela Thurschwell writes, occult transmission 'can be doubly transgressive, disrupting both sense boundaries and traditional codes of behaviour and alliance'.[7] Bowen's

modern ghosts create phantasmic spaces in which intimate sexual, familial and national ties are reconfigured in ways which are very different to
the conventional patriarchal models of inheritance and community via
marriage and the nuclear family.

'Ghost stories are not easy to write', she tells us from the vantage
point of 1952, 'least easy now, for they involve more than they did' (AFT,
p.104). Bowen's ghost stories might be said to begin with 'The Shadowy
Third', originally published in 1923, cluster most thickly during the
'lucid abnormality' of the war years, culminating in The Demon Lover and
Other Stories (1945), and end with 'Hand in Glove', which belongs to the
dwindling trickle of short stories she wrote after the war. Her preface to
The Second Ghost Book is thus a summation of some thirty years of writing
about ghosts in the short story form.[8] However, it is difficult to demar-
cate Bowen's 'ghost stories', or to delimit and define them as a separate
category in isolation from the more general investment in the supernatural of her fiction as a whole. Victoria Glendinning in her preface to
Elizabeth Bowen's Irish Stories (which, oddly, excludes the Irish-set ghost story
'The Back Drawing-Room', discussed below) argues that the absence
of ghosts is the 'big divide' between Bowen's novels and short stories,
citing in support of this claim Bowen's own statement that she felt it
'unethical' to bring the supernatural into her novels, while it is frequently a factor in the short fiction.[9] While this is quite clearly a porous
distinction, given the dependence, to mention only one instance, of A
World of Love (1955) upon the dead Guy's continued uncanny influence
upon the Irish Big House Montefort, Glendinning is presumably – and
understandably – attempting to make a distinction between Bowen fictions that are indisputably ghost stories in the traditional sense (such as
the melodramatic 'Hand in Glove', in which a monstrous husband-
hunter is strangled by an eerily animated glove) and the more diffuse
hauntings and eerie irruptions of the past which are found in the novels.

However, Bowen's writing evokes so inimitably the effects of the dead
on the living, the inexplicable and unpoliceable traffic between consciousnesses, and she is so fascinated by between-states and various forms of psychological Zwischenwelt, whether adolescence, espionage or the unburied
dead of the blitz, that it is difficult to make any hard and fast distinction
between Bowen's 'ghost stories' and her work as a whole. Central to her talent as a writer of fiction is an investment in generic dislocation: a single

work at different times appears to be a thriller, a psychological novel, a genteel comedy of manners – or a ghost story, which, in Bowen's hands, can
contain elements of all of these, uncannily skewed by forms of 'enforced
return' which are at once spectral and psychological. With this caveat, the
remainder of this chapter will restrict its scope to those stories which most
readers of Bowen would agree on as identifiably 'ghost stories'.

'I do not make use of the supernatural as a get-out; it is inseparable
(whether or not it comes to the surface) from my sense of life', writes
Bowen in her preface to A Day in the Dark and Other Stories.[10] R.F. Foster has
influentially linked Bowen to a tradition of Anglo-Irish interest in the
occult. I want to suggest, however, that this inclusion of the supernatural
in one's 'sense of life' suggests Bowen's participation in a more generally
modernist interest in psychical researchers' debates about the possibility
of telepathy, hypnosis and survival after death. Bowen reflects the ways in
which, as Pamela Thurschwell writes, these debates 'contribute to wider
reconceptualisations of the border of individual consciousness and
merge together with new communication technologies such as the telephone and the telegraph, and the beginnings of psychoanalysis'.[11] In the
early twentieth century, psychical research was not yet divorced from
contemporary scientific thinking; the Society for Psychical Research had
been founded by credible scientists, journalists and politicians, and had
links with Bergson and Freud, while William James sponsored an
American association, also concerned with developing a science of the
supernatural.[12] Tele-technologies suggested that contemporary science
could annihilate distances between people, and hence newly dignified
the claims of more occult forms of communication. Talking to the dead
and talking on the phone both held out promises of previously unimaginable forms of contact and modes of propinquity.

Technology, with its enablement of fresh routes to perception, suggests
a new kind of supernatural, undermining old certainties, undermining
the pattern of the past and questioning the impermeability of the mem-
brane between life and death. The aftermath of the carnage of the Great
War contributed to a revival of spiritualism, which itself revived during
the Second World War. Thus various discourses – occult, literary, scientific, psychological and technological – converged to inaugurate shifting
models of the permeability and suggestibility of the individual's mind
and body. Bowen, writing of her own experience of the blitz as a form

of heightened, even hallucinatory collectivity, in the preface to her collection The Demon Lover, does so in images that marry technology, poros-
ity, bodilessness and the collective. The stories of the collection – many
of them ghost stories – are 'flying particles', 'disjected snapshots',
through which the 'high-voltage current of the general' passes.[13]

Victoria Glendinning reports that, church-going Anglican though
Bowen was, she also had a leaning towards less orthodox forms of interest in the paranormal, claiming to William Maxwell that she believed 'in
God and ghosts'.[14] In this she resembles many of her fellow-modernists,
some of whom, most famously Yeats, were professed occultists. Many
modernist notions of writing and influence have their sources in occult
or semi-occult notions of haunting and telepathy, ranging from the links
between modernist anthropology, primitivism and esoteric study, Yeats's
own 'dreaming back' in A Vision and Purgatory, and surrealism's automa-
tism, to Eliot's 'Tradition and the Individual Talent'. While Bowen was no
occult practitioner, she had close spiritualist friends. She knew and
admired Edith Somerville – who believed herself to collaborate still with
her writing partner 'Martin Ross', long after the latter's death – and once
attended, with Rosamund Lehmann, a conference of the College of
Psychic Studies, where, upon being asked to contribute, she spoke
(provocatively?) as 'a staunch member of the Church of England'.[15] An
unwritten section of her autobiography was to be on 'Witchcraft: a
Query: Is anything uncanny involved in the process of writing?'[16]
Bowen's answer to this is of course yes. Certainly, her fictional explorations of various extensions of consciousness relate to questions raised
by psychical researchers about what separates one mind from another,
and what separates the living from the dead. As she writes in The Little
Girls: 'Are not desires acts? One is where one would be. May we not,
therefore, frequent each other, without the body, not only in dreams?'[17]

Her ghost stories abound in tele-technological metaphor, in which
traditional boundaries separating one individual from another are over-
ridden, creating mysterious new forms of 'contact'. A disappointed visiting ghost-spotter in 'Foothold', hoping see the family ghost on his first
night, says 'it was like expecting a phone call' (CS, p.298). In 'The Cat
Jumps', a ghostly facility in interfering with electricity exposes a frightened house party as inherently 'lacking' during a discussion on relativity
(CS). In 'The Happy Autumn Fields' the excluded Henrietta's pain which

'like a scientific ray' penetrates solid matter is also transmitted through time to the sleeping or hallucinating Mary as a 'shock' (CS, p.675). This suggests the dissolving of materiality into the new early twentieth-century scientific categories of energy, field and radiation, in which a flux of force fields and particles in motion replaced the mechanical action of solid bodies, and struck a blow against the idea of a 'hard' universe.[18] In both new developments in telecommunications, quantum physics, electricity and the 'modern' ghost story, notions of mechanical solidity give way to visions of penetrability, and a borderless, accessible subject, potentially connected to others or to alien frequencies or forces. Some of these technologies are domestic, penetrating the previously sacrosanct walls of the home, and bulk so large in Bowen presumably because the modern ghost comes close up, and becomes itself intimate and domestic; others exercise a different kind of intimate relation.

Bowen's supernatural concerns have more often been read as dealing with ghosts considerably less 'modern' and more culturally specific than those of her *Second Ghost Book* preface. Heather Bryant Jordan is typical in linking Bowen's hallucinatory wartime ghost stories to both Irish locations and 'honouring the conventions of the Celtic tradition of the ghost story', yet this is a somewhat eccentric estimation of the stories of *Look at All Those Roses* (1941) and *The Demon Lover* (1945), with their largely English settings and contemporary concerns.[19] The ghosts that implicitly stand behind these collections, particularly the latter, are the London dead of the blitz, who, as *The Heat of the Day* has it, 'uncounted ... continued to move in shoals through the city day, pervading everything to be seen or heard or felt with their torn-off senses'.[20] One can, of course, make a case for Bowen's inclusion in the tradition of Irish Gothic, but her consciousness of that heritage is considerably less evident in her ghost stories than in her 1947 introduction to Sheridan Le Fanu's *Uncle Silas*, and in *Bowen's Court*, her 1942 history of her ancestral home and family from the Cromwellian plantations to the present day.[21] The reader is repeatedly assured that '[t]here is no ghost in the house', and, in the 1963 'Afterword', that '[t]he dead do not need to visit Bowen's Court rooms', but the spectral is in fact reiterated throughout the text, in a manner suggestive – in a way that her fiction is not – of the fantasy explorations of the fears and historical guilts of the Anglo-Irish in the supernatural tales of hauntings, spectral familiars and ancestral curses characteristic of Irish

Gothic (BC, p.451). Alongside the qualified admiration it evinces for the 'humanistic, classic and disciplined' qualities Bowen associates with the Big House, the family history reverberates with the haunting of the present by the weight of the past and traditions; it is in part a conversation with, and in part an attempt to make restitution for, her 'own' dead.

Bowen's Court is saturated with ghosts, beginning with 'the Apparition' (BC, p.39), the family term for the story of the first Bowen in Ireland, whose doppelgänger was said to have appeared to his Welsh wife as a mouldering corpse, while he was still living, though increasingly solitary and mentally unbalanced, on his newly appropriated lands in North Cork (pp.40–8). Bowen refrains from making much of this Puritan cautionary tale, but Neil Corcoran, among other critics, reads its prominent positioning at the beginning of her family history as giving it an emblematic status, implicitly figuring both the 'inherent wrong' (p.453) at the origin of Ascendancy power, and, when she relates the way in which the 'Apparition' revisited her own mentally ill father's mind, a Gothic family curse, in the shape of the 'Bowen doom' of hereditary insanity.[22] Family history dances an uneasy minuet with the supernatural, figured forth in Irish Gothic terms.

However, Bowen's Court also traces the migration of Gothic horror from a threatening outside world to the interior of the mind, from the castles of Maturin and Radcliffe to psychoanalytic theories of the self which draw on the rhetoric of the supernatural. Immediately after the transcription of two documents relating the circumstances of the 'Apparition', Bowen introduces a strikingly modern note, remarking that it 'would make a likely study for the psychiatrist … The hallucination must have been bred of two tormented, tormenting natures – his and hers. Could he have sent that terrible Doppelgänger had she not been awaiting it? Did he really haunt her, or did she haunt him? Who sent those "ghastly ghosts" that, in Ireland, troubled his bed?' (BC, p.48). Bowen's supernatural migrates from the traditional materials of eighteenth- and nineteenth-century literary Gothic – the 'antique manors, castles, graveyards, crossroads, yew walks, cloisters' she lists in her Second Ghost Book preface – to the twentieth-century conception of the 'modern ghost' lodged deep within the self as psychological projection, fear, desire and demand, anchored in the past but nonetheless forming the basis of subjectivity, as theorized by Freud and others. The modern self may, like the uncanny haunted houses of Gothic fiction, be pre-occupied.[23] Here, too, we see the emergence, from the 'official' discourse of dynastic historian, of the materials of the characteristic Bowen ghost story. It is situated in the hinterlands between the supernatural and the psychological – dispersed subjectivity, occult ways of imagining both cultural transmission and individual communication, the capacity for both buildings and minds to house ghosts, variously rehearsed as fantasies or fears of supernaturally enhanced intimacy.

If *Bowen's Court* conjures up the ghosts of the past, with Bowen resuscitating her ancestors – the author as necromancer – it is also traversed by a distinctly modern appreciation of psychological dislocation. The 'Apparition' becomes a hallucinatory insight into an unhappy marriage, in which the distance between 'two tormented, tormenting natures' is not only geographical. Family history can say no more than this, but *Bowen's Court's* inaugural ghost story offers documentation of a familial genesis for the phantom supernumerary third of 'The Shadowy Third', 'Pink May', 'The Apple Tree', 'The Cat Jumps' and 'Foothold'. In each story, ghosts intervene in, or are generated by, a marriage – which, as Maud Ellman shows, both depends on, and is violated by, this 'third presence' – and the supernatural traffic between permeable minds of 'The Back Drawing-Room' and 'The Happy Autumn Fields'.[24] In the 'Afterword', Bowen inscribes herself as another of these porous sensibilities, liable to be traversed by the other; 'sheer information', she writes, did not take her far in the writing of *Bowen's Court*, and she came to rely instead on 'what I do know but do not know how I know ... intuitions that I cannot challenge', communications from the 'extinct senses' of the ancestral dead which permeate the family house (BC, pp.451–2). Here the spectrality which is the legacy of the Gothic novel, the permeable, occulted, haunted Romantic psyche which pre-empts modern psychology, makes the mind a potentially supernatural site – this site in Bowen, almost all of whose ghosts are female, and appear to women, is also strongly gendered, allowing an exploration of the spectres that haunt female psychological terrain.[25] Gothic elements not only invade the mind when it is haunted by memories or obsessive thoughts, but these Gothic elements also structure the world of Bowen's ghost stories, with their insistent enactment of what she terms in the essay 'Out of a Book' the 'enforced return'.[26] This is both what revenants do – ghosts traditionally return to scenes of violence – and also closely resembles the ghostly tropology used by Freud to describe the obsessive recurrence of the repressed impulse or memory, which nonetheless returns, ghost-like, transformed, and makes itself felt in the conscious. Bowen's ghost stories, while at times archly derogatory of psychoanalysis, frequently beg a Freudian reading, her supernatural evoking an 'enforced return' of what is suppressed socially or repressed psychologically – while knowingly comprehending or exceeding this in their effect.

Thus, *Bowen's Court* aside, her brand of Gothic is less concerned with exploring the nightmare of Anglo-Irish history in sombre inheritance, dynastic legacy and the horrors of degeneration, than in relocating occult phenomena within the quotidian spaces of (chiefly) English modernity. Bowen's characters make their way through a middle-class world haunted by reminders of *unheimlich* social and psychological regions beyond their control. Spectral memories of dead inhabitants which haunt the rooms of the house meet the spectres of the contemporary psyche, as the uncanny inhabitants oversee and provoke themes of isolation, sexual betrayal, illicit desire, anxiety and imprisonment. 'The Back Drawing-Room' (1926) and 'The Happy Autumn Fields' (1944), though separated in time by almost two decades, provide fruitful points of entry into the matrix of tropes of which the Bowen ghost story is compounded. Both stories, unusually for Bowen's ghost tales, mediate between England and Ireland at convulsive historical moments. This is the Bowenesque version of 'dreaming back' – subjectivities envisioned as essentially permeable, subject to invasion or imprinting by an other, here specifically the encounter with another's memory.

'The Back Drawing-Room', one of Bowen's earliest ghost stories, embeds an Anglo-Irish story of dispossession, loss and exile within a modish framing narrative of fashionable London drawing-room hermeticism or spiritualism. Most of the attention has gone to this Irish story-within-a-story – a Pooterish English cyclist, stranded by a puncture, encounters a piteously weeping woman in an isolated Anglo-Irish Big House; he later discovers that this house had been burned down by republican forces two years earlier, its family, presumably including the distraught woman whose *doppelgänger* he saw, dispersed and spoken of as though dead – has had most of the critical attention. Maud Ellmann points out the significance of the undead spectral woman belonging to the 'obsolescent Protestant Ascendancy', arguing that Bowen was among those who regarded the Anglo-Irish, after the Actof Union, as 'living ghosts', condemned to extinction.[27] Neil Corcoran highlights the Irish Gothic elements that the 'The Back Drawing-Room' shares with Bowen's Court's originary 'Apparition', though here the Anglo-Irish dispossessors are themselves dispossessed as settlement becomes final siege, and the 'living' ghosthood (which wrong-foots a conventional ghost-story reading), similarly a matter of being in two places at the same time, here becomes emblematic of the ultimate loss of home territory, a 'panic-stricken displacement'.[28] The Anglo-Irish have lost status and home and now must haunt an unbounded world of social and political dissolution – a bleak, ghost-ridden afterlife. To deform the bruising final sentence of The Last September, in 'The Back Drawing-Room' the English ghost story 'opens hospitably' upon the cyclicities of Irish colonial history.

The framing narrative, however, inflects (or infects) the embedded Irish Gothic, as in Bowen's Court, with more overtly modernist concerns. Mrs Henneker, the captivating hostess of the esoteric group debating whether life after death is a matter of 'fitness' or 'tenacity', shrinks from mention of the 'vulgarised' spiritualist manifestations of 'table-rapping, gramophone horns, planchette' but vehemently insists on the 'survival of the soul' in a manner which has suggested to many readers that she is mourning a son lost in the war (CS, pp.210, 200). Initially somewhat ridiculous in her fervent advocacy of 'that finer intercourse, if you like, telepathic' (p.201) over mere 'verbal communication', and her Blavatskyian response to Ireland, the recounting of the encounter with the weeping living ghost with the 'drowning' expression, evokes from her an unexpected depth of response, not to the cyclist's alarm, but to the ghost woman's despair. Her emendation of his account, moving the emphasis from individual experience to 'the whole of a world … the quenching of a world in horror and destruction that happens with a violent death' (p.208), and the pointed and enigmatic silence with which she greets the conclusion of the story, suggests a form of sympathetic, even telepathic communion with both the weeping woman and the death-in-life of which the latter is emblematic.

'The Back Drawing-Room' uses the living ghost in the spectral Anglo-Irish back drawing-room – the English cyclist's stumbling upon someone else's unhealed memory – to haunt the drawing-room of the metropolis, and to figure the ineluctability of spectral returns, whether these are historical spectres not properly laid to rest or the Freudian recognition of the importance of the 'work' of individual mourning for the dead loved one. It also conceives of consciousness as a shared, occult category. In 'The Back Drawing-Room', a male raconteur is only a conduit between forms of female intersubjective contact. Much of the framing narrative is viewed from the perspective of a young woman infatuated by the older Mrs Henneker, and who, during the talk of telepathy between 'closely knit' souls, suggestively strokes a fold of the latter's dress. Written almost twenty years later, during the Second World War, 'The Happy Autumn Fields' presents another instance (this time unmediated) of inexplicable psychic contact between different times, with agreed boundaries (life and death, past and present, self and other) replaced by ideas of uncanny permeability and relatedness between women. Bowen said in a 1950 BBC radio interview that she aimed in her war stories 'to give the effect of fortuity, of a smashed-up pattern with its fragments impacting on one another, drifting and cracking'. She divides this more than usually formally disjunctive story between an eerily all-encompassing sisterly love threatened by the onset of sexual passion, set on a nineteenth-century estate in Ireland, and the bomb-damaged London house where a woman dreams or hallucinates the Victorian story of Sarah and her sister Henrietta (both, incidentally, common Bowen family names, thereby supporting the Irish hypothesis).[29] Mary, alienated from her own life and the lover towards whom she feels only indifference, and unconcerned at the danger of the falling bombs, is wholly given over to the distant past in which she finds an intensity and plenitude missing from the present: 'The source, the sap must have dried up ... So much flowed through people; so little flows through us. All we can do is imitate love or sorrow' (CS, pp.683–4). The past she has 'unburied' in the ruins of her house in the classically Gothic form of a box of old letters brings her into uncanny contact with a moment of threat to an idyllic sisterly symbiosis, in the shape of Sarah's dawning feeling for a neighbouring landowner. This disinterred story of extreme, perhaps more than merely sibling, identification ends in a putatively supernatural moment. It seems that the suitor, whose horse inexplicably throws him before he can make his declaration, has been wished to his death by the despairing younger sister Henrietta, who has earlier declared that 'whatever tries to come between me and Sarah becomes nothing' (p.683).

What appears to have made the horse shy so unaccountably is the weird force of something between 'desire' and 'identification' of women for and with one another. Patricia Coughlan writes that women are bound up together in Bowen's writing with 'an exceptional and even dis-maying intimacy'.[30] The notions of action at a distance and communica-tion in spiritualism are, as Pamela Thurschwell points out, ways of think-ing about intimacy which enter the accounts of desire and identification offered by Freud and others. In particular, Ferenczi's accounts of psychic and physical invasion, and psychoanalytic transference, have been read as the occluded ghost story of psychoanalysis.[31] Adam Phillips, discussing the relationship between psychoanalysis and the psychical, argues that 'sexuality and the unconscious were the new, scientifically prestigious words for the occult, of that which is beyond our capacity for knowl-edge, for the weird, unaccountable effects people have on each other'.[32] In Bowen, desire has a curiously unstable, even spectral, quality, seeming to be imagined – like her Jamesian intersubjective notions of conscious-ness – as not always securely located in individuals. Rather, it is repre-sented as a labile form of energy in itself, for which persons are mere conductors, and to which others of either sex are helplessly attracted. Neither the boundaries between 'appropriate' and illicit sexualities, nor the boundaries between life and death, always tenuous in Bowen's work, can properly oppose the volatile boundary-crossing force of desire, and Patricia Coughlan points out that, in Bowen's work, desire resembles what Sedgwick calls 'an unpredictably powerful solvent of stable identi-ties'.[33] 'Intimacy between people, like occult phenomena, is fundamen-tally bewildering.'[34] Desire itself is occult in Bowen, and the nature of that bewildering 'possession' in her ghost stories – with Le Fanu's lesbian vampire tale 'Carmilla' a frequent textual ghost – often devalues marital plots and heterosexual desire at the expense of women's desire for, or identification with, their own sex. Illicit desire returns as uncanny.

Bowen's work has been read as constitutively lesbian by Patricia Juliana Smith and others, but Maud Ellmann is, I think, right in her assertion that 'outing the heroine is not the point'.[35] However, as Roger Luckhurst notes, the psychical bond, particularly when it involved conventionally 'suscep-tible' female nerves, had sexual valences.[36] A blurring of the lines between same-sex affinity and telepathic connection or spiritual contact is integral to women modernists. For example Radclyffe Hall's extensive spiritualist contact with a dead lover via a medium culminated in a notorious libel trial in 1920. Likewise Hilda Doolittle and her partner Bryher, members of the Society for Psychical Research, received séance messages from dead

RAF pilots and Freud, and, better known to Bowen, Somerville and Ross, conceived of their partnership in explicitly telepathic terms.[37] This perception of common ground between telepathic connection and visionary powers, therefore, and subversive desire, is evident in 'The Happy Autumn Fields', a ghost story organized around notions of uncanny touch and telepathic closeness between women – both that of the sisters Sarah and Henrietta, and Mary's identification with Sarah across time – in which female–female desire is constructed as occult, 'morbid stuff', as the laconic Travis terms it (CS, p.684). Sarah and Henrietta's obsessive mutual love is evoked in terms of a vocabulary of proximity, both mundane and supernatural – of having shared a womb, now sharing a bed and being next to one another at table, as well as the family assumption that 'they knew each other's minds', a closeness culminating in Henrietta's implacable pledge that '[y]ou and I will stay as we are ... then nothing can touch one without touching the other' (pp.681, 672).

Henrietta's pain at her exclusion by the lovers 'penetrates' Sarah and also, across time and space, communicates itself to the finder of the 'dangerous box' of letters, furious at her lover's 'unmeaning' presence as part of the 'conspiracy to keep her from the beloved two', whose disinterred photograph she suggestively covers with her body (p.677). In 'The Happy Autumn Fields' this passionate identification possibly kills a man, who represents a 'fall' outside of the sisters' dyad, and expels the wartime telepath from what her lover calls 'her normal senses' (p.677). Finally, at the moment when Henrietta, in Victorian Ireland, makes her declaration, this literally brings down the house, by causing the final 'dissolution' of the bombed London terrace. The ghost story, and the space of psychical communication, offers Bowen a way of writing about forms of female–female identification and desire without subscribing to a reductively sexological vocabulary of sexual designation, and opens up a space in which occult contacts between women are dominant.

Bowen of course, as well as her conscious sense of her Irish Gothic heritage, and her adaptation of the Jamesian psychological ghost story (her 'Reduced' is clearly a response to his *The Turn of the Screw*) is descended as a writer of ghost stories from those Victorian women ghost story writers who wrote for *Belgravia* and *Cornhill* and used supernatural visitations to expose the secrets of the guilty house, or the private shames of a marriage, not all of them issues of illicit desire.[38] In these stories, the supernatural became increasingly domestic and intimate, the vaults and castles of the Gothic novel contracting to the bounded spaces of urban or suburban petit bourgeois homes. Not all of Bowen's haunted houses are, like Bowen's Court and Kilbarran in 'The Back Drawing-Room', haunted by the impersonal forces of history: there is a preponderance of weekend retreats and suburban villas, traversed by spectres of female alienation and entrapment, among Bowen's most unnervingly haunted houses. They provide the most obvious instances of Bowen's investment in a version of female Gothic in which the domestic hearth is re-envisioned as unheimlich, an uncanny space inhabited by unhappy women and traversed by the supernatural. Bowen's haunted houses continually re-present that moment when all that is associated with the house (the heimlich) becomes the unheimlich, the crucial moment of defamiliarization to which all Gothic returns. This is associated by Freud with 'what is known of old and long familiar' and also 'ought to have remained secret and hidden but has come to light'.[39] Young Mrs Wing in 'The Apple Tree' produces unheimlich effects in the 'unaspiring comfortable sobriety' of her marital home: her husband moves through the haunted library 'as though in a quite unfamiliar room [seeming] to have no sense of space' (CS, p.464).

'Attractive Modern Homes' depicts a housewife unnerved by an undescribed vision of 'something funny' after a move to a raw new house in a 'heartless' half-built suburb, where 'the gored earth round the buildings looked unfriendly with pain', and where her domestic life, ungirded by habit, is revealed as an empty observance of forms, 'like you see in advertisements' (CS, pp.521–2, 526). Here Mrs Watson, deposited there by her husband's 'querulously awaited' promotion (p.522), is herself a ghost, 'semi-detached' from her unknown neighbours and the countryside which 'unknown, edged the estate with savageness': 'Now no one cared any more whether she existed; she came to ask, without words, if she did exist' (p.524). The intimation of 'a ghost's persistent aliveness' (p.525) metaphorizes her death-in-life. Bowen re-visions the cavernous spaces of the Gothic novel as progressively more intimate and petit bourgeois. Ghost stories enact the gender politics of the home, as husbands and wives were brought uncomfortably together in increasingly small, servantless houses.

'The Cat Jumps', however, constitutes Bowen's fullest approximation of domestic Gothic horror, as well as a recognition of the shared roots of the psychoanalytical and the occult. The reader may be reminded of one of the 'abstract or innocent conceptual jokes' from *Jokes and their Relation to the Unconscious*, about a man supremely confident of his rational faculties: 'Not only did he disbelieve in ghosts; he was not even frightened of them'.[40] It concerns a house-warming at Rose Hill, a 'cheerful weekend house' notorious from press coverage of the Bentley murder committed in it, and described in terms explicitly Gothic in their evocation of the *unheimlich*; '[o]n the domestic scene too many eyes had burnt the impress of their horror' (p.362). Against these 'dreadful associations' are posed the 'bright, shadowless, thoroughly disinfected minds' of the Wrights, who 'read their murders only in scientific books' (p.362), who 'set out to expel, live out, live down, almost (had the word existed in their vocabularies) to "lay" the Bentleys' (p.363). Their house-warming is a frightened failure: the electricity fails, the smell of the dead woman's perfume wafts, their admirably rational friends become nervy. All the psychology and sexology of Harold's reference library – 'Krafft-Ebing, Freud, Forel, Weiniger, and the heterosexual volume of Havelock Ellis' (p.366) – proves ineffective against the haunting, which hovers undecidably between auto-suggestion or group hysteria, and the supernatural. Jocelyn Wright and her husband Harold appear near the end of the story to be possessed by the Bentleys: he 'has assumed the entire burden of Harold Bentley', seeing his wife as lying 'like a great cat, always, over the mouth of his life' (p.369), while Jocelyn 'given up to terror', sees in her husband's desire to buy the house an intimation of his hatred of her. The story ends in farce – everyone barricaded behind bedroom doors – but Jocelyn's Gothic moment of terror, an insight into what the story suggests is an insight into a form of living death, a death of the heart – 'if the spirit, dismembered in agony, dies before the body ... in the whole knowledge of its dissolution, drags from chamber to chamber' (p.368) – offers an unnerving insight into the domestic arena re-envisaged as a place of violent death.

Bowen concludes her *Second Ghost Book* preface with that acknowledgement that in seeing ghosts, 'each of us has exposed our susceptibilities, which are partly personal, partly those of our time' (AFT, p.104). This chapter has argued that her ghost stories are less about the irruption of the pre-modern than a supernaturalization of the paradoxically intimate relations generated by the increased speed of communications and the passage of information, and the psychoanalytic spectres of the modern psyche. It is upon precisely the 'hesitation' on a modernist hinterland between the occult, psychology and tele-technology that Bowen's 'modern ghosts' are best understood. Her interest in the supernatural may be seen as deriving in part from the haunting ambiguities of her Anglo-Irish background, and her experience of the altered reality of life under the mass destruction of the blitz, though her ancestors and the dead of the blitz appear only in highly displaced ways in her ghost stories. Psychologically knowing, her supernatural affirms, even while it exceeds, psychoanalytic insight into the 'lunatic giant' within. It also affirms that the individual is traversed, even terrorized, by an excess of feeling, by the impossibility of desire, which returns as a ghost; the supernatural is a figure for the forms of dissolution and dislocation which underlie and afflict the official fiction of coherent identity. However, the ghost story has always offered an apparatus for examining a wide spectrum of anxieties. In Bowen's hands, it allows for an exploration of the blurred boundary between social convention and the 'other world' that lies hidden in the private frustrations and cruelties of marriage, and in particular for the playing out of powerful dramas of gender, whereby ghostly women provide 'company', desired or dreaded, for her protagonists, substituting various forms of female contact for the marriage plot. As she concludes her *Second Ghost Book* preface, as a ghost-story writer she is among the 'twentieth-century haunters of the haunted' (*AFT*, p.104).

NOTES

1. Preface to *The Second Ghost Book*, edited by Cynthia Asquith, 1952, in Elizabeth Bowen, *Afterthought: Pieces About Writing* (London: Longmans, Green and Co., 1962), pp.101–4 (p.101), hereafter referred to in the text as *AFT*.
2. Julia Briggs, *Night Visitors* (London: Faber & Faber, 1977), p.180.
3. Elizabeth Bowen, *Collected Stories*, intro. Angus Wilson (London: Jonathan Cape, 1980), p.512, hereafter referred to in the text as *CS*.
4. 'London, 1940', quoted in Victoria Glendinning, *Elizabeth Bowen: Portrait of a Writer* (London: Weidenfeld and Nicolson, 1977), p.130.
5. R.F. Foster, 'Protestant Magic: W.B. Yeats and the Spell of Irish History', in *Paddy and Mr Punch* (Harmondsworth: Penguin, 1993), pp. 212–32 (p.220).
6. Elizabeth Bowen, *The Death of the Heart* (1938) (Harmondsworth: Penguin, 1962), p.310, hereafter referred to in the text as *DH*.
7. Pamela Thurschwell, *Literature, Technology and Magical Thinking, 1800–1920* (Cambridge: Cambridge University Press, 2001), p.2.
8. Preface to *The Demon Lover*, in *The Mulberry Tree: Writings of Elizabeth Bowen*, ed. Hermione Lee (London: Virago, 1986), pp.94–9 (p.95).
9. Elizabeth Bowen, *Elizabeth Bowen's Irish Stories*, intro. Victoria Glendinning (Dublin: Poolbeg, 1978), p.7.

10. Elizabeth Bowen, *A Day in the Dark and Other Stories* (London: Jonathan Cape, 1965), p.9.

11. Thurschwell, *Literature, Technology and Magical Thinking*, p.1.

12. See Tim Armstrong, *Modernism: A Cultural History* (Cambridge: Polity, 2005), p.123.

13. Preface to *The Demon Lover*, in *The Mulberry Tree*, pp.95, 99.

14. Glendinning, *Elizabeth Bowen*, p.137.

15. Ibid., p.137.

16. Ibid., p.236.

17. Elizabeth Bowen, *The Little Girls* (London: Vintage, 1999), pp.235–6.

18. Armstrong, *Modernism*, pp.122ff.

19. Heather Bryant Jordan, *How Will the Heart Endure? Elizabeth Bowen and the Landscape* of War (Ann Arbor, MI: University of Michigan Press, 1992), p.130.

20. Elizabeth Bowen, *The Heat of the Day* (London: Jonathan Cape, 1949), pp.86–7.

21. Elizabeth Bowen, *Bowen's Court* (New York: Ecco Press, 1964 [1942]), hereafter referred to in the text as BC; and preface to *Uncle Silas*, in *The Mulberry Tree*, pp.100–47.

22. Neil Corcoran, *Elizabeth Bowen: The Enforced Return* (Oxford: Oxford University Press, 2004), pp.29–30.

23. See Nicola Brown *et al.*, 'Introduction', in *The Victorian Supernatural*, ed. Nicola Brown, Carolyn Burdett and Pamela Thurschwell (Cambridge: Cambridge University Press, 2004), pp.10–11.

24. Maud Ellmann, *Elizabeth Bowen: The Shadow Across the Page* (Edinburgh: Edinburgh University Press, 2003), pp.86.

25. See Terry Castle, *The Female Thermometer: Eighteenth-Century Culture and the Invention of the Uncanny* (Oxford: Oxford University Press, 1995).

26. Elizabeth Bowen, 'Out of a Book' (1946), in *The Mulberry Tree*, pp.48–53.

27. Ellmann, *Elizabeth Bowen*, p.15.

28. Corcoran, *Elizabeth Bowen*, pp.33–4.

29. Quoted in R.F. Foster, 'The Irishness of Elizabeth Bowen', in *Paddy and Mr Punch*, pp.102–22 (p.103).

30. Patricia Coughlan, 'Women and Desire in the Work of Elizabeth Bowen', in *Sex, Nation and Dissent in Irish Writing*, ed. Eibhear Walshe (Cork: Cork University Press, 1997), pp.103–34 (p.104).

31. Thurschwell, *Literature, Technology and Magical Thinking*, pp.115ff.

32. Adam Phillips, *Terrors and Experts* (London: Faber & Faber, 1995), p.19.

33. Eve Kosofsky Sedgwick, *Epistemology of the Closet* (Harmondsworth: Penguin, 1994), p.8, quoted in Coughlan, 'Women and Desire'.

34. Phillips, *Terrors and Experts*, p.20.

35. Ellmann, *Elizabeth Bowen*, p.70.

36. Roger Luckhurst, *The Invention of Telepathy, 1890–1901* (Oxford: Oxford University Press, 2002), pp.225ff.

37. Gifford Lewis, *Somerville and Ross: The World of the Irish RM* (Harmondsworth: Penguin, 1995), p.191.

38. See Eve M. Lynch, 'Spectral Politics: The Victorian Ghost Story and the Domestic Servant', in *The Victorian Supernatural*, ed. Brown, Burdett and Thurschwell, pp.67–86.

39. Sigmund Freud, 'The Uncanny', in *The Standard Edition of the Complete Psychological Works of Sigmund Freud*, trans. and ed. James Strachey (London: Hogarth Press, 1955), vol.17, pp.219 (pp.220, 225).

40. Sigmund Freud, *Jokes and their Relation to the Unconscious*, Pelican Freud Library, trans. James Strachey, ed. Angela Richards (Harmondsworth: Penguin, 1976), vol.4, pp.60–1.

CHAPTER SEVEN

'A Time for Hard Writers'

EIBHEAR WALSHE

This chapter deals with that phase of Bowen's career where her centrality within English literary culture in the 1930s and 1940s was confirmed by the critical and popular success of *The House in Paris* (1935), *The Death of the Heart* (1938) and *The Heat of the Day* (1949). Part of that success came from Bowen's increasing confidence in her use of the modernist novel, and her willingness to extend and test her narrative forms, particularly in *The Heat of the Day*. There was also a sense that Bowen caught the imaginative *zeitgeist* of the late 1930s and of the Second World War. In 1941, Ivy Compton Burnett wrote of Bowen that this was 'A time for hard writers and here is one'.[1] These three novels mark Bowen's fictive depiction of the personal within history and the intrusion of history into the personal, and this required 'hard' or skilled writing. In particular, her experience of living in London during the Second World War provided an imaginative atmosphere which enabled and stimulated her as a writer. In her own words:

> During the war I lived, both as a civilian and as a writer, with every pore open ... arguably, writers are always slightly abnormal people: certainly in so-called 'normal' times my sense of the abnormal has been very acute. In war, this feeling of slight differentiation was suspended: I felt one with and just like, everyone else ... We all lived in a state of lucid abnormality.[2]

In this chapter I examine these novels in terms of that distinctive and highly individualized imaginative texture of Bowen's writing, this lucid abnormality.

Each of these three novels reflects Bowen's sense of the increasingly tenuous relation between interior selfhood and societal modes of identity, particularly *The House in Paris*. In her essay on 'English Novelists', Bowen wrote that the primary concern of the European novel, as opposed to the English novel, was 'love's inherent principles of disorder and pain'.[3] To some degree, *The House in Paris* is her most 'European' novel, where the central love affair between the English upper-middle-class Karen Michaelis and Anglo-French-Jewish Max Eberhert has ramifications of disorder and pain for two generations. This novel marks Bowen's maturity and accomplished ease and confidence as a novelist, and it is not surprising that she wrote that 'I don't feel I in any way invented, or, as it were, devised *The House in Paris*', which I suppose really is the ideal feeling to have about a book.[4]

Bowen structures the novel in three episodes, the opening and closing section called 'The Present' set around an afternoon in a house in Paris and the middle section called 'The Past', where all the hidden secrets of the present are uncovered. The novel begins with the arrival of the motherless child Henrietta at the house of Mme Fisher and her daughter Naomi in Paris. Her father has sent her to stay with her grandmother in the south of France and Henrietta must spend the day in Mme Fisher's house, waiting for her train. By an unfortunate coincidence, another child, Leopold, is already there, waiting to meet the mother he has never seen. In flashback, we learn that the novel's heroine, Leopold's mother, Karen Michelis, daughter of an upper-middle-class English family, stayed in this house when in Paris when she was 18 and there she befriended Naomi Fisher. Naomi and her fiancé, Max Eberhart, visit Karen in London, and although Karen is engaged to Ray Forrister, she and Max fall in love and have a short, intense affair.

That affair is, partly, Karen's reaction against her family's conservatism and fear of change and outsiderness. 'She found she had come to hope everything of change ... In her parents world, change looked like catastrophe, a thing to put a good face on: change meant nothing but loss. To alter was to decline. "Poor So-and-so is so changed." You lived to govern the future, bending events your way. If change did break in, you bowed and accepted it.'[5] Max and Karen's affair is at the centre of the novel and is explored in the central section of the novel, outlining the profound consequences for all of the other characters. 'Karen, walking by Max, felt more isolated with him, more cut off from her own country than if they had been in Peru. You feel most foreign when you no longer belong where you did' (HP, p.167). Part of Karen's exhilaration is her sense that she is straying outside her safe, upper-middle-class, resolutely liberal English home and Max's foreignness, his Jewishness, that sets him apart even further. Speaking of her family, she muses, 'They keep me away from everything that has power: they would be frightened of art if I painted really well.' (HP, p.171). When Karen returns home from a meeting with Max, her mother warns her against him in terms that reveals her xenophobia and anti-Semitism. 'I do not like saying this, Karen', said Mrs Michaelis, 'but you have behaved like an infatuated woman, an "easy" woman and he is a very astute man. No Jew is unastute. Apart from being more beautiful and more ... more possible than Naomi, he can see for himself that you are very much wealthier' (HP, pp.188, 189).[6]

There is a sense of despair, of doom, in the connection between Max and Karen. When he returns to Paris to break with his fiancée, Naomi Fisher, he tells Naomi, 'what she (Karen) and I are ... is outside life; we shall fail; we cannot live what we are' (HP, p.194). Mme Fisher revenges herself by poisoning Max's mind and goading him into despair, and he kills himself in her drawing-room. Karen later marries Ray but has Leopold, her son by Max, adopted by a childless couple in Italy. Bowen builds the narrative tension on the anticipated reunion of Karen with her son Leopold in Mme Fisher's house in Paris, and the abrupt, agonizing deferral of that reunion.

Bowen's most characteristic trait as a novelist is her uncanny ability to represent dispossession, apartness, un-belonging, and the novel's other theme, apart from the disorders of love, is childhood dispossession. In Neil Corcoran's words, 'The world becomes a place into which you can never comfortably fit, a place, in which, because you are permanently missing something, you are also missing yourself'.[7] The underlying drive of The House in Paris, as in so many Bowen narratives, is the search by a child for a mother. The child, Leopold, breaks down on hearing the phrase, 'Your mother is not coming today'. Corcoran considers 'The novel's most concentrated expression of the psychological and emotional wounding that is parentlessness'.[8] Bowen's representation of the scenes between the two children, Leopold and Henrietta, stranded in the house in Paris, dramatizes the consequences of this wounding for the unsupervised children. 'With no banal reassuring grown-ups present, with grown-up intervention taken away, there is no limit to the terror strange children feel of each other, a terror life obscures but never ceases to justify. There is no end to the violations committed by children on children, quietly talking alone' (HP, p.25). Yet Bowen does manage to achieve a kind of empathy between these two disposed children. With the traumatic announcement, 'Your mother is not coming; she cannot come' (HP, p.65) a kind of emotional connection is tentatively established between the two children, suddenly aware of their shared fate as abandoned and parentless.

> When she could not speak, Leopold turned round facing the mantel-piece and suddenly ground his forehead against the marble ... Leopold's solitary despair made Henrietta no more than the walls or table. This was not contempt for her presence, no one was there. Being not there disembodied, her so she fearlessly crossed the parquet to stand beside him ... An angel stood up inside her with its hands to its lips and Henrietta did not attempt to speak. (HP, p.208–10)

The novel ends with a reunion, not of mother and son, but rather of son and new father when Ray, Karen's husband, calls at the Fisher house and brings Leopold away to meet Karen for the first time. Unexpectedly, Leopold finds a father when he had been expecting and longing for a mother, 'Their immaterial closeness up to each other, the silence after Leopold had turned around, made their sudden common demand for an understanding tower outside this afternoon and this room' (HP, p.237). The sense of exhilaration, of sudden belonging, makes the ending of The House in Paris an unexpectedly triumphant novel for Bowen. As Neil Corcoran points out, 'in The House of Paris the subjected or subjugated child insists on his release'.[9] The novel closes with Ray's recognition of Leopold as his son, 'Ray had not seen Karen's child in bright light before; now he saw light strike the dilated pupils of Leopold's eyes. Egoism and panic, knowing mistrust of what was to be, died in Ray as he waited beside Leopold for their taxi to come: the child commanded tonight, I have acted on his scale' (HP, p.269).

The theme of parentlessness and of emotional displacement is central to her next novel, The Death of the Heart, published in 1938 and perhaps Bowen's greatest commercial success, a Book Club choice that sold well and made her most money, but, ironically, the one she liked least. Hermione Lee comments that, 'Like *The House in Paris*, this is the story of an education', and goes on to argue that the novel 'ironically exposes the inauthenticity of the English Middle-Class'.[10] Of the three novels considered in this chapter, this is Bowen's most intensive consideration of the private world and one where adolescent displacement is most clearly at the centre of the narrative focus. In the first section of the novel, wealthy young couple Thomas and Anna Quayne, living in Regent's Park, accept the care of Thomas's orphaned half-sister Portia, 16 years old and the child of an illicit affair and late remarriage by Thomas's father. In Hermione Lee's words, 'Portia has invaded a house which is profoundly unconvivial'.[11] Anna resents Portia's presence in her home, and in turn, Portia is clear-eyed about her unwanted status and her emotional marginality within her family. As Portia realizes,

> They were cruel to my father and mother, but the thing must have started even before that ... my father often used to explain to me that people did not live the way we did ... he was quite certain ordinary life went on – yes, that was why I was sent to Thomas and Anna. But I see now that it does not: if he and I met again I should tell him that there is no ordinary life.[12]

The love interest for Portia is introduced when Eddie, Anna's young, unstable protégé, becomes the object of Portia's infatuation and, at the same time, Anna reads Portia's diary. Portia's counterpart in alienation and loneliness is Major Brutt, a casual acquaintance of Anna's, a man out of his time, stranded and lonely, who calls regularly to this profoundly unconvivial house in Regent's Park in the belief that he is welcome and a valued friend. In the second section of the novel, Portia is sent away from London to stay with Anna's former governess in the seaside town of Seale. When Eddie comes to visit Portia, he betrays her with another girl, Daphne.

> The jumping light from Dickie's lighter showed the canyon below their row of knees ... The light, with malicious accuracy, ran around a rim of cuff, a steel bangle, and made a thumbnail flash. Not deep enough in the cleft between their fauteuils, Eddie and Daphne, were, with emphasis, holding hands. Eddie's fingers kept up a kneading movement, her thumb alertly twitched at the joint. (DH, p.195)

Finally, in the third section called 'The Devil', Portia returns to London where she discovers that Anna has read her diary and is in league with Eddie, betraying her secrets and destroying her innocence. Portia confronts Anna's friend, the writer St Quentin, who has been discussing her diary with Anna.

> 'First you said you felt sure I kept a diary, then you told me I mustn't, then you asked me where it was, then you pretended to be surprised when you knew there was one, after that you called me an unkind spy, now you say I love everyone too much. I see now you knew about my diary ... I suppose Anne found it and told you she did?' St Quentin glanced at Portia from the tail of his eye. 'I don't come out of this well', he said. (DH, p.250)

As a result, Portia runs away from her brother's house to Major Brutt's hotel and offers to marry him as an escape from her lonely and betrayed state, but he refuses. Anna and Thomas track her down and send the maid, Machett, to bring her back again. As Anna and Thomas wait for her, Anna muses, 'She and I are hardly the same sex. Though she and I may wish to make a new start, we hardly shall, I'm afraid I shall always insult her; and she will always persecute me' (DH, p.312, 313).

This is Bowen's last use of the voice of the omniscient narrator in her story of a necessary education in duplicity and emotional instability which is the adult human condition. Maud Ellmann comments that 'It is Portia's duty to lose her innocence in order to renounce the wilderness and to come to terms with the world, the flesh and the devil'.[13] Portia, like Eva Trout, is an outsider to social order and identity, emotionally derelict and unwanted, but she is never a victim and learns to fight and to hurt. She tells Major Brutt, her only ally,

> You are the other person that Anna laughs at ... she says you are quite pathetic. She laughed at your carnations being the wrong colour, and then gave them to me. And Thomas always thinks you must be after something. Whatever you do, even send me a puzzle, he thinks that more, and she laughs more. They groan at each other when you have gone away. You and I are the same. (DH, p.288)

Yet the novel is not simply about the tragedy of the loss of innocence and emotional naïvety, and Bowen felt it had been misinterpreted in this way. Maud Ellmann sees that 'Recovering emotion in another place could be described as the prime motor of The Death of the Heart'.[14] Neil Corcoran describes Portia as 'the victim who refuses the role' and argues that the novel is 'more the tragedy of Major Brutt than ... Portia'.[15] In the end, innocence must be lost, and Portia's unravelling of the social structures and pretences around her must stop if she is to survive. As St Quentin describes it: 'I swear that each of us keeps, battened down inside himself, a sort of lunatic giant – impossible socially, but full-scale – and that it's the knockings and batterings we sometimes hear in each other that keeps our intercourse from utter banality. Portia hears them all the time, in fact she hears nothing else' (DH, p.310).

Bowen's next novel, The Heat of the Day, was published nearly ten years later and is her most sustained fictive reflection of her experiences of the Second World War. War made Bowen's writing even harder, in the sense that she extended the scope of her narrative. Times of violence were also times of intense creativity for Bowen, as witnessed by her Irish War of Independence novel, The Last September. When war broke out in 1939, Bowen was living with her husband in London, in Clarence Terrace, and she stayed there for as long as she was able, volunteering as an Air Raid Warden. Their home was first bombed in 1941, but they remained there until the house was seriously damaged in 1944. Between the publication of The Death of the Heart and The Heat of the Day, Bowen produced two short story collections, Look At All Those Roses in 1941 and then The Demon Lover and Other Stories in 1945. She also contributed an essay on 'English Novelists in 1942' to a general patriotic series called Impressions of English Literature in which she wrote: 'We lose much, if we ignore, or honour in name only, so living a part of the English heritage. And now, when the English spirit stands at its full height, to do so now would be a double loss ... It is natural to want our writers beside us as we face this new phase of human experience' (EN, p.7).

Out of this unsettled, abnormal wartime came a flood of writing about Ireland, Bowen's Court in 1942 and Seven Winters in 1943 and, in addition, many of her wartime stories, such as 'The Happy Autumn Fields' in 1945, had an identifiably Irish setting. In all of these Irish writings, Bowen looked homewards to North Cork as a place of stability and loyalty in an endangered and uncertain world and her vision of Anglo-Ireland becomes her talisman, her source of imaginative power and stability in war-disordered London. However this was never a simple process for Bowen. The tensions of being Anglo-Irish at a time when Britain was at war while Ireland remained neutral accentuated her ambivalent attitude towards Ireland. In the words of Heather Bryant Jordan, 'Unable to abandon her colonial training, Bowen found herself in the midst of a battle with institutions that echoed her own skirmishes with herself'.[16]

War led her back to Ireland in another way. In his essay called 'The Irishness of Elizabeth Bowen', Roy Foster details her confidential reporting on the political climate in Ireland for the Ministry of Information in London at the outbreak of the Second World War. Bowen was paid for this work but kept it secret from her Irish connections and friends, and this was, retrospectively, seen as 'spying' in some quarters in Ireland.[17] Clair Wills argues that,

> While 'Espionage' is too strong as well as too narrow a term for what Bowen called her 'activities' in Ireland, they did involve sending secret reports to the Ministry of Information and meetings at the Dominions and the War Office, conveying her sense of the climate of opinion: taking the temperature amongst writers and intellectuals in Dublin, and amongst country people near her home in County Cork ... But it was principally a response to the catastrophic situation for Britain following the fall of France. The stakes could not have seemed higher and the sympathies and loyalties of Allied supporters in Ireland became unbearably stretched.[18]

In these reports, Bowen attempted to defend the Irish decision to remain neutral, but in terms that betray her own clear allegiances. In a report on 9 November 1940 she makes the remark that 'The childishness and obtuseness of this country cannot fail to be irritating to the English mind', but did go on to say,

> It may be felt in England that Ireland is making a fetish of her neutrality. But this assertion of her neutrality is Eire's first free self-assertion: As such alone, it would mean a great deal to her. Eire (and I think rightly) sees her neutrality as positive, not merely negative. She has invested her self respect in it. If the Anglo-Irish would merge their interest with Eire's, they could make, – from

the point of view of England – a very much more solid and possible Eire in which to deal.[19]

After her death, the revelation that she had written these confidential reports did much damage to her name and reputation in Ireland, particularly in North Cork.

This ambivalence was also at the heart of her wartime fictions. At times of violence, Bowen used her learning and her sharp critical intelligence to locate solidity, but her literary imagination was moved by a contradictory impulse to explode permanence. Her underlying desire is to present a sinister threat of extinction lurking somewhere out there in the North Cork landscape. Her fiction reveals a darker version of her anxiously Utopian vision of the fields around Farrahy presented in her memoirs and essays. Roy Forster comments,

> the permanence that Bowen sought, in writing about her Irish past (while the world exploded at war all around her), required an exploration of memory – the only place where, as Proust had taught, permanence resides. A recognised landscape would take her there: that sheltered Farrahy landscape from where, she wrote, 'personal pain evaporates, as history evaporates'.[20]

Writing memoir and personal history were a refuge for Bowen in wartime, but came at a cost. As Heather Jordan comments, 'Bowen's most successful Irish stories undertake to transfer the feeling of war to the neutral country'.[21] To compensate, Bowen's critical writings of the early 1940s show her at her most determinedly optimistic. The best example of this kind of writing comes with her 1940 essay 'The Big House', first published by her friend and lover, Sean O'Faolain, in his pluralist journal, *The Bell*. O'Faolain founded this magazine to counterbalance the oppressive cultural insularity and xenophobia of Ireland in the 1930s and 1940s, and he invited Bowen to speak up, as it were, for the marginalized, antagonistic Anglo-Irish of post-independence Ireland. Bowen seized this opportunity to argue for a valid place for the Anglo-Irish in contemporary Ireland. Thus her essay is a plea for assimilation, a Utopian vision of a harmonious relationship between house and landscape. Her tone throughout the piece is jaunty: 'The loneliness of my house, as of many others, is more an effect than a reality ... When

I visit other big houses I am struck by some quality that they all have – not so much isolation as mystery ... they were planned for spacious living – for hospitality above all.'²² Yet, despite her need to create a place for the Big House in twentieth-century Ireland, her particular sense of the strangeness of the Big House within the countryside inevitably breaks through in this essay. 'The big house people were handicapped, shadowed and to an extent queered by their pride, by their indignation at their decline and by their divorce from the countryside in whose heart their struggle was carried out' (BH, p.197). She concludes her essay with a call for political and cultural accommodation between big house and surrounding towns and villages: 'The big house has much to learn – and it must learn if it is to survive at all. But it also has much to give ... From inside many big houses (and these will be the survivors) barriers are being impatiently attacked. But it must be seen that a barrier has two sides' (BH, p.65).

Bowen's most ambitious wartime writing on Ireland was a history of her family home, Bowen's Court, published in 1942. In this family chronicle she proudly presents successive Bowen patriarchs and landowners as members of a powerful dynasty, and addresses the difficult question of attempted harmonization between house and surrounding lands. However, blankness and non-being threatened to descend on the Big House and the threat of violence is never quite exorcised:

> inside and about the house and in the demesne woods you feel transfixed by the surrounding emptiness; it gives depth to the silence, quality to the light. The land around Bowen's Court, even under its windows, has an unhumanised air the house does nothing to change. Here are, even, no natural features, view or valley to which the house may be felt to relate itself. It has set, simply, its pattern of trees and avenues on the virgin, anonymous countryside.²³

Overall, as Clair Wills writes, 'In Bowen's Court the family history that she had begun in 1939 (presumably while still feeling "wedded" to the country through her "marriage" to Sean O'Faolain), and which she completed during her intelligence-gathering trips in 1940 and 1941, Bowen recorded the "centripetal and cut-off life" of the Protestant ascendancy in Ireland.'²⁴

The Heat of the Day was published in 1948 and sold 45,000 copies almost immediately. Neil Corcoran calls it 'a story about entangled loyalties and treacheries – in war, in love and in relationships across the generations – is itself generated out of a radical sense of the destabilisations or erosions of identity consequent on wartime displacements and disorientations.'[25] The focus of the novel is on Stella Rodney, the same age as her century and a widow with a grown son, Roderick, serving in the army. The action opens in Regent's Park in September 1942, and focuses on the affair between Stella and Robert Kelway, a wartime blitz affair. Harrison, an undercover government agent, shadows Stella and intervenes to tell her that Robert Kelway is under suspicion of being a spy and offers to cover up if Stella has an affair with Harrison. While Stella vacillates and wonders about Robert's possible treason, she discovers that her son Roderick has inherited a house in Ireland, Mount Morris, and travels to Ireland to visit it. There she decides to confront Robert and eventually does on her return to London. Robert, unrepentant and angry, confesses his guilt and dies falling from the roof of her flat trying to escape. By 1944, Harrison returns to find Stella engaged to marry someone else.

Treason is the central theme in The Heat of the Day, both personal and political. Rebecca West, in her 1949 study The Meaning of Treason lays out clear ethical boundaries by which traitors can be unequivocally judged and condemned. West's journalistic coverage of such spectacular treason trials as that of Lord Haw-Haw, the Irishman William Joyce, in 1945, allows her to analyze the motivation for betrayal implicit in Joyce's career. For West's generation, living through two world wars and then observing the emergence of the Cold War, there could be no ambiguities allowed when it came to the classification and the condemnation of treason. In her book, West attempts to analyze the root cause for this corruption of the ideal of nationalism and she did allow that a certain amount of healthy scepticism and individuality was necessary to keep a society vital. 'All men should have a drop of treason in their veins, if the nations are not to go soft like so many sleepy pears',[26] but, ultimately, she deplored any betrayal of country and of national security secrets as signs of moral degeneracy.

The Heat of the Day was published at the same time as Rebecca West's study, and shares the same confident sense of moral forthrightness and lack of ambivalence about treason. Bowen's own wartime experiences as 'interpreter' or confidential agent for England on Ireland and Irish political matters must have shaped her fictive concept of espionage in this novel. (Her own experience of secret reporting may have led her to give the name of Robert to Harrison and Kelway, two central characters – Robert the traditional Bowen first name she would have received if she had been born male.) In Bowen's novel, cultural lines and debates around treason are uncompromising and it is interesting to note that the idea of Ireland operates in this wartime novel as a metaphorical locus for loyalty and stability. Ireland is the place where Stella visits her son's Anglo-Irish Big House and experiences a sense of uncomplicated, liberating allegiance to the allied cause. It is also the locus where she finds proof that Robert is a traitor and she then returns to London to confront him with his disloyalty. Thus, in this fictionalized version of the Irish Big House, Bowen allows a sense of untroubled patriotic love between house and land to predominate. This is of a piece with much of Bowen's wartime sense of Anglo-Ireland as a loyal, stable place, and the Anglo-Irish home becomes symbolically implicated with eventual allied victory. During her stay in Ireland, Stella comes to see this Irish Big House as an oasis of feudal certainty and this certainty is contrasted unfavourably with the suffocating, traitorous suburban villas of the English Home Counties. The Irish landscape around Mount Morris is viewed by Stella in terms of loyalty and stability that contrasts Lois's troubled vision of the rebellious terrain around Danielstown in *The Last September*:

> The river traced the boundary of the lands: at the Mount Morris side it has a margin of water-meadow into which the demesne woods, dark at their base with laurels, ran down in a series of promontories. This valley cleavage into a distance seemed like an offering to the front window: in return the house devoted the whole muted fervour of its being to a long gaze. Elsewhere rising woods or swelling uplands closed Mount Morris in.[27]

In addition, Mount Morris is the place where Stella first hears of Allied victories in North Africa, the turning point of the war. So, it seems as if Anglo-Ireland, and the figure of the Irish servant girl Hannah Donovan, is transmuted into a uniquely loyal, safe and trustworthy terrain by the experience of the Second World War. 'Whenever in the future that Mount

Morris mirage of utter victory came back to her, she was to see Hannah standing there in the sunshine, indifferent as a wand' (HD, p.179).Yet, at the same time, the interior world of the Anglo-Irish Big House is also a place of lurking madness and unhappiness for the Anglo-Irish women, and Bowen does allow this contradictory note to intrude, the one draw-back to this house of peace, loyalty and safety in a time of war and of suspicion. 'After all, was it not chiefly here in this room ... that Cousin Nettie Morris – and who now knew how many more before her? – had been pressed back, hour by hour, by the hours themselves, into cloud-land? Ladies had gone not quite mad, not quite even that, from in vain listening for meaning in the loudening ticking of the clock' (HD, p.166).

Ireland arms Stella for confrontation and, right at the end of the novel, a denouement takes place between the two protagonists, the wartime lovers Stella and Robert, as to the nature of patriotism and its dark opposite, treason. Robert proudly and defiantly confesses that he has been betraying English military secrets to the Germans. The spy Robert, himself the product of a Home Counties family and wounded in the retreat from Dunkirk, has now lost faith in the idea of loyalty and duty to England. His family house, a middle-class villa, is described in these poisonous terms, 'Chiefly Holme Dene had been a man-eating house' (HD, p.237). Robert's decision to spy for the Germans comes not from conviction but rather from despair, a lack of faith, now that all words like *patriotism* are redundant. His sense is that war has rendered any fixed or knowable notions of treason meaningless.

> Country? – there are no more countries left; nothing but names. What country have you and I outside this room? Exhausted shadows, dragging themselves out again to fight ... What is repulsing you is the idea of 'betrayal', I suppose, isn't it? In you the hangover from the word? Don't you understand that all that language is dead cur-rency? (HD, p.268)

On the other hand, his lover, Stella, with her brothers killed fighting for England during the First World War, has a much clearer and uncom-plicated sense of duty to country. She resists Robert's nihilism and coun-ters his sense of despair with her own belief in the tangibility of words like *country* and *loyalty*, connecting her belief in the political structure of war and resistance with her own interior world of love. '"No, but you cannot say there is not a country!" she cried aloud, starting up. She had trodden every inch of a country with him, not least perhaps when she was alone' (HD, p.274). By the end of The Heat of the Day, Robert has been tracked down and is killed, falling from the roof of Stella's house and the novel's open ending suggests eventual Allied victory and a consolidation of the loyal idea of England in time of war. In this, one of the most celebrated novels of the Second World War, Bowen found a voice for an entire generation. As Heather Jordan comments:

> In The Heat of the Day, Bowen depicts the psychological ramifications of the changed landscape ... tackling in a more sustained, and sometimes more agonised, manner, the same questions she had addressed in her wartime short stories: the nature of betrayal, changing concepts of class, the role of Ireland and the Anglo-Irish, and the ramifications of espionage work.[28]

NOTES

1. Quoted in an excellent essay by A.S. Byatt, 'Elizabeth Bowen's The House in Paris' in her collection Passions of the Mind (London: Vintage, 1991), p.249, 191.
2. Elizabeth Bowen, The Demon Lover and Other Stories (London: Jonathan Cape 1945), p.190, hereafter referred to in the text as DL.
3. Elizabeth Bowen, English Novelists (London: Collins, 1945), p.18, hereafter referred to in the text as EN.
4. Victoria Glendinning, Elizabeth Bowen: Portrait of a Writer (London: Weidenfeld and Nicolson, 1977), p.98.
5. Elizabeth Bowen, The House in Paris (London: Vintage, 1998 [1935]), p.130, hereafter referred to in the text as HP.
6. See Jean Radford's excellent essay 'Late Modernism and the Politics of History', in Women Writers of the 1930s: Gender, Politics and History, ed. Maroula Joannou (Edinburgh: Edinburgh University Press, 1999).
7. Neil Corcoran, Elizabeth Bowen: The Enforced Return (Oxford: Oxford University Press, 2004), p.85.
8. Ibid., p.83
9. Ibid., p.94.
10. Hermione Lee, Elizabeth Bowen: An Estimation (London: Vintage, 1999), pp.113, 104.
11. Ibid., p.109.
12. Elizabeth Bowen, The Death of the Heart (London: Vintage, 1998 [1938]), pp.291, 292, hereafter referred to in the text as DH.

13. Maud Ellmann, *Elizabeth Bowen: The Shadow Across the Page* (Edinburgh: Edinburgh University Press, 2003), p.136.

14. Ibid., p.139.

15. Corcoran, *Elizabeth Bowen*, pp.105, 108.

16. Heather Bryant Jordan, *How Will the Heart Endure? Elizabeth Bowen and the Landscape of War* (Ann Arbor, MI: University of Michigan Press, 1992), p.100.

17. See Heather Laird's chapter in this collection and also Roy Foster, *Paddy and Mr Punch: Connections in Irish and English History* (Harmondsworth: Penguin, 1993).

18. Clair Wills, *That Neutral Island: A Cultural History of Ireland During the Second World War* (London: Faber and Faber, 2007), p.117.

19. See National Archives, Kew, Files fp/800/310 Mrs Cameron. Also Jack Lane, 'Introduction', in Jack Lane and Brendan Clifford, *Elizabeth Bowen: 'Notes on Eire', Espionage Reports to Winston Churchill, 1940-2; With a Review of Irish Neutrality in World War 2* (Aubane: Aubane Historical Society, 1999).

20. Roy Forster, *The Irish Story* (Harmondsworth: Penguin, 2001), p.152.

21. Jordan, *How Will the Heart Endure?*, p.142.

22. Elizabeth Bowen, 'The Big House' (1940), in *Collected Impressions* (London: Longmans, 1950), pp.195–196, hereafter referred to in the text as BH.

23. Elizabeth Bowen, *Bowen's Court* (Cork: Collins Press, 1998 [1942]), p.21, hereafter referred to in the text as BC.

24. Wills, *That Neutral Island*, p.176.

25. Corcoran, *Elizabeth Bowen*, p.168.

26. Rebecca West, *The Meaning of Treason* (London: Phoenix Press, 1982), p.7.

27. Elizabeth Bowen, *The Heat of the Day* (London: Jonathan Cape, 1949), p.155, hereafter referred to in the text as HD.

28. Jordan, *How Will the Heart Endure?*, p.153.

CHAPTER EIGHT

'Autobiography As We Know It Now Is Artists' Work'

MARY BREEN

Autobiography always looks slightly disreputable and self-indulgent in a way that may be symptomatic of its incompatibility with the monumental dignity of aesthetic values. (Paul de Man)

In this chapter I consider one of the most neglected areas of Elizabeth Bowen's writing, her 'fragment(s) of autobiography'. I focus on Bowen's negative attitude to autobiography, and seek to explain why, despite this, she does in her 40s and later in her 70s write directly about her own life. I suggest that an analysis of the differences between her autobiography and her fiction will illuminate some of the central concerns of her aesthetic. The main part of the chapter contains a detailed discussion of three texts: *Bowen's Court*, *Seven Winters* and *Pictures and Conversations*.

Throughout her writing career, Bowen expressed such serious reservations about autobiography and its place in her own writing, and indeed in any literary endeavour, that it is surprising to discover that she did at two specific periods in her life turn to what was for her a type of writing that was 'fraught with aesthetic problems, difficulties and tests'.[1] During the Second World War, while living in London, she wrote *Bowen's Court*, published in 1942, a large family history, and *Seven Winters*, published in 1943, a very short childhood memoir, detailing the first seven winters of her life, which were spent in Dublin. During the last years of her life she wrote the early chapters of an autobiography, *Pictures and Conversations*, published posthumously in 1974.

There are many challenges facing the reader of *Bowen's Court*, *Seven*

Winters and *Pictures and Conversations*, the most daunting of which is Bowen's often stated resistance to autobiographical writing. We have three pieces of writing and attached to each are very serious cautions about the limitations of autobiography put in place by Bowen herself, in prefaces, outlines of work, an afterword, and most of all in her separate essays on autobiography. In these she attempts to protect herself from her own awareness of the weakness of the genre.

One of Bowen's main concerns about autobiography is its reliance on memory. She repeatedly voices her distrust of her own ability to record anything that has happened in the past: 'The past is veiled from us by illusion over illusion. It is that which we seek, it is not the past but the idea of the past which draws us.'[2] In her essay 'Out of a Book', Bowen again voices her reservations about the nature of memory: 'I know that I have in my make-up layers of synthetic experience, and that the most powerful of my memories are only half true. Reduced to the minimum, to the what did happen, my life would be unrecognisable by me.'[3]

Bowen's views on the complex nature of memory are shared by many writers and critics of her generation. The critic Philippe Lejune reminds us that it is because of its overt claims to a reality outside the text that writers of autobiography are obsessed with the nature of memory and its versions of the past.[4] Bowen is so concerned with the difficulty of accessing the past through memory that she rarely uses it in her fiction. All of her novels with the exception of *The Last September* are set in the present. Even in *The Last September* she is concerned to remind us that the events she records happened a decade before.[5] Her fiction embodies a series of testings and evaluations of memory. For example, her anxiety that memory may be 'more than half a fake' is echoed in *The Death of the Heart* by St Quentin Millert, who likes writing novels because 'what's in them never happened' and finds memory slightly distasteful:

> Memory is quite unbearable enough, but even so it leaves out quite a lot. It wouldn't let one down as gently, even, as that if it weren't more than half a fake – we remember to suit ourselves. If one didn't let oneself swallow some few lies, I don't know how one would carry the past. Thank God, except at it's one moment there's never any such thing as a bare fact. Ten minutes later, one's begun to glaze the fact over with a deposit of some sort.[6]

A further complication that Bowen recognizes when trying to record past experience is her belief that life for her is always overlapped and haunted by fiction. For her, it is almost impossible to separate the details of life from those of fiction as writers and readers traditionally tend to. She fears that all she writes or has experienced she has encountered before in fiction. 'Almost no experience, however much simplified by the distance of time, is to be vouched for as being wholly my own – did I live through that, or was I told that it happened, or did I read it? When I write, I am re-creating what was created for me' (MT, p.53).

In the following passage Bowen explains why, when she does venture into the self-constrained area of autobiography, she never deals with her adult life. When she does write autobiography, however indirectly, and however qualified, it is concerned almost exclusively with childhood.

> The overlapping and haunting of life by fiction began of course, before there was anything to be got from the printed page; it began from the day one was old enough to be told a story or shown a picture book ... Happily, the Eden, like a natal climate, can be unconsciously remembered, and the magic stored up in those years goes on secreting under today's chosen sensations and calculated thoughts. What entered the system during childhood remains; and remains indistinguishable from the life of those years because it *was* that greater part of the life. (MT, pp.48–9)

Unable to believe in its powers of truth-telling, Bowen must seek for the importance of autobiographical writing elsewhere; she vests all of its significance in its aesthetic value. In her 1951 article 'Autobiography', Bowen categorizing it as 'self expression only at one remove' (SW, p.71), anticipates what Paul de Man refers to as 'the distance that shelters the author of autobiography from his experience'.[7] She also makes a plea for autobiography as literature, not as truth: 'It is as literature not as a private document that autobiography makes its claims,' (SW, p.70). And again, appealing to its aesthetic value she writes: 'It is the product of disciplined concentration, not a licensed ease, no longer an amateur affair' (SW, p.70). Bowen wanted her autobiography to surpass the genre as she knew it; for her literary style transcends concerns with truth. Critic Richard Coe in his 1984 book, *When the Grass was Greener*, defines the autobiographer as, 'a solipsist, an individualist, a poet above all, whose truth, like that of the poet, is essentially independent of the evidence of facts'.[8] It seems to me that Bowen's serious reservations about autobiography have their roots in her fear that it is not art, that at best it is history, at worst the self-indulgent confession of personal details that should not be spoken about in public or noticed in private. This helps to explain, at least in part, why her autobiographical writing is so slight and fragmented and why she turns to it only at times of crisis in her life. But the desire to see autobiography as art causes Bowen to recognize other difficulties: 'art out of the very necessity to compose a picture, cannot but eliminate, edit – and so falsify'(MT, p.57). So by insisting on autobiography as literature she further limits its ability to tell any kind of truth. In a very awkward phrase she tells us 'Autobiography as we know it now is artists' work: though pegged to one man's story it has as its subject Life as by one man this has been found to be' (SW, p.75).

Bowen's reservations about autobiography dovetail very neatly with her ideas about what she terms her own 'race', the Anglo-Irish. The self-revelation that autobiography implies is totally at odds with her own construction of the ethos of her class, The reserve, the good manners and the hiding of feelings behind a surface display of style, that for her epitomizes them, has strong echoes of her autobiographical style. The life that holds itself together by the inner force of its style is not going to be revelatory, 'life with the lid on' restricts itself to a surface display of style. Summing up her article, Bowen suggests that autobiography is 'a task which, while it might seem humanly straightforward, is fraught with aesthetic problems, difficulties and tests' (SW, p.73). However, she does admit that part of its value lies in the fact that, 'above all, to study the contrast, the interplay between the inner and the outer I may be fascinating' (p.73). Her hesitation – 'may be fascinating' – should alert us to her uncertainty about this possibility and indeed as far as her own autobiographical writing is concerned, this interplay between the inner and the outer I is replaced by a focus on the interplay between the present and the past self.

For Bowen, autobiography is above all narrative and like any other story she feels it ought not to be 'clogged by too much analysis' (AT, p.203). This definition of autobiography as literature is questioned by critics like Paul de Man, who in his 1979 essay 'Autobiography as De-facement' resists any attempt to define autobiography as literature: 'Autobiography always looks slightly disreputable and self-indulgent in a way that may be symptomatic of its incompatibility with the monumental dignity of aesthetic values'.[9] Bowen, in her insistence on autobiography as literature, is clearly apprehensive of accusations of self-indulgence like those expressed by de Man. However, Bowen and de Man do have in common the belief that all writing is determined by books that have been read. But de Man takes the argument a step further than Bowen by suggesting that all autobiography is determined by the structures of autobiography:

> We assume that life produces the autobiography as an act produces consequences, but can we not suggest, with equal justice, that the autobiographical project may itself produce and determine the life and that whatever the writer does is in fact governed by the technical demands of self-portraiture and thus determined, in all its aspects, by the resources of his medium.[10]

De Man suggests that 'The interest of autobiography, then, is not that it reveals reliable self-knowledge – it does not – but that it demonstrates in a striking way the impossibility of closure and of totalization (that is the impossibility of coming into being) of all textual systems made up of tropological substitutions.'[11] Although Bowen does not use the language of de Man, in her discussions of autobiography they share the view that autobiography does not offer the possibility of constructing a fixed identity. The genre is unequal to such a task.

This brings us to the vexed area of Bowen's literary style. Most readers encountering Bowen's fiction for the first time, even the second, experience difficulties with the clotted nature of the narrative techniques that make her writing style so distinctive. Ellmann details some of these difficulties: 'Her syntax – with its double negatives, inversions and obliquuities; its attribution of the passive mood to human agents and the active mood to lifeless objects'.[12] Even her friends and admirers expressed certain reservations about her style: Sean O'Faolain describes it as 'Bowen 707, take off style'. Does she carry her fictional style into her autobiography? Yes and no is the answer to this: many of the stylistic traits are carried forward, but there is a clear attempt to make the style more easily accessible, particularly in *Seven Winters* where she adopts, what is for her, a simplistic style. In an attempt to explain the reserved nature of her style Bowen asserts that 'Autobiography is more detached, and less impassioned than writing the life of another man' (SW, p.71)

Bowen's autobiographical writing can not be read simply as a record of her life, or a history of her family; it is a self-conscious invention. Declan Kiberd in 'The Dandy in Revolt' states: 'Bowen wrote not so much to record as to invent herself',[13] thus making the general point that the self does not pre-exist the text but is constructed by it. Bowen constructs an identity, not just for herself but for her family and her class, the Anglo-Irish. For her, they are a race, a people set apart, a little society. This identity is based on the myths and fictions of the past, her own knowledge, her received notions and her desire for a glamorous, stylish identity. Having constructed this identity she does not question it. She supports it and finds in this construction something to be proud of. She presents her family as part of a race, a glamorous, courageous race, living up to the ideal she creates for them. She constructs an ideal, insists on its foundations in hundreds of years of occupation of the same place, while at the same time acknowledging its insecure foundations. Because of their insecurity, Bowen reasons, the Anglo-Irish construct a stylish façade and in the end this is all that is left.

Despite the many reservations about autobiography that Bowen puts in place, her writing is haunted by things that even she has not taken into consideration. Her autobiographical writing belongs to a tradition of Anglo-Irish writing that has sought to record, with varying degrees of valorization, the Anglo-Irish way of life. She does not question whether the historians she uses and credits with the best credentials may be determining the patterns she imposes on her family and personal history. She must also have been driven by the need to justify the Anglo-Irish presence in Ireland. It is not enough to admit that the whole façade that is Anglo-Irish culture is constructed on a wrong. She needs to invest this small elite group with importance, now that they are on the eve of extinction. She finds this in highlighting their courage in the face of this decline, and in their adherence to a code of behaviour that is stylish and glamorous despite the fact that there is little money to sustain their way of life: 'To live as if living gave them no trouble has been the first imperative of their make-up: to do this has taken a virtuosity into which courage enters more than has been allowed. In the last issue, they lived at their own expense.'[14] Ironically Bowen's autobiographical style is limited by her understanding of the identity she constructs for her class. To a certain extent her own identity is derived from this as is her theory of autobiography. Much of Bowen's discomfort with autobiography as a mode of self-expression may stem from her ambivalence towards her own identity as Anglo-Irish. Commenting on the relationship between Bowen's sense of herself as Anglo-Irish and her writing, Hermoine Lee states that she 'never records a simple response to being Anglo-Irish, either as a child or later'.[15] It is also worth noting that although Bowen recognizes that memory and language are very different mediums, and appreciates that experience is not just difficult to recall but is always mediated by representation, she remains confident in the power of language to create; she does not question it in any overt way in this writing.

There are several reasons why Bowen, so conscious of the difficulties in writing autobiography, actually turns to it in the late 1930s and early 1940s. She tells us in her essay 'The Bend Back' that 'Contemporary writing retreats from the present-day'.[16] Reflecting on the reasons why writers have taken to writing 'novels set back in time, picturesque biographies, memoirs, diaries dated long ago, books about old homes, collections of family letters from generations back', she states that they are responding to 'a universal demand' for writing set in the past (MT, p.54). This is fuelled, she suggests, by the identification of the past with 'the better days'. She also suggests that the 'Imagination finds it [the past] a golden terrain' (p.54). The war made everything unstable, so only versions of the past could be relied on; this encouraged many writers to turn to autobiography as a way of accessing a secure past. Ironically, in Bowen's case, the home she had feared would be burned out during the 1920s becomes her imagined refuge in the 1940s and in the 1960s is torn down, when she feels that she has left it in safe hands.

Kristine Miller in her essay on Bowen's wartime writings, '"Even a Shelter's Not Safe"', sees Bowen's Court as representing 'a conservative, elitist retreat from the problems of war'.[17] This reading underestimates the complexity of the text. Having inherited Bowen's Court in 1930, Bowen found it a huge financial and psychological burden. Bowen's Court as a physical structure was expensive to maintain, and as its owner and the last member of her family she became the custodian of the family history and identity. Bowen also recognized the unstable foundations of the family occupancy of the Bowen's Court estate, admitting that it was 'founded on a wrong' (BC, p.453). This feeling of unease is never allowed to disappear, it lurks just beneath the stylish and amusing family history. Her publisher Alfred Knopf, recognizing in wartime England the mood and demand for this kind of writing, encouraged Bowen to turn to family and personal history at this time. There are good reasons for this: the proceeds from the sale of the books would certainly help to support a large country house that was in constant need of repair, and it would also allow Bowen to escape, in imagination at least, the horrors of wartime London. During this time of uncertainty Bowen wrote *Bowen's Court* and *Seven Winters*; both, as Hermoine Lee reminds us, are written 'from a distance in place and time'.[18] There is also the challenge involved in doing something that she perceived as difficult, a challenge that she certainly would have risen to. She began to write *Pictures and Conversations* during another difficult time in her life. Having at last very reluctantly sold Bowen's Court and retired to live in the small village of Hythe in Kent, she faced her last illness with courage and fortitude and when she was in difficulties with her fiction turned to look back at her life and to reconstruct her past.

Before we begin to look in detail at the texts it is useful to note, as Laura Marcus reminds us, that for many critics what is important is not whether what the autobiographer remembers is true, but the way she now sees her past self. So 'the accuracy of recall is less important than the reconstruction of the past in the present of memory and/or writing'.[19] Although Bowen was obsessed with the inability to recall her past accurately, in reading her writing this will not be our main concern. Bowen in these three works is not searching for a true version of her past self, but is attempting to create a self through writing. It is this self that we are now going to examine.

Bowen's Court, at over 460 pages, is a substantial text. It consists of ten chapters, opening with a description of the house in Chapter 1, with each of the succeeding chapters named after one of Bowen's male ancestors. Chapter 2 tells the story of the first Bowen to come to Ireland. Colonel Bowen arrived with Cromwell's army and was granted lands in North Cork in return for his services in 1650. The following chapters detail the lives of each of the succeeding Bowens, ending with Henry VI, Bowen's father. The chapters are not of equal length, the Henrys and

Roberts of the nineteenth century getting much more space than their ancestors in the seventeenth and eighteenth centuries. There are practical reasons for giving her male ancestors numbers, like Henry VI, as there are two Johns and six Henrys, but this also has the effect of associating the family with royalty. Bowen's Court has a substantial para-text: a map of the Farahy lands, a family tree and twenty family photographs. The map, family tree and photographs point to a reality outside the text; they are a way of grounding it in history, of vouching for its authenticity. These are the firm footholds of the text, the scaffolding that allows Bowen to build the sometimes factual sometimes fanciful history of her family. In 1963 she wrote an afterword to accompany the text, which contains an explanation of why autobiography should be approached with such caution.

Bowen's Court is a family story, not a personal one. Bowen does use it, however, to place herself securely in a long and well-established background of Anglo-Irish landed gentry. If she feels displaced and insecure in London at the time of writing, then this tracing of family history over several hundred years resident in the one place may offer the promise of a safe and familiar sense of identity and belonging. But this is not quite how the text reads. There is a constant undertow of insecurity in the narrative, no matter how elaborate the structure she builds for the Anglo-Irish, as represented by her family. She explains: 'The stretches of the past I have had to cover have been, on the whole, painful: my family got their position and drew their power from a situation that shows an inherent wrong' (BC, p.453). She begins with a detailed account of the landscape of North Cork; it is very beautiful, but the beauty is tinged with a pervasive sense of loneliness. The landscape has 'an inherent sense of emptiness of its own' (p.5). The text is haunted by the future, not just the future that will be revealed in the chronological movement forward that is the structure of the text, but the future that it anticipates but is not known at the time of writing. (We as readers know what the future holds: Bowen's forced abandonment of the house and its destruction.) Bowen then places the house firmly at the centre of this very Irish landscape. The house is described in minute detail. Over seven pages of text are devoted to it, from attention to the classical simplicity of its architecture to the height of the ceilings and the number and details of the rooms on each of its four floors. Bowen's Court, completed in 1776, is a 'high bare Italianate house' (p.21), from the front door, which 'stands open all day on to the steps', to the bedrooms whose 'open windows let in the smell of woods and country and often of mown grass' (p.28).

The identification of Bowens with Bowen's Court is an important element in her construction of their identity as a family: 'Each member of each of these isolated households is bound up not only in the sensation and business of living but the exact sensation of living here'(pp.19–20). She invests Bowen's Court not just with atmosphere but with the ability to shape the Bowens themselves. The members of the family are formed and in turn form not just a way of life but leave their mark on the landscape in which Bowen's Court is set. 'Their eyes left, also, prints on the scene'(BC, p.451) and the house in turn returns their gaze: 'The house, not unkindly, eyed them' (p.239). John Banville, commenting on Bowen's evocation of the lifestyle of the Big House, emphasizes the charm of Bowen's writing when he suggests that no writer would ever 'catch with such wistful accuracy the languid yet curiously valiant mode of life at the Big House just as its demolition was at hand'.[20]

Bowen has a very definite readership in mind when she is writing this text, her intended reader is English, not Irish. For example when describing the gardens around Bowen's Court she explains: 'It must be said that in Ireland a "lawn" does not mean turf subjected to fine mowing; it means that grass expanse that in England is called a Park' (pp.20–21). We should remember that she is writing during the Second World War, living in England and working undercover for the British Ministry of Information, gathering information about attitudes to the war in Ireland. Her attitude to Ireland at this period is troubled by her failure to understand the official Irish attitude to the war. This places Bowen in a long line of writers who attempt to explain Ireland to an English readership.[21]

Bowen's Court is based on research into family papers, reports of the substantial number of law cases the Bowens were involved in, family lore and some well-known historical sources. These are all stitched together into a lively and entertaining version of her family's history in Ireland. Vouching for the reliability of her historical sources she claims: 'My transcripts of history have, at least, been drawn from source beyond reproach: I have relied upon no authority who did not place fact above passion or interest' (p.453). But these are just the scaffolding around which Bowen constructs her version of the family history. These sources provide a very incomplete story; Bowen invents much detail to fill in the gaps. The reader is alerted to moments when the narrator is diverging from known fact into speculation. The narrative rings with qualifications: 'it must have been', 'I hope', 'perhaps', 'Was she pretty? For my pleasure she had to be', 'pure supposition' (pp.149 and 115). Bowen has fun with the facts, filling in what she would like to have happened in place of unknown material. Occasionally she calls attention to her own lack of knowledge: 'I must leave one of those blanks by now usual in my narrative'(p.281). For her, 'the boldly left gaps, the admitted lacunae in the narrative' are not a mistake, they 'guarantee the veracity of what has been written down' (AT, p.204). In an attempt to balance the obvious lacunae, she does call on other writers to give authority to her text. Arthur Young is a good example of this: 'I think that I can do no better than quote from Arthur Young' (BC, p.170).

In an attempt to underpin her family history without making claims for its historical accuracy she claims that Bowen's Court is the version of the family story that she likes. 'It has a psychological, if not a strictly historical, likeliness' (BC, p.67). In her 1963 Afterword to Bowen's Court she acknowledges her 'ignorance' of her family's past and goes on to say: 'In the writing of this book, sheer information would not have taken me very much of the way – only a little displaced by my researches, the greater part of that ignorance still remains; it is natural' (p.452). It seems to me that it is this ignorance that sets her free in Bowen's Court to 'colour their outlines in' (pp.451–2). Her lack of knowledge acted as an invitation to invent, an excuse to cross over into fiction, thus valorizing de Man's contention that 'The distinction between fiction and autobiography is not an either/or polarity but that it is undecidable.'[22] This admission of the strong fictional strain in Bowen's Court further distances it from mere facts: it is not history, it is a work of art.

Looking back on the reasons why she wrote Bowen's Court, Bowen claims that she was partly motivated by a search for truth. Not the possibility of finding a truthful past, but the possibility of finding some truthful explanations for the present in a reconstruction of the past, no matter how fictionalized that may be: 'that disparity or contrast between the time I was writing in and my subject – only acted upon my subject as to make it, for me, the more important. I tried to make it my means to approach truth' (BC, p.454). Developing this idea further, Bowen states that her analysis of the Bowens' way of life may help her to understand the issues of the war period. 'Also, the idea of the idea of power governed my analysis of the Bowens and the means they took – these being in some cases emotional – to enforce themselves on their world' (p.455). This reinforces the point that what matters is when the autobiographer is writing, and how they see themselves at the time of writing, and the uses they make of their search for the past.

Bowen's Court is at times a fanciful and amusing text. Many of the characters Bowen creates are romanticized, drawn larger than life, and are an important component of her presentation of the Anglo-Irish as charming, stylish and loveably eccentric. Her deliberate construction of her class as elegant and polite lends itself persuasively to her reserved autobiographical style. She tells us in her essay 'The Big House': 'In the interest of good manners and good behaviour people learned to subdue their own feelings', and again, 'why not be polite – are not humane manners the crown of being human at all?'[23] Those who knew Bowen repeatedly commented on the contradictions in her character, at once gregarious and sociable and yet intensely private. This is how *Bowen's Court, Seven Winters* and *Pictures and Conversations* read. Although the narrator is friendly, and at times even seemingly communicative, she is more often secretive and always very reserved.

One of the qualities Bowen admires most in her ancestors is their toughness, a quality she believes she herself has inherited from them.

> They honoured, if they did not justify, their own class, its traditions, its rule of life. If they found a too-grand idea of themselves, they did at least exert themselves to live up to this: even vanity involves one kind of discipline. If their difficulties were of their own making, they combated these with an energy I must praise. (BC, p.456)

Using this toughness as a yardstick, she laments the weakness of the nineteenth-century Anglo-Irish writer Dorothea Herbert; commenting on her writing and her life she states: 'She was a clergyman's daughter, fatally well-connected, she broke her own heart, failed to marry and writes through a mist of queerness: she could not stay the course' (p.204). Bowen's position is clear, Herbert destroys herself, she is singled out as an exception to the rule. In Bowen's construction the Anglo-Irish do not give up, they continue to keep up appearances even when times are hard. This also reads as a kind of aspiration for the future: if the Anglo-Irish are to survive they must remain tenacious, and continue to espouse the identity she has created for them.

Bowen closes the narrative in 1914, as news of the outbreak of the First World War is announced at a garden party in Mitchelstown Castle. She sees this as a final scene: 'Ten years hence, it was, all to seem like a dream – and the Castle itself would be a few bleached stumps on the plateau' (BC, p.436). She says goodbye to her own people on the terrace of Mitchelstown castle. From then on the history of her people and Ireland becomes too complicated. She fears that to cover the years between 1914 and 1941 'would make a book that should be as long again as the book I have written by now' (p.437).

What makes Bowen's autobiographical writing so poignant, particularly *Bowen's Court*, is that 300 years of family history end with her. She is an only daughter, and is herself childless, she is the first woman to inherit Bowen's Court and she has married and changed her name. Having for years struggled to keep up the house that made all the Bowens she eventually sells it; shortly afterwards it is demolished. The experience of viewing the ruins of Bowen's Court is haunted by Bowen's writing, just as she believes that all her experience is haunted by books she has read.[24]

Seven Winters is that rare delight: a book about childhood written for adults, which successfully avoids being sentimental, one of the major pitfalls of this kind of writing. *Seven Winters*, very short, episodic and picaresque, has a simple structure. It is divided into twelve sections, each with a chapter heading that centres the piece and allows Bowen to illuminate a single aspect of her childhood. Each begins with a detailed description of the setting. So structure is dictated by place: house, room, dance studio. Each is a separate and complete narrative. The text is also very static, there is no progress, or very little; it is not chronological. Yet the text appears much more substantial than its length would suggest. The effect is produced by introducing a childhood activity like dancing lessons, devoting a chapter to describing one in great detail and then telling the reader that they happened twice a week during her childhood. Thus we get one representative sample of a particular scene, and we know that the same scene happens over and over again. The same effect is created by the chapter titled *Sundays*, where Bowen describes a typical Sunday: 'On Sundays we went to St Stephen's'.[25] The very detailed description that follows creates for the reader an endless vista of Sundays, all repeating each other in tone and detail throughout Bowen's childhood. This technique has the effect of increasing the feeling of timelessness in the text, creating depth in the narrative, and it confirms Bowen's belief that memory is fragmentary and disjointed. Memory here is very still, it works like a set of photographs or paintings. Given Bowen's addiction to the detailed description of places and things and her art school training, it is not surprising to find her using pictorial images. There is constant reference to the tools of pictorial art, canvas, artist and brush, in the three texts. Bowen also suggests that memory has planes, some memories are much closer and clearer than others and it is these that surface in the text and form the pattern that emerges.

It can be argued that autobiography has no plot, that at best it contains a pattern that is held together by the narrator's single point of view. This is certainly true of *Seven Winters* and also of *Pictures and Conversations*. If the focus in *Bowen's Court* is on family history, in *Seven Winters* it is on the physical life of the child and the child's sensory responses to the world. Dress, food, manners, heat and cold, all that is physical play a dominant role in the narrative. On the surface *Seven Winters* seems to be about children's parties, dresses, dancing classes and walks through Dublin with a succession of governesses, but behind these material things lie a whole series of questions about the nature of memory, the search for identity and the haunting of life by fiction.

In a preface to the 1962 edition of *Seven Winters* Bowen wrote: '*Seven Winters* could be called a fragment of autobiography. At the same time, I look on it as a self-contained work for it is as much of my life story as I intend to write − that is to write directly' (*SW*, p.vii). She goes on to claim, in contradiction to many of her beliefs about the unreliability of almost all autobiography, that 'The happenings in *Seven Winters* are those that I shall remain certain of till I die' (p.vii). Yet in the text itself all the 'happenings' are hedged in with qualifications; the only thing we are left certain about is the topography, and even that has large holes and gaps, places that she cannot see, things that she has to assume that she has seen. 'On the whole, it is things and places rather than people that detach themselves from the stuff of my dreams' (p.9).

Why does Bowen express confidence about her ability to recall in *Seven Winters*, at least in the Preface, when she has expressed such doubts about it in her other writing? The answer is that she sees childhood differently. In 'Out of a Book' she suggests that the sensations of childhood 'can be unconsciously remembered, and the magic stored up in those years goes on secreting under today's chosen sensations and calculated thoughts' (MT, p.49). Richard Coe argues that the autobiography of childhood is a separate genre, with its own rules: the child self has an autonomous existence. This is why, he explains, it is one of the most popular forms of autobiography. Bowen suggests that children have access to knowledge that is denied to adults. In *Seven Winters*, commenting on her negative reaction as a child to the Georgian façades of Dublin, she reasons: 'Perhaps a child smells history without knowing it – I did not know I looked at the tomb of fashion' (pp.32–3). Personal emotions are not recorded, but the landscape of Dublin becomes increasingly menacing as the text progresses; there is no explanation of this, the child senses it and is afraid: 'It was a charnel fear, of grave-dust and fungus dust' (p.17). In 'Out of a Book' she argues: 'I feel certain that if I could read my way back, analytically, through the books of my childhood, the clues to everything would be found' (HT, p.51). On a much more pragmatic note the reason that Bowen can be so sure about the events in *Seven Winters* is that she herself is the only authority, her parents are dead at the time she is writing and there are no records.

Unlike most childhood autobiographies, Bowen does not finish *Seven Winters* with adolescence or adulthood. Just seven years are detailed, brought to an abrupt end when her father's mental illness forces him into a period of rest and Bowen and her mother leave Dublin and go to live in the south of England. The abrupt ending of the narrative makes *Seven Winters* very unlike the childhood autobiographies of her two contemporaries, James Joyce and Edmund Gosse, where the young protagonists as they reach adolescence experience the anguish of failed faith, and where religion is a very important theme. There is no anguish of failed faith in *Seven Winters*, as there is in Joyce's *The Portrait of the Artist as a Young Man* or Gosse's *Father and Son*. In fact religion plays no role at all. There is no rebellion in *Seven Winters*; instead the adult narrator is now aware of how unusual her family is: 'I had been born, I see now, into a home at once unique and intensive, gently phenomenal' (p.9). Bowen looking back does not see herself as at odds with her family, or with society at large and its cherished institutions. If anything she is their guardian, their champion, who recognizing their worth, enshrines it in her consciousness and her writing. If Bowen turned to writing family history during the 1940s as a way of finding security in the evocation of a strong sense of family identity, she turns to childhood as a way of accessing 'the purest time'. As she tells us in her essay 'The Bend Back': 'The demand is, that writers should re-instate the idea of life as liveable, loveable' (MT, p.55).

Seven Winters begins with feelings of dislocation: 'I felt that I had intruded on some no-place' (*SW*, p.4). In a similar technique to that used in *Bowen's Court*, this openly stated unease remains just below the surface of the rest of the short text. We should be alerted by the fact that it is place, one of the few firm footholds Bowen seems to have, that is questioned in this opening section. She paints a vivid picture of family life, one where her parents live in a vague dreamlike state that forces her into a similar position, isolated and lonely. She does not learn to read or write until she is 7 and this is where the narrative ends, before their acquisition. Her mother, fearing that she may inherit the Bowen tendency to mental instability, does not let her read as it could overtax her brain. Bowen also believes that her first nurse doped her milk, so she laments how few memories she has of her first years. In *Seven Winters* she sees herself as a solitary child, conscious of being alone. Elizabeth Grubgeld, in her book *Anglo-Irish Autobiography*, highlighting the fact that Bowen is an only child, sees this as disfiguring. She backs up this statement by making the general point that 'Western cultural tradition has ... attitudes that subtly or blatantly pathologies the only child'.[26] However, this misses two points specific to Bowen and Ireland: Bowen at no time expresses any regrets about being an only child, and in Ireland, a family of one or two children had a certain social cache, as it distinguished the Anglo-Irish elite from the very prolific Irish Catholic families they lived among but from whom they wished to be distinguished. This is not to deny the importance of the representation of only children in her fiction.

What is the relationship in *Seven Winters* between the self who writes and the self who is remembered? Bowen contemplates her former self indulgently, the stance is from maturity looking back at a more innocent time, a time of sensation but not of interpretation. She also stands back from, and comments on, her younger self. 'I can see now' 'Her beauty, for I know now it was beauty' (SW, p.30). As in Bowen's Court, her story is hedged around with disclaimers and blanks: 'If I could see the Dublin Quays as I must have seen them', and 'It seems likely' (p.13). Unlike Bowen's Court however, she does not attempt to fill in these gaps in Seven Winters, the elisions are left, even fore-grounded as part of the nature of the genre she is using. She constantly repeats 'I see now' and highlights failure in memory: 'I cannot remember any house where he lived' (p.19). She does not fill in the missing pieces in Seven Winters; however, she does continue to offer many asides which are usually generalizations. Commenting on the vagueness of one of her governesses, she remarks: 'Like so many other young women, she slid through her hours in a narcissistic dream' (p.16).

As in the works of Proust and Joyce, two writers Bowen greatly admired, there are a number of moments of insight in Seven Winters. In an attempt to understand the ways in which we perceive the past, she suggests that 'We perceive the past in terms of vital glittering moments' (MT, p.59). These moments, or epiphanies, are associated with physical sensation. Unlike in Proust, however, where to taste a madeleine as an adult is to open a vast avenue of memory stretching back to early childhood, Bowen's description of her first taste of ice-cream leads to a staged moment of insight, but we do not learn what that insight is: 'At the Fane Vernon's I ate my first strawberry ice. I also remember, in connection with this party, my first real disconcerting sight of myself' (SW, p.46). Bowen had worn a dress that she had been given by a cousin, one she admired, but on catching sight of herself in a mirror she discovers how unflattering it is: 'Above the ornate white satin collar I saw my face harsh and brick-pink, my top-knot an iron whorl. The dress had done to my being what the ice was doing to my inside ... For years I would not eat an ice again' (p.47).

I hesitate to include Pictures and Conversations in this study as, firstly, it is incomplete, secondly, it was published after Bowen's death, and thirdly, Bowen tells us directly that it is not autobiography. 'The book is not an autobiography. It will differ in two ways 1 It will not follow a time

sequence 2 It will be anything but all inclusive.'[27] Her literary executor
Spencer Curtis Brown describes it as 'descriptive non-fiction' in his
introduction. But there are many similarities between this and *Bowen's
Court* and *Seven Winters*, in terms of structure and content. Bowen explores
similar debates about the nature of memory and the relationship
between living and writing that throw light on her construction of her
identity through her writing about herself. These make a brief analysis
of this unfinished work a useful place to conclude this chapter. Also,
Bowen, justifying the purpose of this text, and expressing dissatisfaction
with many of the things written about her, tells her publishers: 'if anybody must write a book about Elizabeth Bowen, why should not
Elizabeth Bowen?' (PC, p.62).

Intentionality, always a problem with literary texts and particularly
with autobiography, poses a slightly different problem when we come
to read *Pictures and Conversations*. Here we are concerned with what Bowen
might have intended, as she had only completed the first two and the
beginning of the third section of the planned five sections of the book
at the time of her death. Spencer Curtis Brown tells us that she did give
permission for its publication in the days before her death. Given the
fact that the text is incomplete, we have no way of knowing what
changes or additions might have been made that would totally have
altered the nature of it. Curtis Brown in his foreword to the book tells
us that the title comes from *Alice in Wonderland*, and points out that its significance lies in the fact that Bowen never intended to write about her
adult life but only about 'images that her eyes had seen and with memories of things said to her' (PC, p.viii).

Pictures and Conversations was published in 1974. Like *Seven Winters*, it is
short and episodic. There are three sections, the first 'Origins', by far the
longest, is followed by 'Places' and the first few pages of 'People'. In
Bowen's notes to her publisher about the book's structure she explains
that she intends the book 'sparking its way along by free association –
"recalls", and the ideas a recall brings with it' (PC, p.61). This she has
remained faithful to, it is the organizing principle of the text.

The opening section 'Origins' begins with a five- page description of a
walk she takes on a 'slightly hysterical sunny' May Saturday morning in
Kent, where she lived for the last years of her life (PC, p.5). It is set very
firmly in the present, and she describes the various places she passes and

uses them as a gateway to the past. Each place evokes memories of the childhood years she had spent there. These are presented as pictures: they are static and very detailed: 'Among my pictures of here' (p.6). The landscape she describes is not so much like itself as like a depiction of itself: 'Inland, the steep, overhanging scenery took on the look of a painted backdrop: one had the sensation of gazing up not so much at trees, rocks and bastions of evergreen as at depictions of them' (pp.7–8). In this opening section, as in *Bowen's Court* and *Seven Winters*, memory is questioned, and the large gaps in it fore-grounded: 'some things are as clear as day or at least as yesterday' while others are blank. Trying to recall a childhood friend she comments: 'her only I cannot identify, either by face or name. She is blotted out' (p.7).

In *Pictures and Conversations* we begin to get glimpses of the interiority Bowen has denied access to in *Bowen's Court* and *Seven Winters*. Describing the beauty of a particular landscape where 'flowers erratically scattered their way' and 'Vetches wove themselves into the longer grass', she refuses to be affected by this profusion of beauty and explains that 'I registered what I loved with such pangs of love (that is to say, registered what was around me) only out of the corner of an eye, only with an unwilling fraction of my being.' In a rare analytical moment she concludes: 'This was the beginning of a career of withstood emotion. Sensation, I have never fought shy of or done anything to restrain' (PC, p.9). But there are limits to this revelation, as while she does tell us about withholding emotions, she does not tell us what they are. As the title of this section suggests, she moves from the time she is writing to her childhood in Kent and then further back to her parents' marriage in Ireland. Describing the time she spend in England with her mother she realizes: 'the dominance of my more or less synonymous race and family: the Anglo-Irish – with their manner of instantly striking root into the interstices of any society, and in their own way proceeding to rule the roost, One could be perpetually vouched for' (p.14).

Bowen begins the next section, 'Places', with a declaration of the importance of place in her own and other writers' work. 'Am I not manifestly a writer for whom places loom large?' she demands (PC, p.34). She goes on to detail her concern with place when reading other writer's work, and the questions that she would like to ask. The questions she poses are practical ones, beginning with: how many places are 'actual' how many 'imagined'? (p.35) She believes that 'Bowen topography will die' with her. This she sees as a grave mistake for those who read her writing, as for her, landscape makes stories, in fact it determines them (p.37). In this section she uses many references to, and passages from, her novels and autobiography to illustrate points she is making. She tells us how sometimes her novels bring back to her events of the past, when her fiction writing functions as an aid to memory, in her own words an 'unearther of memory'. Literally in this case, as she goes on to tell us: 'This attempt I had completely forgotten till it was returned to me by *The Little Girls*' (p.57). Here in a complete reversal of roles she sees her own fiction as a way of accessing the past. The complexity of the relationship between experience, fiction and memory shifts yet again and, rather than competing with experience, fiction here gives direct access to experience that has faded from memory. Bowen's suggestion to her publisher that she was the most suitable person to write a book about Elizabeth Bowen is worth noting again, as this chapter reads more like an essay on Elizabeth Bowen than a piece of personal writing.

The third and last section, 'People', is only three pages long and ends abruptly. It shows Bowen concerned to the end with the differences between fiction and life, something that has intrigued her all through her writing career. However, despite its brevity there is an interesting point to make about this short section. Thinking about herself as a writer, she wonders about her 'make-believe about people'. 'But I ask myself, could these early dodges of mine queer the pitch for me as an autobiographer? What was, as opposed to what I choose to imagine' (PC, p.59). Highlighting her difficulties with illuminating characters in her autobiography, she reasons: 'To the fraction of the past that is in my keeping, I should like to give the sobriety of history: facts, events, circumstances demand to be accurately recorded: that is my aim. But people? – the denizens of those times and places? With people the impossibility of "accuracy" begins' (p.59). But, she continues: 'With the characters in my stories it has been otherwise, Between them and me, exists no gulf. I could say, they have made themselves known to me – instantly recognisable, memorable from then on' (pp.59–60). Here at the very end of her life she explains why she is so at home in fiction and so apprehensive about autobiography. In her proposal for this work written for her publisher she does describe *Pictures and Conversations* as a work of retrieval, if not of introspection: 'A considerable – in fact, probably the greater-part of what it is to be about is still fairly deep down in my consciousness, waiting to be brought to the surface' (p.63). Unfortunately this is where much of it remains, as Bowen dies before completing what might have been her most revealing piece of writing about herself.

In her critical writing Bowen anticipates many of the modern debates about autobiography, in particular the work of Philippe Lejune and James Olney. Olney, echoing Bowen's concern about stories she has heard before, tells us: 'For better or worse, we all exist and only exist within the circumference of the stories we tell about ourselves.'[28] Bowen's anxiety about referentiality and the status of truth in autobiography have become some of the central debates surrounding the vexed areas of genre, and truth versus fiction, that preoccupy many critics. Her recognition of the value of investigating the relationship between writing and life anticipates many late twentieth-century debates about writing, and particularly about autobiography. Elizabeth Grubgeld in her work on Bowen's autobiographical writing argues that 'Taken together her writings present both the recollecting narrator and the recollected past self as the most tentative of entities'.[29] This is only partly true. Bowen manages, despite the many reservations she expresses about autobiography in the texts themselves and in her other writing, to construct a very developed self, one that is reserved and sometimes withdrawn, but none the less intact.

NOTES

1. Elizabeth Bowen, 'Autobiography' (1951), in *Seven Winters and Afterthoughts: Pieces about Writing* (London: Longmans, 1962), pp.68–76 (p.73), hereafter referred to as *SW*.

2. Elizabeth Bowen, *The Mulberry Tree: Writings of Elizabeth Bowen*, ed. Hermoine Lee (London: Virago, 1986), p.48, hereafter referred to in the text as MT.

3. Elizabeth Bowen, 'Out of a Book' (1946), in *The Mulberry Tree*, pp.157–60 (p.48).

4. Philippe Lejune also suggests that all autobiography rests on an act of faith as the reader has no way of knowing if the autobiographer is relying on memory or on imagination. Philippe Lejune, *Memory and Narrative* (Chicago, IL: University of Chicago Press, 1998).

5. See preface to *The Last September* (Alfred A. Knopf, 1952). Here Bowen explains how she is haunted by the fear that readers will miss the viewpoint of the novel: 'from the start the reader must look, be conscious of looking backward – down a backward perspective of eight years' (*SW*, p.200).

6. Elizabeth Bowen, *The Death of The Heart* (London: Jonathan Cape, 1938), p.300, here-after referred to in the text as DH. Matchett, the voice of common sense in *The Death of the Heart*, tells Portia that 'those without memories don't know what is what' (p.98). She also explains how furniture has memories: 'furniture is knowing all right, good furniture knows what's what' (p.98).

7. Paul de Man, 'Autobiography as De-facement', *Modern Language Notes*, 94, 5 Comparative Literature (Dec. 1979), pp.919–30 (p.919).

8. Richard N. Coe, *When the Grass was Greener: Autobiography and the Experience of Childhood* (New Haven, CT: Yale University Press, 1984), p.15.

9. De Man, 'Autobiography as De-facement', p.919.

10. Ibid., p.920.

11. Ibid., p.922. Of course De Man is here making a much more general point about the limitations of language.

12. Maud Ellmann, *Elizabeth Bowen: The Shadow Across the Page* (Edinburgh: Edinburgh University Press, 2003), p.7.

13. Declan Kiberd, 'The Dandy in Revolt', in *Sex, Nation and Dissent in Irish Writing*, ed. Eibhear Walshe (Cork: Cork University Press, 2002), p.138.

14. Elizabeth Bowen, *Bowen's Court* (London: Longmans, Green and Co., 1942), p.456, hereafter referred to in the text as BC.

15. Hermoine Lee, *Elizabeth Bowen* (London: Vintage, 1999), p.15.

16. Elizabeth Bowen, 'The Bend Back' (1950), in *The Mulberry Tree*, pp.54–60 (p.54).

17. Kristine A. Miller, '"Even a Shelter's Not Safe": The Blitz on Homes in Elizabeth Bowen's Wartime Writing', *Twentieth Century Literature*, 34, 2 (Summer 1999), pp.138–58 (p.139).

18. Lee, *Elizabeth Bowen*, p.17.

19. Laura Marcus, *Auto/Biographical Discourses: Theory, Criticism, Practice* (Manchester: Manchester University Press, 1994), p.196. See Jean Starobinski, who reinforces this point: 'What is of primary importance is not historical veracity but the emotion experienced as the past emerges and is represented in consciousness.' Jean Starobinski, 'The Style of Autobiography', in *Autobiography: Essays Theoretical and Critical*, ed. James Olney (Princeton, NJ: Princeton University Press, 1980), pp.73–83 (p.198). (For a discussion of Starobinski, see Laura Marcus.)

20. John Banville, 'Shades of Elizabeth Bowen'. The Dublin Film Festival, a supplement to the *Irish Times*, 3 April 1999.

21. See Richard Stanihurst, *Treatise containing a Plaine and Perfect Description of Ireland*, 1577; Edmund Spenser, *A View of The Present State of Ireland*, 1586–96; Arthur Young, (1742–1820) *A Tour of Ireland* (Belfast: Blackstaff Press, 1983). Bowen relies heavily on the work of Jonah Barrington (1760–1834), particularly on *Personal Sketches and Recollections of His Own Times* (Dublin: Ashfield Press, 1997).

22. De Man, 'Autobiography as De-facement', p.55.

23. Elizabeth Bowen, 'The Big House' (1940), in *The Mulberry Tree*, pp.25–30 (p.29).

24. At the time of writing this chapter all that now remains of Bowen's Court is an untidy mound of limestone, and semi-exposed foundations that gape at a deserted

landscape, a landscape denuded of the once sheltering trees that surrounded the house. Only the Ballyhoura Hills now guard the spot where for 300 years the Bowens lived.

25. Elizabeth Bowen, *Seven Winters and Afterthoughts* (New York: Alfred A. Knopf, 1962), p.47, hereafter referred to in the text as *SW*.

26. Elizabeth Grubgeld, *Anglo-Irish Autobiography: Class, Gender and the Forms of Narrative* (Syracuse, NY: Syracuse University Press, 2004), p.278.

27. Elizabeth Bowen, *Pictures and Conversations* (Harmondsworth: Penguin, 1975), p.61, hereafter referred to in the text as *PC*.

28. Olney (ed.), *Autobiography: Essays Theoretical and Critical*, p.23. For critics like James Olney, autobiography is the purest form of a literature of consciousness.

29. Grubgeld, *Anglo-Irish Autobiography*, p.38.

CHAPTER NINE

'Half Different': The Vanishing Irish in *A World of Love*

CLAIR WILLS

Her time, called hers because she was required to live in it and had no other, was in bad odour, and no wonder. Altogether the world was in a crying state of exasperation, but that was hardly her fault: too much had been going on for too long. Like someone bidden to enter an already overcrowded and overcharged room, she paused for as long as possible on the threshold, waiting for something to subside, for the floor to empty or the air to clear. The passions and politics of her family so much resembled those of the outside world that she made little distinction between the two. It was her hope that this might all die down, from lack of recruits or fuel, or, most of all, if more people were to take less notice. She did what she could by adding no further heat.[1]

The young, innocent idealist on the threshold of adult society is a favourite character in Elizabeth Bowen's fiction. Crossing the frontier between adolescence and adulthood is fraught with disappointment and danger, not only for these girls (Lois, Portia and Emmeline, for example) but also for the society into which they enter. As Barbara Seward put it, in a 1956 review of *A World of Love*, 'Appalled by the tragic inability of our world to meet the demands of the innocent romantic, Miss Bowen has throughout her career been still more appalled by the romantic's inability to meet the crying demands of our world'.[2] *A World of Love* turns this loosely tragic plot upside-down with all the panache and sprightliness of a Shakespearian comedy. In this novel the romantic illusions of the young woman, Jane, are played out in an Irish version of the enchanted forest. A victim of puckishness, with a packet of letters playing the part of the love juice, Jane's misdirected romance with a man more then thirty years dead helps to break the atrophying spell which the 'passions and politics' of her family have laid over the present. Her stagey romance destroys the fetters tying the adults to the past, and – exuberantly and improbably – makes way for love.

The novel opens soon after 20-year-old Jane has discovered an Edwardian dress and a packet of letters in the attic of her family home, a 'small mansion' on a run-down estate in Ireland. The letters have been written by her cousin Guy before his death in France in the First World War, but to an unknown addressee. As they circulate around the members of the household, at moments hidden, stolen, lost, found and eventually burnt, the letters conjure in each of their many recipients a series of reactions which begin to shake the certainties of the family's narrative of the past. The story of the (not always beneficial) help and protection given by Guy's cousin Antonia to his fiancée Lilia after Guy's death is well known – too well known – in the family. But the passage of the letters through the house and garden uncovers a suppressed history of entanglements between Guy, Antonia, Lilia (Jane's mother), and Guy's 'half' cousin Fred, who has married Lilia on Antonia's insistence. All have loved Guy, and all have been cauterized by his sudden death. It is not, as Antonia realizes, that Guy is a ghost with the power to haunt the present. His death has never really been accepted, and 'the continuation of the apparently cut off life' has left them bereft and at the same time subject to an absent presence: 'It was simply that these years she was living belonged to him, his lease upon them not having run out yet. The living were living in his lifetime; and of this his contemporaries – herself, Lilia, Fred – never were unaware. They were incomplete' (WL, p.45). This half-life lies at the core of the novel.

As Bowen suggests, however, the passions and politics uncovered here are not only those of Jane's family's legacy, but of the whole 'outside world'. In fact it is impossible to disentangle one from the other. In The Heat of the Day Bowen had described the pressure of history on the individual as a kind of haunting. The lovers Stella and Robert Kelway cannot shake off the spectre of the war in which they met, and which defines their relationship: 'Their time sat in the third place at their table. They were the creatures of history ... The relation of people to each other is subject to the relation of each to time.'[3] Despite the fact that A

World of Love appears to take place in a timeless world, the enclosed and isolated arena of fairy-tale convention, Jane knows that she is defined by the 'crying state of exasperation' of her society as a whole. And the novel poses the question of the boundaries of this exasperated world. Jane's time is the early 1950s; the world's tears include those of her parents' generation, living a half-life after the slaughter of the First World War, but also those who must live in the aftermath of the Second.[4] Bowen here addresses the links between a faltering and embattled Anglo-Ireland and the 'outside world' which expands to include Ireland, England and the 'bad odour' of her whole historical moment. That moment is defined by the Cold War, as Bowen makes clear in the passage I have quoted. Jane feels 'bidden to enter' this arena but lingers on the threshold – it appears that there is no space for her. The room is overcrowded, filled up with the 'passions and politics' of previous inhabitants who won't go away. Guy and his contemporaries have not yet left the room, and the legacy of the First and Second World Wars ensures that the siege-like state of war continues. Jane's attempt to assuage the rising tensions by adding 'no further heat' is designed to maintain the cool temperature of a war which is already quite overcharged enough.

Turning down the heat on a cold war even further, R.F. Foster has suggested that the novel depicts 'the ice-age Ireland of the 1950s'.[5] It is ironic, then, that the action takes place in a summer of unnatural, almost supernatural, warmth. The heat is oppressive, the air close, the light glaring, the river dry. The uncanny weather is one catalyst for the long-suppressed battle. It is a conflict between good fairies and evil demons, manifesting themselves as the witch-like Lady Latterly, or the child Maud's 'familiar' Gay David, who provoke the battle between family members.[6] Jane gets drunk, Lilia cuts her hair, Antonia goes to sea, but the cuts and bruises sustained by Maud in her fight with her father are the most concrete sign of the end of the emotional freeze.

In a 1951 broadcast for the Third Programme on 'The Cult of Nostalgia', Bowen analyzed the contemporary vogue for comforting representations of the past, and of childhood, as a response to unsettling times. Although she did not specify the causes of the disturbance which, she argued, sent people back to the past in search of reassurance, it is clear that the post-war political dispensation, and Cold War realities, were aspects of the contemporary upheaval:

> The unfamiliar: really, it may be argued, these days we are having
> enough of that. Its cold breath meets us at every turn, not only in
> art, which we may eschew, but in everyday life, which is unavoid-
> able. To live at all, to conduct oneself through a day, week, year, is
> a matter of shocks, incredulities, then adjustments ... The past,
> now, seems to be the repository of all treasures.[7]

The broadcast focused on the harmful effects of nostalgic fantasies ('our
perpetual dwelling on the past'), which she saw as most dangerously
associated with idyllic scenes of pre-war England: 'Everything was,
apparently, nicer then: more vivid, less monotonous, more important'.
She recorded her wish to see the young break free of this overpowering
Edwardian idyll: 'I should like to see a whole generation keep the power
of taking its moments "straight" – not half-overcast by fantasy, not
thinned-down by yearning'.[8]

She might have been describing the plot of *A World of Love*, except that
it is through fantasy that Jane (unwittingly aided by her little sister Maud)
helps to break the hold of the past on an entire generation. As a young
girl she has indulged a natural aversion to the past ('Oh, there lay the
root of all evil! – this continuous tedious business of received griev-
ances, not-to-be-settled old scores' [*WL*, p.35]). It is only when she
becomes bewitched by the past, and in particular the pre-war 'gay days',
hugging the letters to herself as she imagines they have been addressed
to her as 'Guy's latest love', that her parents are able to let it go. In the
same way Bowen had written of her excavation of familial and political
history in *Bowen's Court*, that her aim was not 'to drag up the past but to
help lay it'.[9]

Many critics have noted that this past is a specifically Anglo-Irish one
(as it is in *Bowen's Court*). Montefort, the decaying smallish Big House
which now appears as little more than 'the annexe of its farm buildings',
encapsulates the 'virtually posthumous life' of the Anglo-Irish after the
First World War and the Irish revolution.[10] The house has turned in on
itself; with its Venetian window sealed up (tracing what the novel elsewhere calls a 'ghost of style') it presents a 'blind end' to the gorge. With
the gentry now making their living as farmers, the house is described as
as good as closed up and abandoned: the front door 'no longer knew
hospitality'; the avenue 'lived on as a rutted track'. The house is sealed

too against the passage of time, possessing 'none of the innovations' such as plumbing and boilers. If it weren't for Maud's obsession with the chiming of Big Ben on the wireless, the entire house would echo the massive range, the lack of plumbing, the faded calendars, the stopped clock, in proclaiming 'the almost total irrelevance of time, in the abstract, to this ceaseless kitchen' (*WL*, p.21).

Part of the problem is lack of money (sharply contrasted with the English Chatelaine's profligate schemes for heating and plumbing), and part of it is lack of society. In *Bowen's Court* (published in 1942) Bowen had analyzed the 'centripetal and cut-off life' of the Protestant Ascendancy in Ireland, lamenting the isolation of the Anglo-Irish from contact with the world outside the Big House demesne. Their aloofness began from the moment of their arrival in Ireland, she argued, but increased with the Act of Union in 1800. From this moment Anglo-Irish culture was, by necessity, directed politically and economically towards England, though a social life centred in Ireland continued. As Hubert Butler later suggested, the withdrawnness increased again with the Anglo-Irish war: 'For our parents of the ascendancy it was easy and obvious to live in Ireland, but we of the "descendancy" were surrounded in the 'twenties by the burnt out houses of our friends and relations. England beckoned us and only an obstinate young person would wish to stay at home.'[11] The Montefort inhabitants in *A World of Love* are not so much obstinate as without alternatives. The word 'loneliness' echoes through the novel, along with descriptions of a 'bereft' and 'abandoned' landscape. The Hunt Fête, which has occurred the day before the novel opens, is 'now the sole activity of the lonely year' for this forsaken family. But for Lilia it is social agony, as she stands isolated in the field in uncomfortable shoes, or begs a lift home from a stranger: the event can only emphasize her loneliness, not cure it.

'No idea anyone was living there', says the man who eventually drives Lilia home. It is not simply Guy who has gone, but the fabric of Anglo-Irish society, and with it the 'social idea' upon which the Big House was built.[12] As Neil Corcoran has pointed out, *A World of Love* itself is in hoc to the past. The plot of the novel repeats much of the action of *The Last September* in comic mode, with Jane a latter-day version of Lois, and Kathie a diminutive of Kathleen.[13] Taking up Butler's hint in the term 'the descendancy', we can think of the theme of the novel as in part about the survival of a species, and its costs. The spectral half-life of the war generation is also the half-life of the Anglo-Irish. What happens, Bowen asks, when the house doesn't burn (as it burns at the end of *The Last September*)? Like Beckett's tragi-comic depiction of the latter-day Big House in his wartime novel *Watt*, in which the decrepit Watt and Knott live isolated from the world outside the demesne and tied to each other as master and slave in an endless, sterile series, Bowen's query concerns the impossible future for those who live on after the rest have gone.[14]

One result of isolation is fear. The 'historical' fear of being burned out appears in the novel as Lilia's fear that the attics, stuffed with the rubbish of the past, will catch light. In the end it is Jane herself who sets a torch to this material, as she rummages there to find the letters, for she has 'an igniting touch'. 'Tell 'em to go to blazes', counsels her father. Later at the dinner party at the castle she drunkenly imagines herself passing through the burning building unscathed. And if revolutionary fires have turned inward, to be lit by the Big House inhabitants themselves, violent intruders also now appear on the inside. The fear of outsiders is noticeable in all Bowen's depictions of the Anglo-Irish in Ireland, but here it reaches fantastic proportions. Montefort is fiercely gated and chained. The novel is punctuated by the repeated scene of fumbling with the chain on the gate at the end of the avenue. So far from the gracious outward-looking ideal of the eighteenth-century Big House, Lilia now lives in fear not of night-time marauders, but of 'any comer at all'. When a car arrives with a party invitation for Jane, Lilia backs herself against a wall and Maud scuttles across the living-room floor on her hands and knees, to peer out of the window without being seen. There is an echo here of the hysterical Aunt Fran in Bowen's wartime story 'Summer Night', who can't rest until the house has been locked up at night and who prays for deliverance from unseen foes. But the irony in that story of marital betrayal is that the source of the trouble is already on the inside: 'Not a benediction falls on this apart house of the Major: the enemy is within it, creeping about. Each heart here falls to the enemy.'[15] In *A World of Love* a similar internal rottenness renders futile Antonia's elaborate barricading of the house:

> Not since Montefort stood had there ceased to be vigilant measures against the nightcomer; all being part of the hostile watch

kept by now eyeless towers and time-stunted castles along these rivers. For as all land knows, everywhere is a frontier; and the outposted few (and few are the living) never must be off guard. (WL, p.79)

It matters little whether the fear of invasion is from the dead, so vastly outnumbering the living, or from the hostile life outside the Montefort gates, for the door has 'gone into dissolution: shut out nothing'. Guy has already slipped in as, later in the novel, he slips into the walled garden where Lilia is sitting. In both instances the apparition of Guy is displaced by, or merged with, the real-life Fred; the distance and difference between the two men collapses. After all Fred has acted, for the past twenty years, as a substitute for Guy. This is the ur-substitution which leads to a series of substitutions and shared identities in the novel – a mode of existence signalled in Maud's struggling relationship with her 'other half', her familiar Gay David. At different points in the novel Antonia and Guy change places (aided by Jane's recollection of a photograph which brings out the family resemblance), Jane substitutes for Lilia in the eyes of her father, and Lilia stands in for Antonia at Montefort, where she is 'half the hostess, half not'. Antonia has stood in for Lilia as one of Guy's loves, as has another, unnamed girl whose letters have somehow found their way into the attic. Jane stands in for the imaginary daughter of Guy and Lilia, or of the cousins Guy and Antonia. Guy stands in for all men.

This doubling of parts, with its gesture towards the cross-gendering of Shakespearian romance, signals the incestuousness of the relationships within this dwindling group. They are living off themselves. However, this is not merely a condition of Anglo-Irish life. It is true too of the English 'displaced rich' who form the party staying at Lady Latterly's castle. These characters, described as black and white cardboard cut-outs, are sterile, hollow versions of human beings. Lady Latterly invites old Terence, a still-living relic of the pre-war 'gay days', and Jane to lend the group substance. Guy comes too, or is conjured by the party themselves. He is the original 'guy' without whom the party would be in danger of disappearing altogether.

With their halved and twinned identities, none of the inhabitants of Montefort are complete in themselves (except possibly Kathie the servant[16]). But the fact of their being 'half different' is also a key to their survival. I have described half-life as an aspect of the characters' belatedness, their having been sundered from a part of their lives which continues its ghostly existence elsewhere. But it is also a sign of their ability to adapt. In *Bowen's Court* Bowen had argued that the isolationist and protectionist impulses of the Anglo-Irish were a mark of a 'breed' fast becoming extinct:

> Isolation, egotism and, on the whole, lack of culture made in them for an independence one has to notice because it becomes, in these days, rare. Independence was the first quality of a class now, I am told, becoming extinct ... I recognise that a class, like a breed of animals is due to ... become extinct should it fail to adapt ... The gentry, as a class, may or may not prove able to make adaptations ... To my mind, they are tougher than they appear.[17]

Thirteen years later, in *A World of Love* she explores the adaptations that have been made. After Guy's death extinction for Montefort has been staved off by bringing the English Lilia to Ireland to marry the half Anglo-Irish, half 'Irish' Fred. They live in the house not as landlords but as farmers, not as tenants but not as owners either. Though the ritual of chains and bolts and barricades continues (as does the barrier implied by 'the Protestant van' which takes Maud to school), Fred makes a living for the family as any other local farmer. Antonia meanwhile halves her life between Ireland and London, along with her part Anglo-Irish, part English, part cousin, part daughter Jane.

This version of cross-breeding has rendered them invisible. Compared to the stark yellows and blacks and whites of the castle, Montefort – its paths greening and outhouses crumbling – does not exist. 'Pity that's gone', says Terence. To Jane's insistence that 'I live there', Terence returns a confused, 'I heard it had got into farmer's hands'. For the house to have become a farm is as good as its having disappeared, as far as Terence is concerned. But as the hay seed lodged in Jane's hair signifies, the family at Montefort are not sterile like the hollowed-out creatures at the castle. 'Died out, have you?' asks Harris the chauffeur, when he learns that there are no more men in the family. But Bowen allows Jane to carry the seed, and the end of the novel gestures to the next adaptation the family will make, as she falls for a man from Colorado.

Harris's question is posed of the family but once more the family mirrors the 'outside world' and in particular the depopulated world of rural Ireland. As so often in Bowen's fiction, the condition of the isolated Anglo-Irish does not simply contrast with, but reflects, the broader condition of Ireland as a whole. In her wartime Irish stories and *Bowen's Court*, for example, the isolationist 'house-islands' created by the dwindling number of Anglo-Irish in Ireland share with the neutral Irish state a desire for protective 'immunity' from the violence of the war. (In her most hard-hitting stories, such as 'Summer Night' and 'A Love Story', they also share a penchant for betrayal.[18]) And in *A World of Love* it is noticeable that the stagnation, abandonment, loneliness and incompleteness of the Montefort domain mirrors the territory outside its gates.

For the novel also describes the 'virtually posthumous life' of the Irish, which at the time almost seemed on the cards. By the mid-1950s concern over extinction and survival was by no means limited to the Anglo-Irish in Ireland. The post-war wave of emigration to Britain had reached such overwhelming proportions by 1948 that the new inter-party government set up the Commission on Emigration and other Population Problems to investigate the causes of the massive 'exodus' of the working population, and to recommend policies to forestall it. As the report pointed out, over the course of a century (and including the consequences of the famine) the overall population of the country had halved. The commissioners heard evidence from government bodies, independent organizations and interested individuals, in addition to interviewing groups of would-be emigrants at Labour Exchanges around the country. They reported their findings in 1954.[19] Much of the report focuses on the problems facing rural areas, and in particular the failure of small farms (often in the west of the country), which were increasingly being abandoned as farmers' children and labourers chose to take up paid work in England rather than continue the subsistence-level economy of their parents. The majority of the commissioners were happy to acknowledge that the primary causes of emigration were economic – and put the situation principally down to the lack of constant employment at a decent wage. But in addition to this overwhelming 'push' factor, the report also suggested that various 'pull' factors were at work, including the desire to improve material conditions, the attraction of urban life, dissatisfaction with poor living conditions on farms lacking electricity and running water, and so on. Women emigrants were seen as especially susceptible to these 'lures', partly because of a general belief that women were less likely to emigrate because of want of work than a desire for a husband and a more comfortable way of life. The more conservative submissions, from interested individuals as well as some members of the Commission, liked to blame the love of luxury characteristic of young Irish women, which led them to covet the cinemas, dancing, high-heels and modern hairstyles available in Dublin and English towns and cities above the frugal living waiting for them at home. But despite the tendency to moralizing (noticeable too in responses to the report published in national and local newspapers), the principal mood of the report was one of regret – that the parlous state of Irish economic life meant the structure of traditional Irish rural society was being undermined.[20] 'Pity that's gone', says Terence of the house whose survival as a form of tenant farm has been enabled by Fred's mixed inheritance. Terence is wrong about Montefort, but being a farmer and having disappeared were equivalent not only for those of the 'descendancy', but for Irish farmers in general.

Bowen's description of the empty yard at Montefort could be a description of any abandoned Irish farm, perhaps excepting the dovecote:

> The slate roofs sent shimmers up; the red doors ajar all seemed caught by a spell in the act of opening; white outbuildings tottered there in the glare. Grass which had seeded between the cobbles parched and, dying, deadened her steps: a visible silence filled the place – long it was since anyone had been here. Slime had greenly caked in the empty trough, and the unprecedented loneliness of the afternoon looked out, as through eyelets cut in a mask, from the archways of the forsaken dovecote. Not a straw stirred, or was there to stir, in the kennel; and above her something other than clouds was missing from the uninhabited sky. (WL, p.43)

The idea that it is long since anyone had been there is odd, since this yard stands directly outside the back door of the house. This is one sign that in these descriptions of abandonment Bowen meant to gesture towards a more general condition facing rural Ireland. It is repeated in the picture of the local town, Clonmore. In its juxtaposition of the tourist traditional and practically modern ('cars parked askew, straying ass-carts, and fallen bicycles') the main street echoes the make-do modernizations at Montefort. Above all, the town echoes the feeling of having been left behind which overshadows the house: 'Dung baked on the pavements since yesterday morning's fair; shop after shop had insanely similar doorways, strung with boots and kettles and stacked with calicoes – in eternal windows goods faded out' (*WL*, p.88). Home of a faded out existence, Clonmore 'not only provided no place to be, it provided no reason to be at all' (*WL*, p.88). In a strange echo of Flann O'Brien's *The Third Policeman* (though this hadn't yet been published) Bowen describes the town as flattened out by the heat:

> deadly glazed into a picture postcard such as one might receive from Hell. Gone was the third dimension; nothing stood behind anything – opposite Lilia, a hillful of holy buildings appeared to weight down the slated street roofs below. And worst, wherever she turned her eyes movement could be seen to expire slowly – a bus, it was true, came punting in, but only to be at once deserted: why and how again should it ever start? She could have pitied the bus. But, like everything else, it was absolute in its indifference to her.
>
> 'You know, Jane, this is a place where one could not even be run over.' (*WL*, p.88)

In this place where nothing can happen the hairdresser's salon alone possesses 'the art of reviving the life-illusion'. But even here existence is halved. Not only is Miss Francie's 'reputed partner' perpetually absent, but Miss Francie herself is prone to 'mysterious total vanishings'. On this occasion she flits off in the middle of cutting Lilia's hair, leaving her with one side only shorn. This gives rise to Lilia's 'Already I feel half different'. Bowen's use of the term 'vanishing' (*WL*, p.90), a term which repeats her earlier description of Kathie as 'vanished', as well as the 'faded out' condition of the town as a whole, itself echoes the title of a controversial book on the problem of Irish depopulation published while Bowen was writing *A World of Love*, and a few months before the publication of the Emigration Commission Report. *The Vanishing Irish: The Enigma of the Modern World*, a collection of essays edited by John O'Brien, included contributions by writers and commentators such as Sean O'Faolain, Paul Vincent Carroll, Arland Ussher, Bryan MacMahon and Shane Leslie, many of whom had been associated with *The Bell*.[21]

The Vanishing Irish was criticized by members of the Commission, and of the government, for the melodramatic way in which it posed the problem of national decay and the coming 'extinction' of the race. But the publication of two significant works on population decline in the same year does point to the general concern over emigration in the early 1950s. An estimated 43,000 men and women left the country in 1954, rising again after a minor drop in 1956, to a new high of 54,000 in 1957.[22] As Mary Daly has suggested, although the national newspapers tended to produce guarded reports on the problem, provincial newspapers regularly printed regional stories about the high rates of emigration, and its costs to the community, indicating local levels of concern.

The wartime and post-war needs of the British labour force had decisively altered the shape of Irish emigration. Large numbers of men were needed in construction, mining and factory work, while women were employed as trainee nurses, domestic servants and factory workers – setting a pattern of migration of unskilled and semi-skilled labour to the Midlands and south of England. Because of housing shortages in Britain, many men left dependants in Ireland, returning at Christmas and for summer holidays. What developed was a regular two-way traffic for many migrants, which differed markedly from earlier phases of emigration to the United States, for example, and which meant not only that the idea of England was kept in mind, but confirmed the continuing close ties between the British and Irish economies.[23] So, for example, the 'Rural Survey for Clonmel, Arklow and Wexford' conducted by Commissioner William Honohan as part of the Commission on Emigration, described the local population not merely as halved by emigration, but in large part as made up of individuals who themselves were 'half' emigrants. Mr Murphy, the manager of the Exchange in Clonmel, described the town as having a large 'floating population – those who spent half the year in Britain and half here. He estimated them at 15,000, and he thought they didn't really know their own minds.'[24] On the other hand Murphy's own evidence suggests that they knew their minds very well. As Honohan reported, 'Mr Murphy told me that Clonmel was always an emigrating centre and England (especially London) was their spiritual home. On occasions of Rugby Internationals, a large percentage of the excursionists from Clonmel did not return.' If sport offered an occasion for emigration, leisure and the freedom to do as one liked offered an incentive: 'even though the cash margin in Britain was slight, the emigrants felt they could spend it with freedom as they like. It was to be feared that over here such diversions as sing-songs in pubs would, to say the least, be frowned upon.'

This summary of the social and economic landscape of the area is repeated across the rural surveys, although the detailed pattern of migration differs considerably between the poorer rural counties such as Mayo and Sligo, and provincial centres such as Kilkenny. Commissioners often stressed that it was the impact of modern forms of leisure and lifestyle on the local area (rather than the complete absence of modern influences) which caused dissatisfaction with the quality of life which could be had at home. In other words, it was the links with the wages and leisure to be had in England, rather than the distance from them, which encouraged emigration. There is more at issue here than the emigrant remittances, visits from returning and holidaying migrants, and emigrant letters, which traditionally provided the link between life at home and in England. In contrast to some who argued that emigrants left because of the 'dullness' of rural life, Honohan suggested that it was, paradoxically, the presence of new leisure activities (along with insufficient money to take advantage of them) which attracted people to life in English cities:

> It may be that, in the past, when standards were lower and perhaps opportunities for spending money not so great in certain areas (no cinema, no dance hall, not so much smoking), many of those now emigrating were satisfied with work in large or short spells from time to time. The modern requirement, however, is a pay-packet of definite dimensions every week, and I think the Commission might well comment of the fact that we are moving away from the time when employers of labour can count on getting men for a couple of days or a couple of weeks at a time and then laying them off. The day of the casual and purely temporary worker – employed directly and not through a contractor – is, to all intents and purposes, passing – a matter which is, of course, aggravated by the attractiveness of full employment in Britain at the present time.[25]

As Honohan pointed out, the growth of the cash economy particularly affected the 'large unpaid pool of relatives assisting'. (He estimated them as 243,000 – 61,000 men and 182,000 women.) These men and women, who in the past would not have worked for a wage, could now claim work in Britain.

> It may be that, in years gone by, such persons have been content to live virtually on a subsistence basis, but the cinema, radio, newspapers and friends are now luring them into the attitude that they should not be satisfied with this but should leave home to raise their standards, get married and have homes of their own. Who can blame them?

Although Honohan is sympathetic to the young emigrants, his use of terms such as 'luring' suggests the broadly moral terms in which he understands this process. By contrast, Bowen presents the problem as structural: one half of life is already in England. Just as Maud's obsession with hearing the chiming of Big Ben over the wireless creates a standard of measure for Montefort, so too the British economy has created the conditions against which Irish economic prospects are measured. Despite the repeated images of isolation, the community is the opposite of self-sufficient.

In this context it is fitting that Lilia suddenly decides to go to London after having her hair cut in Clonmore's 'magic oasis of tinted mirror, enamel and bakelite'. Miss Francie's salon is the locus for the 'lure' of modernity in the town, a modernity equally appealing on the average farm and at Montefort with its 'ceaseless kitchen'. The spectral other half of the salon does indeed exist in another realm, and certainly in another country, and, according to the Commission report, it is partly responsible for Clonmore's deserted bus. The glossy magazines resting on the gilded table in Miss Francie's salon are precisely the type of literature frowned on by the more conservative members of the Commission. 'Prototype Woman' stares out at Lilia from the cover of her magazine, and she would undoubtedly be blamed for creating unrealistic expectations of life among local girls. But in fact nearly everything the women encounter in Clonmore brings London to mind. The tins of Russian salad in the grocer's remind Jane of delicatessens in London. The warm weather causes the grocer to comment that they are 'demented with the heat in England'. Most of all, the sheer bareness of the town, mirrored in the abandoned Montefort, and the 'empty' castle drawing-room, conjures up London, where life had once been possible and still might be.

Although cousin Guy is principally a figure for a lopped-off part of Anglo-Irish life, he also alludes to the figure of the migrant. Half of life at Montefort lies in the past, but in Clonmore more generally half of life is in England. (As Bishop Cornelius Lucey pointed out in a melodramatic Memorandum to the Commission, death and emigration are equivalent as far as population is concerned – they have the same demographic effect.[26]) Guy is repeatedly described as 'more' than other men – 'The whole of a man!' exclaims Lilia, marking him off from the incomplete men still living. This echoes the common lament about mid-century emigration that 'the best are leaving' or 'the cream of the population is gone'. Moreover, in his sudden reappearance Guy is a version of the returned emigrant – still trapped in the past, but with the power to unsettle the present with expectations. In both cases – the 'continuation of the apparently cut-off life' (*WL*, p.44) and the shadow existence of the migrant – the effect on those who remain is that they too are also only half there. 'If you call it going; you're all the time somewhere else' (*WL*, p.26), complains Antonia of Jane's abstraction. Lady Latterly echoes this charge: 'So that's where you've always been, is it – not here?' (*WL*, p.56). The whole community is 'breathing in wronged air – air either too empty or too full, one could not say which' (*WL*, p.44).

While everyone else continues to focus on England, and London in particular, Jane re-orientates west. In the final sequence of the novel Harris the chauffeur (playing the part of the good fairy who disappears in the final lines of the novel, his job done) drives Jane, Maud and with them, the reader, through the Limerick countryside to the emphatically modern airport at Shannon. Bowen wonderfully evokes the precarious position of the technological and the new in this grassy territory. The airport appears as a sort of mirage, made of 'magnetic little buildings' which appear 'to circle' as the van approaches. The terminus is both part of the landscape and emphatically a route to another world at the same time – it is, after all, accessed via 'the Turn Off', the 'vast taut cemented causeway' which 'looked like the future and for some was'. Inside the buildings the muffled, 'glassed in' world, and conditioned air replicate this sense of non-belonging. And the passengers themselves, stopping *en route* to elsewhere, make their lack of connection with Ireland abundantly clear as they troop off to be fed and plied with duty-free goods: 'indifferent to the earth they were to know for so short a time'.

This unlikely ending, in which Jane's rescuer drops in from the new world, has gathered its share of criticism. Yet it is not only exact in its portrayal of Shannon as a locus of possibility and hoped-for change in the Ireland of the 1950s, it also dovetails with Bowen's own increasing orientation to the United States in this period, partly as an escape from pressing financial difficulties in Ireland, and partly as a result of 'coming unstuck' from the post-war political dispensation in England.[27] Moreover, as Bowen appreciated, Cold War realities insisted that it was not only the decaying Anglo-Irish family which found its protector in America, but also the 'outside world' of Ireland, and indeed Britain too.

NOTES

1. Elizabeth Bowen, *A World of Love* (London: Viking, 1999), p.34, hereafter referred to in the text as *WL*.
2. Barbara Seward, 'Elizabeth Bowen's World of Impoverished Love', *College English*, 18, 1 (1956), pp.30–7.
3. Elizabeth Bowen, *The Heat of the Day* (London: Viking, 1998), p.194–5.
4. See for example p.45 of the novel: 'Meantime, another war had peopled the world with another generation of the not-dead, overlapping and crowding the living's senses still more with that sense of unlived lives.'
5. R.F. Foster, 'The Irishness of Elizabeth Bowen', in *Paddy and Mr Punch: Connections in Irish and English History* (Harmondsworth: Penguin, 1993), p.121.
6. On the fairy-tale, magical and other-worldly plot devices in the novel, see Robert Tracy, *The Unappeasable Host: Studies in Irish Identities* (Dublin: University College Dublin Press, 1998), pp.242–55, and Lis Christensen, *Elizabeth Bowen: The Later Fiction* (Copenhagen: Museum Tusculanum Press, University of Copenhagen, 2001), pp.174–85.
7. Elizabeth Bowen, 'The Cult of Nostalgia', *The Listener*, 9 August 1951, p.225.
8. Ibid. It was these conditions which encouraged a number of Bowen's friends to seek homes in Ireland, a group satirized in the character of Lady Latterly. See Victoria Glendinning, *Elizabeth Bowen: Portrait of a Writer* (London: Weidenfeld and Nicolson, 1977), pp.194–5.
9. See Elizabeth Bowen, *Bowen's Court and Seven Winters* (London: Vintage, 1999).
10. See Neil Corcoran, *Elizabeth Bowen: The Enforced Return* (Oxford: Oxford University Press, 2004), p.63.
11. For Bowen's essay, 'The Big House', first published in *The Bell*, 1, 1 (October 1940), p.453, see Hermione Lee (ed.), *The Mulberry Tree: Writings of Elizabeth Bowen* (London: Virago, 1986), pp.25–9. I also quote here from Hubert Butler, 'The Bell: An Anglo-Irish View', *Irish University Review*, 6, 1 (1976), pp.66–72. For a comic (and largely unsympathetic) treatment of this isolation, see Henry Green, *Loving* (London, 1949).
12. For a discussion of Big House sociability see Foster, *Paddy and Mr Punch*, p.112.

13. Corcoran, *Elizabeth Bowen*, pp.66–7.
14. For an extended analysis of comparisons between Bowen and Beckett see Sinéad Mooney, 'Bowen's Beckettian Affinities', *Modern Fiction Studies*, 53, 2 (Summer 2007), pp.238–56.
15. Elizabeth Bowen, 'Summer Nights', *Elizabeth Bowen's Irish Stories* (Dublin: Poolbeg, 1978), p.83.
16. Kathie is in a sense the final recipient of the letters – when they are burnt she 'saves' the ribbon and ties up her hair with it. While the other characters' encounters with the letters allow them to move on, Kathie may have the least 'future' of those at Montefort. She will meet no lover and ends the novel still 'tied' to the past, even though it is to a past not her own.
17. *Bowen's Court*, p.456.
18. See Clair Wills, 'The Aesthetics of Irish Neutrality during the Second World War', *boundary 2*, 31, 1 (Spring 2004), pp.119–46.
19. See *Commission on Emigration and Other Population Problems, 1948–1954, Reports* (Dublin: Stationery Office), P.25411; R.63. See also the Arnold Marsh Papers, Papers of the Commission on Emigration (Trinity College Manuscripts). On emigrant numbers to Britain, see Enda Delaney, *Demography, State and Society: Irish Migration to Britain, 1921–1971* (Liverpool: Liverpool University Press, 2000), pp.161–8.
20. Numerous essays in the journals *Studies*, *Irish Monthly* and *Christus Rex* throughout this period testify to the pervasive anxiety about the death of rural Ireland. See also the publications by Muintir na Tire and Macra na Feirme on the need to protect and develop the small farm, for example, Jerome Toner, *Rural Ireland: Some of its Problems* (Dublin: Clonmore and Reynolds, 1955).
21. The essayists agreed that the primary factor cause of the country's population problems was emigration, but a disproportionate amount of the emphasis in the book was on the low marriage rate and the fact that 'all is not well in the relations between the Irishwoman and the Irishman' – an impressionistic but strongly held view. *The Vanishing Irish, The Enigma of the Modern World*, ed. John O'Brien (London: W. H. Allen, 1954).
22. See Mary E. Daly, *The Slow Failure: Population Decline and Independent Ireland, 1922–1973* (Wisconsin: University of Wisconsin Press, 2006), p.185.
23. Ibid., p.143.
24. Marsh papers, Rural Surveys, S5. See James Ryan, *Home from England* (Dublin: Phoenix, 1995) for a novelistic treatment of the migrant father who leaves his family in Ireland.
25. Marsh Papers, Rural Surveys, S5. See Delaney, *Demography, State and Society*, pp.168–76 on patterns of migration across the country, and the changing perceptions of acceptable standards of living.
26. Marsh Papers, 8304/41 14.
27. See letter to William Plomer, 24 September 1945, reprinted in Lee (ed.), *The Mulberry Tree*, pp.266–7.

CHAPTER TEN

'A Sort of Lunatic Giant'

EIBHEAR WALSHE

In this chapter I argue that in her last two works, The Little Girls and Eva Trout, Bowen radically reinvents and remakes her version of the modernist novel. In her previous writings, Bowen's representation of the past was often figured as a possible, frail source of security or stability for an insecure self. However in The Little Girls the past is revealed as empty and forlorn, while in Eva Trout the self becomes monstrous. In The Death of the Heart, one of her characters says, 'I swear that each of us keeps, battened down inside himself, a sort of lunatic giant – impossible socially, but full-scale – and that it's the knockings and batterings we sometimes hear in each other that keeps our intercourse from utter banality'.[1] In this chapter I want to consider Bowen's last two novels, where this 'lunatic giant' is released into full-scale narrative expression.

Critically these last Bowen novels have been somewhat under-valued. In her study of Bowen, Hermione Lee argues 'That Elizabeth Bowen's highly charged, contrived and controlled style should have been reduced to the clumsy procedures of The Little Girls can be attributed to more than obvious reasons of old age and dissatisfaction with out-dated formulae.'[2] Patricia Craig writes of Eva Trout that 'it goes even more awry than The Little Girls'.[3] Neil Corcoran expresses a more measured appreciation of the novels to some degree, when he writes:

> Since the novels which eventually followed, The Little Girls in 1963 and Eva Trout in 1968, are notoriously difficult to attach in any unproblematic way to the remaining canon of her work, we may feel that in A World of Love, by ending Bowen's fictional engagement with Ireland once and for all, but also by ending, as it were, nowhere at all, pitches Bowen the novelist towards the most unsettling kinds of further writing.[4]

It is the unsettling nature of this final writing that I want to explore, continuing the work of other recent critics such as Patricia Coughlan, Rene Hoogland, Tina O'Toole, Claire Connelly⁵ and others who have argued for these novels, particularly *Eva Trout*, as crucial within Bowen's canon. Connelly calls *Eva Trout* 'A neglected and misunderstood novel, which confronts contemporary readers with a memory of an in-between space in literary and cultural history'.⁶ Likewise Rene Hoogland writes that 'In those final, dislocated years, Bowen wrote two further novels ... both represent radical departures from her earlier stylistic methods and narrative techniques. While far less well received than any of her previous work, these texts, in which powerful subversive forces can be felt to be cracking through the surface, reveal the abiding strength of her creative and critical imagination.⁷

In this chapter I draw on this renewed critical interest in her final novels and suggest also that circumstances from her own personal life contributed to the starkness and directness of the abiding strength of these last writings. Throughout her writing life, Bowen had the security of her London home in Clarence Terrace, her family home, Bowen's Court, in North Cork, and the stabilizing presence of her husband, Alan Cameron, organizing her life in both homes and providing her with a secure work and social environment. In early 1952, due to Cameron's ill-health and early retirement, they gave up their London flat to return to live permanently in Ireland. Alan Cameron died in August 1952 and, bereft of his help, Bowen struggled unsuccessfully to maintain Bowen's Court. By 1959 she was forced to sell her family home. The security and reassurance that her home had afforded her was considerable, particularly during the Second World War. 'I suppose that everyone, fighting or just enduring, carried within him one private image, one peaceful scene. Mine was Bowen's Court. War had made me that image out of a house built of anxious history.'⁸ Yet financial necessity meant that the house had to be abandoned and this decision had, for Bowen, something of a shameful renunciation of an inherited trust and responsibility. In an afterword to a reprinting of *Bowen's Court* in 1963, she wrote:

> The house, having played its part, has come to an end. It will not, after all, celebrate its two hundredth birthday – of that, it has fallen short by some thirteen years. The shallow hollow of land, under the

mountains, on which Bowen's Court stood, is again empty. Not one hewn stone left on another on the fresh-growing grass. Green covers all traces of the foundations. Today so far as the eye can see, there might never have been a house. One cannot say that the space is empty ... It was a clean end. Bowen's Court never lived to be a ruin. (BC, p.459)

The loss of this house was a central moment for Bowen, both as a sorrow and a failure in responsibility. Curiously, at the same time, it afforded her an imaginative release from the burden of the past, Bowen's Court's anxious history. This imaginative release is reflected in her last novels. During this time of transition after the death of her husband, when Bowen was undecided about the future of her family home, she spent some months in Rome as writer-in-residence at the American Academy in Rome in the autumn of 1959. She had been visiting Rome throughout the 1950s and the result is her only travel book, *A Time in Rome*, published in 1960.[9] This text is crucial, I would argue, as a key insight into the process of Bowen's demolition and subsequent remaking of her own style, and marks the period of transition for the experimental style of narration in her last two novels. As she herself remarked, half in jest: 'I must look out or Rome would ruin my style' (ATR, p.71). Although Bowen characterizes her time apart in the Eternal City as 'Partly ... a liberation from the thicket of the self' (ATR, p.239), in fact the book seems less of a liberation. More than anything, it is an account of a breakdown within a city laden down with history. At the point of abandoning her own Anglo-Irish past, the oppressive historical weighting of Rome seems to disorientate and confuse her (indeed one chapter is called 'The Confusion'). In this account of her time in Rome, part travel guide and part impressionistic diary, Bowen records her sense of loneliness and apartness. She keeps losing her way and her comic relationship with her map is characteristic of this narrative of urban alienation.

> Difficulties with the map ... the one I bought, the Nuovissima Pianta, had been impossible to avoid, pressed upon me at every counter, by every vendor. Very newest it may have been, but not satisfactory. It is large, and I was in a constant state of needing to unfurl it in its entirety. Not canvas-backed, it is printed on brittle paper which disintegrates almost before you touch it. Rome

throughout February into March is windy, draughts if there are not gusts, gusts if there are not outright gales: the Pianta forever was rearing up to wrap itself blindingly round my face. My struggles with it were acute in the early days when I needed its guidance at every corner. (*ATR*, p.12)

Bowen's search is for meaning, belonging and solidity, yet Rome constantly evades her attempts to know and understand it. As she remarks, 'I was looking for splinters of actuality in the shifting mass of experience other than my own' (*ATR*, p.11). Part of that search is a desire to sweep away the past and start again, dispensing with the accreted burdens of the past. 'What is the shape of the ground underlying Rome? How would it look, I wondered, stripped of the city?' (*ATR*, p.10).

Ireland is conspicuous in its absence from this travel book and from her last two novels, but an Anglo-Irish sensibility appears again and again in Bowen's reading of the remains of Imperial Rome, the Rome of the new ruler, Augustus. In her account, Augustan Rome is reconstructed as a garrison culture and the Imperial women as the chatelaines of this newly imposed, insecure, brutalizing regime. In particular, in this description of a statue of Livia,[10] the wife of Augustus, she is now re-made as an Anglo-Irish conqueror's wife, a chatelaine in the years after Cromwell. Yet, like the Anglo-Irish woman, this wife of a powerful man finds her identity under pressure.

What did she look like? She must have been the subject of many portrait-busts, of which some must be in the museums seen by me, but I have forgotten them. My sense of her physical being comes from a statue, said to be of her, I saw it in a villa – the figure sits slid forward, almost reclining, on a low low-backed chair, in great ease, indolently at peace with its own beauty. It is young-mature. The plisse dress, having fallen vaguely around the breasts, flows on, moulding the narrow thighs, down the longer stretch between knee and sandal-tip. The repose suggests rest after something done, so well done or pleasurable in itself that it is to be thought over with a smile, in so far as the lady is thinking at all. The smile is in the attitude, or is a sort of effluence from the body: there is no head. (*ATR*, pp.190, 191)

The loss of the head, the woman who smiles in the absent space where her head once was, must stand for Bowen's maddened Anglo-Irish chatelaines, like Cousin Nettie in *The Heat of the Day*, pressed inexorably into cloud-land by the isolation and loneliness of their Big Houses, set in hostile and unloving Irish landscapes. In another section of the travel book, Bowen finds another Anglo-Irish connection in Rome, now in the Protestant Cemetery, and allows the lost daughters of a County Waterford Big House to upstage Keats in his unmarked grave, a sacred place of pilgrimage in Rome.

> The pair of Englishmen have few neighbours in this fresh, desultory grassy stretch; it is natural to wander to see who the few are. Among them, two let us imagine beautiful Irish sisters, Miss Moores, from and of Moorehill, County Waterford – Helen, dying in Rome at eighteen, was three months later followed by Isabella, aged twenty-nine. The elder nursed the younger, then caught it, too? 1805, Moorehill lost its daughters; sixteen years later, Earth lost Keats. No, lost he could not be! Death does nothing to poetry. The loss, for us, is that of the 'more': otherwise does it matter whether a poet, being what he is, is alive or dead? It could be said that the Miss Moores, being nothing but themselves, were the greater loss. (*ATR*, p.229)

At the end of the travel book, Bowen leaves Rome but in that moment of departure, again, as her biographer, Victoria Glendinning, suggests, she deconstructs her own self-possession. 'Nevertheless the last two sentences of the book, after describing the pain of departure, come as a slight shock. What she wrote, and what she had the panache to leave written, is the controlled, undirected cry of the displaced person': "My darling, my darling, my darling. Here we have no abiding city."" [11]

In her last two novels, dispossession comes to the fore as a thematic preoccupation, but now without the stabilizing context of an Anglo-Irish past. Hermione Lee writes that 'In one way, then, *The Little Girls* marks the culmination of a central preoccupation, the uncontrollable activity of memory and the disabling legacy of the past.'[12] This novel comes nine years after the publication of *A World of Love* and opens up to what Maud Ellmann sees as not so much difficulty of the past, rather the anguish and ultimate emptiness of calling it up. Bowen divided her narrative into three parts, the first and third sections set in the 1960s and at the centre of the novel, a flashback to a girl's school in 1914. Dinah Delacroix, a well-preserved wealthy widow, asks friends for items to fill a cave in her garden, to be sealed up, thus allowing a future generation to understand the England of the 1960s. 'We are putting these things in here to be deduced from.'[13] This sets Dinah's memory in train, reminding her of a childhood incident from her girls' boarding school, St Agatha's, where she and two other little girls, Sheikie and Mumbo, buried a coffer full of items. Dinah advertises to meet them again and to attempt to dig up the treasure, thus reclaiming their past. The three women reunite, Sheikie now Mrs Sheila Artworth and Mumbo a successful businesswoman running a chain of gift shops throughout the Home Counties. In searching for the past, they discover that St Agatha's had been bombed during the Second World War. In a farcical night-time scene, the three women dig up the long-buried coffer, now in the garden of a suburban villa, but find it empty. 'It was there. It was empty. It had been found' (LG, p.182). This lead Dinah to a breakdown. As Bennett and Royle comment, 'Dinah's ultimate seizure bears witness to the dreadful sense that the past cannot be known and cannot be spoken: it is irrevocable, it cannot be recalled, it is no longer vocable'.[14]

Later, towards the end of the book, as her mind and health is unravelling because of the coffer, Dinah complains about the hollowness of contemporary life, the very life she was attempting to commemorate and preserve for the future in her cave.

> There's a tremendous market for prefabricated feelings ... and I'll tell you one great centre of the prefabricated-feeling racket, and that is, anything to do with anything between two people: love or even sex ... So many of these fanciful ways people have of keeping themselves going, at such endless expense of time and money, seem not only unnecessary but dated. (LG, p.193)

At the end of the novel Clare muses: 'And now, nothing. There being nothing was what you were frightened of all the time, eh? Yes. Yes it was terrible looking down into that empty box' (LG, p.277). In this novel about the emptiness of the past, the imminence of death predominates. Hermione Lee notes: 'When the three schoolgirls bury their most precious possessions in the coffer with a proclamation written in Mumbo's invented "Unknown Language", they ask each other whether it matters that posterity won't understand them.'[15] Ellmann sees the past incubating within the novel as a metaphorical force disentombing the secrets of the dead, and goes on to describe the novel as 'Proust without sex'.[16] By characterizing the past as dangerously empty, Bowen is extending her earlier preoccupations with isolation and unrootedness to a point of uncompromising bleakness, even nightmare, in this penultimate novel, a prelude for Eva Trout.

This notion of 'a future without language' as Lee terms it,[17] permeates Bowen's last novel, Eva Trout, a novel termed a 'reflection of cultural anxiety and a vehicle for social criticism' by Liz Christensen.[18] Eva Trout is Elizabeth Bowen's last completed novel, the story of a young girl and woman, the unloved heiress, Eva Trout and her fruitless search for a selfhood, a home and a child. Some of Bowen's most arresting fiction centres on orphaned, place-less, un-needed children and adolescents; Lois in The Last September, Portia in The Death of the Heart, Leopold in The House in Paris . Aside from this, there is no doubt that Bowen draws on her own life for her representation of the orphaned heiress. When Elizabeth Bowen was 7, her father's mental illness necessitated a removal from Bowen's Court and her mother took her to live in Kent, the setting for much of Eva Trout. Her sense of loss was intensified with her mother's death from cancer when Bowen was 13. Imaginatively she draws on this sense of dislocation caused by her father's mental illness and her mother's early death, and her representation of Eva owes something to these early experiences.

But Eva Trout is not simply a self-portrait or a work of veiled autobiography. This is the novel in which Bowen uncharacteristically abandons social comedy and observation to extend her interest in fictionalizing the incompatibility between self and society. By the time she came to write Eva Trout, Elizabeth Bowen had settled in Hythe in Kent, the same place where she had lived with her mother over fifty years previously, and this return to the scenes of her adolescent wanderings and dispossession was, in her own words, 'a back-to-the-wombishness'.[19] Writing without the secure base of her homes and without the protection of her domestic life with Alan Cameron, Eva Trout is starker than her other writings. The two parts of Eva Trout's life, her derelict childhood and her alienated adulthood, owe much to the landscapes of these two phases in

Bowen's own life. 'In a sense, the plot of Eva Trout too may be considered a disfiguration of the plots of the orphan child in the earlier books.'[20] Eva Trout is an extreme, nightmarish novel where, in the words of Ellmann, 'In the figure of its colossal heroine, with her vast wealth and unbridled imagination, Bowen asks how far fiction can go without ethics, or without forsaking any aspiration for the truth.'[21] Eva Trout is a story of innocence and vulnerability and the betrayal and exploitation that such unprotected innocence attracts.

Eva's childhood is one of neglect and disinterest and, as the only daughter and heiress of the business genius Willy Trout, she lives the life of a wealthy vagrant, moving from country to country. Her father has left his marriage for another man, Constantine, and her mother is killed in a plane crash with her lover, just after Eva's birth. The consequent disruption and homelessness, combined with her physical largeness, leaves Eva rootless and alienated. 'Perpetual changes of milieu attendant on being the Trout daughter had left her with no capacity to be homesick – for, sick for where?'[22] Her upbringing is haphazard and intermittent under the baleful guardianship of her father's lover, Constantine, and, almost too late, she is sent to an experimental boarding school for a 'normal' education. The adolescent Eva's physical largeness contributes to her alienation and serves to underpin her sense of difference.

Bowen structures the novel in two parts, and in the first part she explores Eva's derelict upbringing. The second part of the novel deals with Eva's adult life, where the consequences of this upbringing are ultimately tragic. Through this structure, Bowen examines what Glendinning calls 'a tension between the clarity of innocence and its destructiveness',[23] and the narrative follows this tension. Eva is physically and emotionally marked, a large, sexually ambiguous, conspicuous girl who attracts exploitation, attack and betrayal in her dealings with almost every other character in the novel. Eva's rearing or lack of rearing at the hands of her father Willy, her guardian Constantine, and her teacher Iseult, is an education in rejection and exploitation. Yet somehow, as Bowen constructs her, Eva retains a kind of innate integrity and honesty that survives into her adult life. Bowen's compassion and empathy for her protagonist is one of the strongest narrative elements within the novel.

The result of this displaced upbringing is alienation and outsiderness for Eva, and much of the novel centres on Eva's attempts to find a place and a selfhood in a perpetually unaccommodating world. Schooled out of selfhood, Eva's quest is for acceptance at any cost. Thus Bowen's presentation of houses throughout *Eva Trout* is without the habitual imaginative weighting that she gives them in her other writings. Usually, in Bowen's imaginative landscape, houses take on a life of their own; have personality and an emotional life, often providing an implicit moral commentary on the characters in the narrative. (One example is Holme Dene, the family home of the spy Robert Kelway in *The Heat of the Day*. Holme Dene is a house made for surveillance, a man-eating house.) In *Eva Trout*, houses are themselves dispossessed, without character, alienated. Eva's temporary homes, the rented Cathay, the Castle, Larkins, are all implicated in her failure to settle, to find a place. The novel is filled with reference to the vagrant aspect to Eva's hotel life, and Bowen carefully details the clutter of her luggage as testament to her homelessness. Eva's own sense of actual and emotional homelessness is central to the novel.

Her teacher Iseult complains: 'What caused the girl to express herself like a displaced person? The explanation – that from infancy onward Eva had had as attendants displaced persons, those at a price being the most obtainable, to whose society she'd been largely consigned – for some reason never appeared: too simple, perhaps?' (ET, p.17). In a novel where Eva is exploited and betrayed by men, and where many of the male characters – her father Willy, her guardian Constantine, her teacher Kenneth – are gay, Bowen does present her protagonist with two possibilities for love and emotional connection. Both of these possibilities are with other women. Firstly the adolescent Eva falls for her schoolmate, the 'fairy-like near albino who had for some reason been christened Elsinore'. Elsinore is taken ill and Eva keeps vigil by her bedside.

> To repose a hand on the blanket covering Elsinore was to know in the palm of the hand a primitive terror – imagining the beating of that other heart, she had a passionately solicitous sense of this other presence. Nothing forbade love. This deathly yet living stillness, together, of two beings, this unapartness, came to be the requital of all longing. (ET, p.56)

Later, in adult life, Eva accidentally meets Elsinore again. Despite the interval of the years and the obstacle of other relationships, they are both connected by the memory of their shared past – 'The tower room in the castle, the piteous breathing. The blinded window, the banished lake, the dayless and nightless watches. The tent of cobwebs. The hand on the blanket, the beseeching answering beating heart. The dark: the unseen distance, the known nearness. Love: the here and the now and the nothing-but. The step on the stairs. Don't take her away ... She is all I am. We are all there is' (ET, p.133). This moment of connection, Eva's vital moment of love, passes and an opportunity is lost. Much of the later tragedy of Eva's later life can be read in the light of her loss of Elsinore and her inability to respond to Elsinore is, in many ways, her undoing.

The other moment of possible connection with another comes to Eva from her teacher, Iseult. As Patricia Coughlan writes, 'Her capacity for intense, helpless love, as for her mentor Miss Smith, has the effect of revealing the limitations of its objects. She strongly recalls the monster in *Frankenstein*, abandoned by its maker, righteously angry, and at first totally innocent.'[24] Iseult takes Eva up, makes her a special case and as a result Eva falls in love with her: 'Love like a great moth circled her bed, then settled' (ET, p.63). However, Eva's trust in Iseult is not justified (Bowen refers to Iseult's 'vivisectional interest' in Eva) and Iseult withdraws, in fright, another lost chance for connection during Eva's adolescence.

In the light of these lost opportunities, Eva pursues the course of her adult, independent life travelling restlessly and erratically, isolated yet empowered by her vast wealth. She breaks with Iseult and Constantine, disappears to America where she encounters the adult Elsinore and finally returns to England with her 8-year-old adopted son, the deaf-mute Jeremy. All of her important decisions are the consequences of her upbringing, where, as she tells Iseult, 'Anywhere would seem strange to me that did not' (ET, p.59). Throughout, Bowen highlights Eva's quest for the appearance of normality at all costs, and thus at considerable cost to herself. Eva, so unhappily reared, wants the appearance of marriage and of motherhood, when the reality is denied her. She wants to seem the same, not to seem different. Only once is it suggested to Eva, by her French doctor, Bonnard, that her upbringing has harmed her, deformed her sense of self and that she might eventually escape. 'The way one is envisaged by other people – what easier way is there of envisaging oneself? There is a fatalism in one's acceptance of it ... Choice – choice of those who are to surround one, choice of those most likely to see one rightly – is the only escape' (ET, p.223). Such escape seems impossible for Eva.

When, in the final scene, Eva stage-manages an illusionary marriage for herself, she is transformed and beautified by this illusion, not just for herself but also in the eyes of those who surround her. Radiant pathos is achieved by Eva at this moment of dangerous illusion:

> Not far off, in one of those chance islands of space, she stood tall as a candle, some accident of the light rendering her luminous from top to toe – in a pale suit, elongated by the elegance of its narrowness, and turned-back little hat of the same no-colour; no flowers, but on the lapel of the jacket a spraying-out subcontinent of diamonds: a great brooch. A soft further glow had been tinted on to her face; her eyes were increased by the now mothy dusk of their lashes. (ET, pp.261–2)

Eva Trout is the culmination of Elizabeth Bowen's work. Here, Bowen presents her most uncompromising portrayal of the gap between self and society in her story of the heiress, Eva Trout. The heroine embodies Bowen's lifelong themes of dispossession and emotional dereliction. Maud Ellmann writes that 'In a review essay called "The Shadow Across The Page" (1937) Bowen argues that "Every artist adds year by year to a major unwritten work". Eva Trout embodies that unwritten work: she represents the silence of the worlds that Bowen never lived to rescue from the deep.'[25]

NOTES

1. Elizabeth Bowen, The Death of the Heart (Harmondsworth: Penguin, 1962 [1938]), p.310, hereafter referred to in the text as DH.

2. Hermione Lee, Elizabeth Bowen: An Estimation (London: Vintage, 1999), pp.205–6. Hermione Lee is one of a number of critics who view Bowen's last novels in this light, including Neil Corcoran, who in his recent study of Bowen confesses that he sees The Little Girls as 'deeply flawed' although he admires Eva Trout greatly and writes perceptively of her last novel.

3. Patricia Craig, Elizabeth Bowen (Harmondsworth: Penguin, 1986), p.135.

4. Neil Corcoran, Elizabeth Bowen: The Enforced Return (Oxford: Oxford University Press, 2004), p.78.

5. See P. Coughlan, 'Women and Desire in the Work of Elizabeth Bowen', in Sex, Nation and Dissent in Irish Writing, ed. Eibhear Walshe (Cork: Cork University Press, 1997),

pp.103–35; Rene Hoogland, *Elizabeth Bowen: A Reputation in Writing* (New York: New York University Press, 1994); Claire Connolly, '(Be)longing – The Strange Place of Elizabeth Bowen's Eva Trout', in *Borderlands: Negotiating Boundaries in Post-Colonial Writing*, ed. Monika Reif Hülser (Amsterdam: Rodopi, 1999), pp.135–43. Also see Tina O'Toole's chapter in this collection.

6. Connolly, '(Be)longing', p.137.

7. Hoogland, *Elizabeth Bowen*, p.13. Also see Tina O'Toole's chapter in this collection.

8. Elizabeth Bowen, *Bowen's Court* (Cork: The Collins Press, 1998 [1942]), p.457, hereafter referred to in the text as BC.

9. Elizabeth Bowen, *A Time in Rome* (New York: Alfred A. Knopf, 1960), hereafter referred to in the text as ATR. I am very grateful to Eamon O'Carragain for allowing me to read his unpublished essay on Bowen and Rome, and to Graham Allen for his insights into this text.

10. To some degree, Bowen must have been reacting to the violently misogynistic view of Livia in Robert Graves' 1934 novel, I *Claudius* in her reading of Livia as adept, loyal and successful.

11. Victoria Glendinning, *Elizabeth Bowen: Portrait of a Writer* (London: Weidenfeld and Nicolson, 1977), p.215. This, again, brings Rome back to Bowen's Court; the quote from the Epistle to the Hebrews also appears on the memorial table to her grand-parents in the family church in Farrahy in North Cork.

12. Lee, *Elizabeth Bowen*, p.199.

13. Elizabeth Bowen, *The Little Girls* (New York: Alfred A. Knopf, 1964), p.10, hereafter referred to in the text as LG.

14. Andrew Bennett and Nicholas Royle, *Elizabeth Bowen and the Dissolution of The Novel* (Basingstoke: Macmillan, 1994), p.138.

15. Lee, *Elizabeth Bowen*, p.199.

16. Maud Ellmann, *Elizabeth Bowen: The Shadow Across the Page* (Edinburgh: Edinburgh University Press, 2003), pp.178, 191.

17. Lee, *Elizabeth Bowen*, p.197.

18. Liz Christensen, *Elizabeth Bowen: The Later Fiction* (Copenhagen: Museum Tusculanum Press, University of Copenhagen, 2001), p.206.

19. Glendinning, *Elizabeth Bowen*, p.222.

20. Corcoran, *Elizabeth Bowen*, p.134.

21. Ellmann, *Elizabeth Bowen*, p.204.

22. Elizabeth Bowen, *Eva Trout, or Changing Scenes* (London: Vintage, 1999 [1968]), p.50, hereafter referred to in the text as ET.

23. Glendinning, *Elizabeth Bowen*, p.226.

24. Coughlan, 'Women and Desire in the Work of Bowen', p.128.

25. Ellmann, *Elizabeth Bowen*, p.224.

CHAPTER ELEVEN

Angels and Monsters:
Embodiment and Desire in *Eva Trout*

TINA O'TOOLE

'Books continue each other', Virginia Woolf suggests, 'in spite of our habit of judging them separately'.[1] Elizabeth Bowen's final work *Eva Trout* (1968) is a case in point in that, in order to fully realize the dissident potential of this novel, it is necessary for the reader to revisit some of her earlier experiments with gender and sexuality. It is evident that the transgressive knowledge available to the writer (and reader) of *Eva Trout*, specifically in relation to issues of female masculinity and same-sex desire, stretches back in place and time to foundations laid in *The Last September* (1929). Here, the connection made between the adolescent Lois and the older, more sophisticated, Marda, who keeps to herself a deeper awareness of such transgressive knowledge particularly in relation to sexual desire, prefigures the central relationship in *Eva Trout*. This pattern of constructing identity and writing desire between women is reworked and worried throughout one seam of Bowen's fiction, and is particularly evident in 'The Jungle', *Friends and Relations*, *The Hotel* and *The Little Girls*, as has been discussed in some depth by scholars such as Rene Hoogland and Patricia Coughlan.[2] In addition, while continuing to address key questions raised in Bowen's earlier work, I link her project to the experiments ongoing in the work of her contemporaries, which I address below. I will contend that in *Eva Trout*, Bowen 'continues' the cultural and social work of other twentieth-century novelists, including Radclyffe Hall (among others) and, arguably, contributes to the kinds of engagement of feminist writers, such as Monique Wittig, whose first novel *The Opoponax* was published in 1964, in relation to gender and sexual identities. Thus, by reading Bowen's fictional experiments in tandem with those of her peers, we may gain more insight into the cultural and social experiments relating to gender and sexuality during the period.

As *Eva Trout* has been discussed in the previous chapter, I will briefly sketch in those episodes relevant to my chapter. The novel is concerned with the eponymous Eva, and in particular, her involvement with, and attachment to, an influential teacher, Iseult Smith, at the boarding school she attends briefly as an adolescent. Dealing with these episodes retrospectively, the novel opens with Eva, heiress to a large fortune, wanting to escape from the home of her now married teacher, Iseult Arble, where she has been placed by her guardian Constantine until she should come of age. Her disaffection with Iseult, who concludes that Eva has now 'fallen in hate' with her,[3] is tangible in the early passages of the text. Finally setting up home independently for the first time, Eva propels herself into a peripatetic existence, spending many years living in a variety of North American cities where she adopts a baby, Jeremy, by illegal means. My discussion chiefly relates to Part One of the novel, suffice it to say that she later returns to England and begins a liaison with a young man, whom she persuades to marry her. However, on the morning of the wedding, Eva is shot dead by her young son, who uses a gun left behind by Iseult in their luggage.

In *Pictures and Conversations*, Elizabeth Bowen, discussing her removal from Ireland to England as a child, comments: 'At an early, though conscious age, I was transplanted. I arrived, young, into a different mythology – in fact, into one totally alien ... Submerged, the mythology of this "other" land could be felt at work in the ways, manners and views of its people, round me.'[4] As any reading of Bowen's work, whether fiction or memoir, illuminates: for Bowen *what* you remember and *how* you remember it are central tenets of identity formation. In this particular instance, she is discussing her national identity, and the dawning of an awareness in her child self that in different places, there are different 'mythologies' at work, as she describes them. However, it strikes me that this perspective could be summarized to discuss identity formation more generally, and it becomes clear in reading her fiction that Bowen's delineation of the 'mythologies' in relation to gender and sexuality was equally incisive and divided in the same binary fashion. Thus, in several of her fictions, but in particularly in *Eva Trout*, Bowen constructs the central character as an outsider in a gender-divided and heteronormative environment, who struggles to understand the dominant culture as evinced in the ways, manners and views of its people around her. I will contend that Eva, with no access to an alternative model, nonetheless struggles to recover something 'submerged' in this culture, to gain access to a 'different mythology' to which she was once (perhaps) privy, and which, it is clear, she was then conditioned to forget if she was to survive. Thus when her teacher exclaims 'What caused the girl to express herself like a displaced person?' (ET, p.18), the reader may observe that this is precisely because she *is* displaced, although not quite in the same way as her teacher uses the term. As the novel progresses, Eva's efforts to re-member herself, to match her own 'submerged mythology' with that of the social world she moves through, result in a series of disjunctures, or ripples, in the surface of the dominant culture.

To focus, then, on this 'outsider' figure as it is realized in *Eva Trout*, it seems to me that Braidotti's work on monsters can usefully inform our reading of Eva: 'The monstrous or deviant is a figure of abjection in so far as it trespasses and transgresses the barriers between recognisable norms or definitions.'[5] Everything about Eva is larger-than-life and it is obvious from this first description of her that her large frame is some-how out of kilter in relation to those around her:

> The giantess; by now, was alone also … shoulders braced, hands interlocked behind her, feet in the costly, slovenly lambskin bootees planted apart. Back fell her cap of jaggedly cut hair from her raised profile, showing the still adolescent heaviness of the jawline … Monolithic, Eva's attitude was. It was not, somehow, the attitude of a thinking person. (ET, p.13)

More than just her size and shape, it is suggested, are monstrous. In atti-tude, she is 'monolithic', which suggests a being inflexible or immune to the environment around her. Furthermore, her physiognomy is indicative to Mrs Dancey, whose perspective this is, of someone who does not (*cannot?*) think as others do. This is later echoed in Eric Arble's view of Eva: 'there she sat, twisted against the window, keeping fanati-cal watch on the Channel skyline. Uncomprehending? Dumb, anyway, as a rock' (ET, p.99). The use of comparisons with immutable objects to describe Eva's thought processes continues throughout the text. We are told that at school, her teacher Iseult Smith had made an effort to 'induce flexibility' but in terms of both language and thought, these attempts came too late: 'her outlandish, cement-like conversational style had set. Moreover – the discouraging fact emerged – it was more than sufficient for Eva's needs. She had nothing to say that could not be said, adequately, the way she said it' (ET, p.18). To return to the opening scene, something of Mrs Dancey's awe, or perhaps even fear, of this 'giantess' is transmitted in the following lines, suggestive of a Gothic narrative:[6] 'sure enough, Eva *was* coming back! Purposeful strides could be heard returning over the turf made iron by black frost. They passed the car, not a pause, and continued onward. Going after the children?' (p.13). Continuing in the same vein, Eva is referred to as the Danceys' 'captor', an accurate description of their sense of her power over them – all, that is, except for 12-year-old Henry who, we are told, was 'qualified to deal with Eva ... treating her on the whole as he might an astray moose which when too overpowering could be shooed away' (p.15). Thus, the outsized Eva is introduced in the text, with later accounts describing her as an 'Amazon at bay' (p.85) and a 'she-Cossack' (p.93), this from Mr Denge, following Eva's 'attack' on him.

Discussing the genesis of the monster in European texts from the sixteenth century on, Braidotti tells us that the 'monstrous birth' is commonly attributed to the sinfulness or guilt of the parents: 'The most common form of parental transgression concerns the norms for acceptable sexual practice ... sexual excess, especially in the woman, is always a factor'.[7] Of course, in the case of Eva Trout it is her father, Willy, who is more obviously 'to blame' in terms of a breach of 'acceptable' (read: 'normative') sexual practice. Willy's homosexuality, and more specifically his relationship with Constantine, is the cause of much that is out-of-order in Eva's social context. We are told that Willy 'passed' in the dominant culture: 'The entire cut of the jib of Eva's father could have given the lie to that obsession ... Big in height and frame and in a big way easy in movement, stalwart and open in countenance ... he looked what he otherwise was: a crack polo player, with a pretty wife. He had been popular' (p.19). Thus, despite having fulfilled all of the necessary obligations of happy heterosexuality – a wife, a child, friends, a large physical (manly) presence and success at sport – Willy's 'obsession' with Constantine, that is his homosexual identity, is his downfall: 'It was in him to deviate' (p.19). It is this 'rocky side' of his nature which causes his wife and child to be 'defrauded' (p.19). The pretty wife, Cissie, flees the scene, allegedly with her lover, two months after the birth of Eva. However, her escape bid is not a success as she is killed in a plane crash. It is suggested thus, that both Eva's parents are guilty of the kind of sexual excess outlined by Braidotti. Constantine, not necessarily truthfully, later suggests that Cissie was 'unhinged' (p.122), which increases the shadow over Eva's genesis.

With regard to socialization, we only later learn that Eva has an extended family from whose influence she is removed by her father, who has 'violently quarrelled' with them following events in which they 'rais[ed] heaven and earth, writing insulting-denouncing letters and wielding threats, in efforts to get Eva away from him, out of contamination-range. Some even charged him with Cissie's death, that having arisen from her flight' (pp.223–4). Their central objection to Willy is his relationship with Constantine and more specifically his insistence on rearing his child himself with his new partner. Allowing free reign to homosexual domesticity in this way has a destabilizing effect on the social order within (and perhaps also without) the text, as it suggests flaws in the ideological construction of heteronormativity and the family institution. The surrender of patriarchal authority – Willy loses his right to rule in the heterosocial order by revoking his investment in the law of the father – is made all the more striking by the fact that homosexual desire is never actually named in the text. Willy is something of an absent presence in this text at every level. At no point does he give voice to his own sexual identity – it is outlined only through the eyes of Eva, his daughter, and Constantine, his lover. As such, Eva occupies the unusual position of being the spectator, as a child, of two men involved in a love affair, overturning the more typical configuration of same-sex desire between women as a spectacle for the male voyeur. Parallels may be drawn between this central triangle and that of an earlier Irish novel The Land of Spices (1941), by Bowen's countrywoman and contemporary, Kate O'Brien.[8] As with Willy Trout, the homosexuality of Henry Archer in The Land of Spices causes him to relinquish patriarchal authority and this breakdown is a central strategy through which O'Brien empowers her main characters. This strategy, the deployment of male homosexuality as an enabling factor which ultimately frees her central characters from the rigidities of heteronormativity in O'Brien's text – could conceivably have lent itself to Bowen's construction of this novel. Comparatively however, as we shall see, Eva's encounters with the dominant culture are not hived off into a women-only space, as they are in the convent at the centre of *The Land of Spices*, and her efforts to make her way in the world outside such a liminal space are met with considerable opposition.

While Eva does not criticize her father's sexual identity, as her counterpart in *The Land of Spices*, Helen Archer, implicitly does, it is clear that she hates Constantine and blames him for her father's early death. As such, sexual deviance between men is the initial wild card, or disruptive sign in this text, a point which has tended to be neglected by critics of the novel to date. The impact of this same-sex relationship on Eva's upbringing is clearly indicated as the 'cause' of her being at odds with the codes of the dominant social world later in her adolescence. Following the barrage of letters from her extended family, Eva situates herself in opposition to these, her father's 'enemies', thus rejecting the social world on terms her father would approve of. She later realizes that 'She had first been withheld from, then forfeited her birthright of cricket matches and flower shows' (pp.223–4). In this way, we come to understand Eva's liminal position, her outsider status is cemented.

To return to Eva's construction within the novel, having established a monstrous social identity for her central protagonist, Bowen demonstrates Eva's oddity in a number of key episodes. People Eva encounters outside her charmed circle tend to either fear or pity her, but certainly 'Other' her. This is evidenced in particular when she moves into a new neighbourhood and rents a house from Denge, a local estate agent. His version of this episode, as passed on by telephone to Iseult, is later recounted by her:

> That a violent outbreak had caused him to flee the premises, into which you then barricaded yourself, *as* violently; that a messenger subsequently sent out by him with a kettle had turned tail, leaving the kettle to its fate, on being grimaced at 'hideously' from a window, and that no further sort or kind of any communication has been had from you since; though sallies into Broadstairs, in incomplete control of a powerful bicycle, have been reported. (p.118)

Fears of 'mania', and more specifically, pyromania, are hinted at in Denge's account of his encounters with Eva, and his fear of her extends to this manifestation of woman and bicycle somehow moulded together into a monstrous organism, or perhaps a cyborg, to use Donna Haraway's formula.[9] Jennifer González points out that

> The image of the cyborg has historically recurred at moments of radical social and cultural change ... In other words, when the current ontological model of human beings does not fit a new paradigm, a hybrid model of existence is required to encompass a new, complex and contradictory lived experience.[10]

It seems to me that Bowen, particularly in episodes such as this, is attempting to forge a new paradigm, as I will discuss below.

While the perception of Eva's body is central to this text, she is rarely herself presented as one who is 'centred' in her own body, to the extent that in some episodes she does not appear to be at home within a human body at all. Eric Arble is the first person to come into close physical contact with this creature, but his alcohol-fuelled attack on her heightens, more than anything else, the sense that Eva is somehow not human. There is a strong suggestion in this passage that treating Eva badly, even violently, is not quite the same thing as abusing another human being.

> Eric got hold of Eva by the pouchy front of her anorak and shook her. The easy articulation of her joints made this rewarding – her head rolled on her shoulders, her arms swung from them. Her teeth did not rattle, being firm in her gums, but coins and keys all over her clinked and jingled. Her hair flumped all ways like a fiddled-about-with mop. The crisis became an experiment: he ended by keeping her rocking, at slowing tempo, left–right, left–right, off one heel on to the other, meanwhile pursing his lips, as though whistling, and frowning speculatively. The experiment interested Eva also. Did it gratify her too much? – he let go abruptly. 'That's all' he told her. 'But mind your own business next time.' (p.101)

Crucially, even in such an acutely physical scene, where one person lays hands on and violently shakes another, our attention is drawn not so much to Eva's physical body, as to her inanimate aspects. She is shaken by the pouchy front of her anorak (manufactured, modern and mundane) and when shaken, she clinks and jingles, suggesting a robot or again a cyborg, but certainly not something composed of human hair or flesh and blood, but rather fabric, metal and mop-hair. If anything, she is transformed here into a large rag-doll, and like a child, Eric 'experiments' with the effect of his shaking her, apparently with no complaint from his human doll. Having sustained this for quite some time without any cry from her, Eric concludes that this abuse in some way gratifies Eva and it is only at this point that he stops abruptly, telling her sternly 'that's all'. In the aftermath of this violent scene, as both Eric and Constantine leave her alone in the house once more, we are told that there is 'not a trace left [of these various visitors] but for damage to Eva's frame ... She now yawned: so dismissive a yawn that it distended her rib-cage to cracking-point, just not dislocating her jaw by the grace of heaven' (p.126). Again, the reference to 'frame' suggests the woman/bicycle cyborg, but her yawn, travelling as it does down through her body tissue and her bones, has quite a different effect. Both the flippancy of this gesture in the wake of the departing men, and Eva's ability to wrack her own body by the simple introduction of air into her lungs, is suggestive of someone reasserting herself bodily. That this effect is produced deep inside her rib-cage demonstrates the impact of Eric's actions as having merely affected the surface of her body – which could be said to be indicative of the effect of the opposite sex upon Eva throughout the novel.

Rather than being contrasted in bodily terms with Eva, Iseult Smith seems no less 'embodied' in this text than does her devoted pupil. This is partly due her being rendered in Eva's memory as someone with 'a face already becoming unearthly' (p.78), whether because she has already assumed, in Eva's mind, the role of goddess, or more simply because Eva is beginning to forget her exact features, is not made clear. In the same passage, Eva thinks of her as having had an 'involuntary beauty' (p.78), which we may link with what Iseult herself constructs as the involuntary nature of her attachment to Eva. Bowen deftly juxtaposes this memory of Iseult's ethereal beauty with her rather more mundane appearance on her 'present-day' arrival at the train station, where she's met by her husband: 'Make-up staled and caked on her face by the long day gave her the feel of wearing her own death-mask. The feathered turban irked like an iron circle' (p.78). Moreover, this appearance demonstrates the hobbling of the divine Iseult, who is now buried under a cake of make-up and imprisoned in a feather hat, by all of the trappings of contemporary femininity, in fact. However, reflecting back to a time long before this, Eva describes her 'Miss Smith' as a being 'disembodied': 'neither then nor later did Eva look upon her as beautiful or in any other way clad in physical being. Miss Smith's *noli-me-tangere* was unneeded in any dealings with Eva – who could have touched her?' (p.70). Comparing this with Eva's own untouchable character in later episodes, and in particular with the scene outlined above where Eric shakes Eva, might we conclude that the pupil has constructed her own *cordon sanitaire* within which she may be handled, but never really *touched*? Unlike Eva, however, whose disembodied nature is studied (possibly partly as a reaction to her father's investment in the bodily), Iseult's '*noli-me-tangere*' results from her devotion to a life of the mind. Iseult's intellectual depth is gestured to on a number of occasions, her ability as a teacher is attested to by many pupils, the books 'mustered on the low white shelves' in her room, the desk holding fragments from tombs and temples which she uses as paperweights; and she can unerringly take down any needed volume from the school library without looking. This retreat into intellect, it is suggested, has the effect of removing her from the material world. Describing her room, we are told that 'But for a cherry-coloured cardigan – which, tossed away, had fallen short of the divan on to the floor – and Miss Smith herself, little betrayed the fact that anybody inhabited this room' (p.74). Interestingly, 'Miss Smith herself' is something of an afterthought here, which suggests that perhaps there is no-body really there to inhabit the space. Feeding only her intellect, Iseult has neglected to develop herself bodily and emotionally, and the effect this neglect has upon her in later life, as well as on the rest of Eva's life, is catastrophic:

> that particular spring at Lumleigh, the young teacher was in a state of grace, of illumined innocence that went with the realisation of her powers. They transcended her; filled her with awe and wonder, and the awe and wonder gave her a kind of purity, such as one may see in a young artist. No idea that they could be power, with all that boded, had so far tainted or flawed them for her. About Iseult Smith, up to the time she encountered Eva and, though discontinuously, for some time after, there was something of Nature before

the Fall. (pp.70–1)

Of course the Fall, when it comes, will have far-reaching effects on the lives of almost everyone in the novel, as well as perhaps on the social world the text represents, as Hoogland and others have discussed.

As I mentioned at the outset, it is difficult to disconnect Bowen's interrogations in *Eva Trout* from the experiments of other twentieth-century writers such as Radclyffe Hall. While *The Well of Loneliness* was first published in 1928, due to censorship it was in fact only made available to the wider reading public in a popular edition in 1968, the same year as *Eva Trout*. Some elements of *The Well* are clearly echoed in Eva's struggles with her body and identity, such as Iseult's comment that Eva's child had to be a boy, because '"Girl" never fitted Eva. Her so-called sex bored and mortified her; *she dragged it about after her like a ball and chain*. Why should she wish to reproduce it when she chose a child?' (p.287; my emphasis). This is almost a direct reflection of Stephen Gordon's perspective on her body: 'She hated her body with its muscular shoulders, its small compact breasts, and its slender flanks of an athlete. All her life *she must drag this body of hers like a monstrous fetter imposed on her spirit*. This strangely ardent yet sterile body' (my emphasis).[11] Nor, regrettably, is it possible to look back at these twentieth-century fictional writings on female masculinity from a post-revolutionary perspective, as Halberstam reminds us: 'despite at least two decades of sustained feminist and queer attacks on the notion of natural gender, we still believe that masculinity in girls and women is abhorrent and pathological'.[12] Eva Trout's aberrant body image creates just such a reaction in those about her. One of her school-fellows asks 'Trout, are you a hermaphrodite?', to which she responds 'I don't know' (p.58). This scene is not rendered negatively, however, as her classmates immediately begin to discuss the case of Joan of Arc, who was 'supposed to have been' a hermaphrodite. In other words, the possibility of having a transgender identity is dealt with in positive terms here, from the perspective of the young Eva, made consistent with the identity of an idealized role model – albeit one who dies a tragic and untimely death (as will Eva). However, this episode causes us to examine more scrupulously our earlier impressions of Eva's bodily form: 'the giantess' described by Mrs Dancey now appears less 'monolithic' or monstrous, than masculinised. Halberstam suggests that one reason for the kinds of reaction to female masculinity produced in the Mr Denges of contemporary society is that its manifestation undermines traditional notions of masculinity and thus patriarchal power. Furthermore, she notes that the masculine woman has tended not to be read as a 'historical figure, a character who has challenged gender systems for at least two centuries'.[13] This is a timely reminder in the context of our reading of *Eva Trout*, a novel now forty years old, enabling us to situate this discourse at the centre of a series of ongoing struggles in the arena of female masculinity.

Unlike Stephen Gordon, however, who struggles to adjust or 'fit in' to the heteronormative social context, Eva takes the opposite course – striving to bring the social context around to her way of seeing the world. Beginning with her removal to Cathay, the house in Broadstairs, she attempts to construct a life for herself on her own terms, refusing any interference from friends or family, and rejecting any imposition from the local community into her new world. This separatist desire is clearly viewed with suspicion by others: '"Mr Denge has gone", Eva told [Eric], with the utmost complacency. Her euphoria had for Eric, for the first time, almost an overlap of insanity' (p.100). She chooses a remote suburban desert for her new life, one which even the locals have trouble finding, as Constantine tells her:

> I had trouble finding Cathay. My taxi driver maintained it did not exist, and one drew a blank wherever one stopped to ask. One can only think it has faded from human memory ... Is it *your* aim to fade from human memory? From the way you've been going on one supposes so'. (pp.115–16)

Having rid herself of Denge, Eric Arble and Constantine, Eva sets about constructing her own Utopian space within the house, which becomes a decidedly non-domestic space. Unlike Iseult's retreat from the material into a world of books, Eva fills the house with the most up-to-date audiovisual equipment. This is later a motif in her life with Jeremy, her deaf-mute son, with whom she moves from one North American city to another; the only cohesion given to this existence comes from the time they spend together watching movies and newsreel in hotel rooms. Thus, these 'heavenly twins' become voyeurs, lookers-on at the material world through the filters of contemporary media, which they have the means to switch on and off at will.

Eva's time in North America is delineated by these visual encounters at a remove from the material world, rather than an investment in local community or adult relationships. This is hardly surprising, given that her efforts to construct a space within the social world where she might have a relationship with another woman were all doomed to failure. As a schoolgirl, shortly after the 'hermaphrodite' discussion, Eva forms her first attachment to a young girl, Elsinore, who is gravely ill. When finally Elsinore is taken home by her mother, presumably to die, Eva, who has not even been recognized as the primary carer for this girl over many months, suffers her first experience of heartbreak and loss.[14] Her later love for Iseult is not simply spurned by her teacher, but quashed by an inability to admit the possibility of lesbian desire at all. Iseult's reaction is read by Smith as a classic case of 'lesbian panic': 'the panic evoked by presence of the lesbian or even the perception of lesbianism [which] has long functioned as a pervasive narrative strategy in literature representing women's lives and consciousnesses'.[15] In retreat from Eva, or lesbian possibility, Iseult 'throw[s] herself away' (p.18) in marriage to Eric Arble, a man who is clearly not her equal on any terms:

> Iseult Smith's abandonment of a star career for an obscure marriage puzzled those for whom it was hearsay only – but the reason leaped to the eye: the marriage was founded on a cerebral young woman's first physical passion. The Arbles had been the Arbles for some years – so far, no children. (p.19)

Eva's later hold over Iseult cannot be understood by Eric Arble, although his efforts to find the root cause of his wife's unhappiness threaten to destabilize Eva's new-found security:

> 'Old Eva – what can she do to you? Or what *does* she do?' She turned again in the chair – he received a sudden, as it were stolen, view of her face: its bereftness, its unresigned weariness of its exile. He took a leap in the dark. 'Remind you of what you *could* do? – of what you used to be, when you liked?' (p.28)

Iseult's terrified response: 'What do you mean?' ... 'Don't go away from me – don't!' (p.28) is really very revealing. For all that her 'exile' has transformed her from a woman at the height of her powers to a 'marionette' housewife (p.25), her fear of abandoning the known social world for a 'sapphic relationship' (p.216) will keep her in her place.

Eva, on the other hand, will not seek to reconstruct herself within the terms of the heterosexual contract, but instead, by adopting Jeremy, she attempts to construct a family for herself without entering into marriage or domesticity. Nor do her efforts to define herself take the form of a nostalgic reflection of the past – she does not, for example, model herself upon a projected image of her mother or of her teacher/surrogate mother, Iseult. Rather, her struggle to re-member herself derives from her own, sometimes mistaken, reading of the 'mythologies' which surround her and thus, as Hoogland points out, Bowen's text 'depicts what happens when a (female) subject does not effectively enter the phallogocentric order' (p.209). In fact at times Eva's 'readings' of the social code turn out to be more prescient than that of those around her, effectively disturbing the hegemony in ways which threaten even those, such as Iseult, who would appear to have much to gain from its disruption: 'expos[ing] that not only her own subjectivity, but subjectivity generally is no more than a necessary fiction with no meaning or essence'.[16] This is threatening to Iseult, of course, because she – as a mature adult with a successful teaching career – realizes the potentially fatal consequences of claiming either a dissident social identity or worse, a transgressive desire, within the prevailing climate. As Hoogland's work has masterfully demonstrated, these struggles with same-sex desire and sexual identity are a central force field within this text and thus the main tensions are here produced as a kind of ripple effect from Eva's re-constructions of her narrative of desire and development.

Earlier, I suggested that *Eva Trout* derives from some of the same philosophical and critical interventions developing in the work of other *avant garde* writers of the mid-century. I would contend, for example, that we may see Bowen's work as being coterminous with the early work of radical feminist thinkers such as Monique Wittig, particularly in *Les Guerrillères*, which was published the following year. This is not to suggest that Wittig's earlier texts directly informed Bowen's writing of *Eva Trout*, or vice versa, but rather that both authors were involved in comparable experiments during the same period using a similar knowledge base and, arguably, with some of the same aims in mind. At the centre of *Les Guerrillères*, for example, is an attempt to overturn the symbolic order, as the women declare that they have 'no need of myths or symbols'.[17] Wittig asserts that a lesbian is not a woman: 'for what makes a woman is a specific social relation to a man ... a relation which lesbians escape by refusing to become or stay heterosexual'.[18] Based on this, her theory of the 'lesbian sign' used to dismantle the binary codes of heteronormative discourse discloses the act of social construction implicit in the label 'woman'. Offering a radical analysis of Rousseau's social contract, which Wittig reads as a 'heterosexual contract', she argues that Lévi-Strauss's theory of the exchange of women 'exposes heterosexuality as a political régime', a social contract from which benefit women are explicitly excluded.[19] Set beside this discourse, Eva's rejection or 'misreading' of the social code or, as Hoogland frames it, her 'failure to enter the phallogocentric order', perhaps does not seem quite such a radical move on Bowen's part. However, we can see that in fictional mode it contributes to and continues this feminist dialogue interrogating the construction of the social order. In a later essay, Wittig observes: 'Whether we want it or not, we are living in society here and now, and proof is given that we say "yes" to the social bond when we conform to the conventions and rules that were never formally enunciated but that nevertheless everybody knows and applies like magic.'[20] By rejecting a 'normal' heterosexual relationship (even her later relationship with Henry is characterized by its performativity rather than its intimacy) as well as the family unit constructed around her by the Arbles, and, finally, by rejecting a normative approach to motherhood, we can outline a range of ways in which Eva Trout rejects the social bond.

While these rejections may perhaps be constructed as deriving from her ignorance of the 'conventions and rules' or 'mythologies', of the social bond, nonetheless, Eva struggles to reshape the social contract to conform to an ethic she sets about constructing for herself. This may be compared to the way in which, in *Les Guerrillères*, the community works to develop a territory outside patriarchy, clearing ground for the development of a whole range of other social and sexual identities. Thus, it seems clear to me that a redefinition of the social contract is a central concern of both texts.

Furthermore, both Bowen and Wittig operate from a position which sees gender roles as socially constructed within the material world. While Eva tries for a time to remove herself totally from the material world, both by moving to the house in Broadstairs and subsequently through her various removals in the USA, this separation is never quite complete. To follow Wittig's statement above, whether Eva wants to or not, it becomes clear that she must engage with the hegemonic order if she is to disrupt its codes. Throughout the text, constant flux reshapes notions of a fixed family institution, and to some extent, redefines family as a communal commitment, the components of which are inclusive as opposed to exclusive, distinct units. Thus, in the later work of Bowen and the early work of Wittig there is a clear commitment to a gendered world in flux, rather than a static account of immutable patriarchal oppression, and, arguably, both propose concrete strategies for change. However, unlike Wittig, whose project is the construction of a counter-culture or alternative social world, Bowen reimagines an affective life only at the level of the individual. Thus, when Wittig later declares that her aim is to effect 'a whole conceptual reevaluation of the social world, its whole reorganisation with new concepts',[21] we can clearly see how an Eva might benefit from such a Utopian space. Bowen, however, will never be amenable to the revolutionizing of the social world on a grand scale, and, like her predecessor Radclyffe Hall, her reactionary political views and complete lack of interest in state social development are indicative of this. Nonetheless, bringing to mind Halberstam's comment that figures such as Eva Trout (and Stephen Gordon) have 'challenged gender systems for at least two centuries', it seems to me that Eva has been deliberately constructed as a challenge to the status quo, albeit in something of an exceptionalist way.

To return to Braidotti, whose 'monstrous other' encompasses both the divine and the abject,[22] we might read the figure of Eva Trout as a harbinger, as Bowen's attempt to reconfigure notions of fixed gender and sexual identities and to open up a space for new forms, redefinitions. As Henry Dancey points out, 'Here's another thing about you, Miss Trout: you leave few lives unscathed. Or, at least, unchanged ... Ethically perhaps you're a Typhoid Mary. You also plunge people's ideas into deep confusion ... you only have to pass' (pp.209–10). In the final scenes of the novel, Eva is described thus:

> Not far off, in one of those chance islands of space she stood tall
> as a candle, some accident of the light rendering her luminous

from top to toe – in a pale suit, elongated by the elegance of its narrowness, and turned-back little hat of the same no-colour; no flowers, but on the lapel of the jacket a spraying-out subcontinent of diamonds; a great brooch. (pp.309–10)

Irigaray posits the role of the angels, divine messengers, as a strategy to move beyond the prescribed roles allotted to sexual identity in Western culture. She reminds us that in Judaeo-Christian mythology, the angels act as mediators who 'circulate between God, who is the perfect immobile act, and woman, whose job it is to look after nature and procreation'.[23] Within this discourse, the angels open up the closed nature of the worlds of identity, action and history. Here, this luminous Eva could be described as taking up the role of angel in the text, rejecting the use of woman-as-signifier to determine place (motherland, *alma mater*) language (mother tongue) and project a moving-beyond the text into unknown and unknowable spaces.

NOTES

1. Virginia Woolf, *A Room of One's Own* (Harmondsworth: Penguin, 2002), p.80.
2. Patricia Coughlan, 'Women and Desire in the Work of Elizabeth Bowen', in *Sex, Nation and Dissent in Irish Writing*, ed. Eibhear Walshe (Cork: Cork University Press, 1997); Rene Hoogland, *Elizabeth Bowen: A Reputation in Writing* (New York: New York University Press, 1994).
3. Elizabeth Bowen, *Eva Trout, or Changing Scenes* (London: Jonathan Cape, 1989 [1968]), p.37, hereafter referred to in the text as ET.
4. Elizabeth Bowen, *Pictures and Conversations*, ed, Spencer Curtis Brown (London: Allen Lane, 1975), pp.23–4, hereafter referred to in the text as PC.
5. R. Braidotti, *Nomadic Subjects: Embodiment and Sexual Difference in Contemporary Feminist Theory* (New York: Columbia University Press, 1994), p.65.
6. See also C. Connolly, '(Be)longing – The Strange Place of Elizabeth Bowen's Eva Trout', in *Borderlands: Negotiating Boundaries in Post-Colonial Writing*, ed. Monika Reif Hülser (Amsterdam: Rodopi, 1999), pp.135–43.
7. R. Braidotti, 'Signs of Wonder and Traces of Doubt: On Teratology and Embodied Differences', in *Feminist Theory and the Body*, ed. J. Price and M. Shildrick (Edinburgh: Edinburgh University Press, 1999), pp.290–301 (p.291).
8. Kate O'Brien, *The Land of Spices* (London: Heinemann, 1941).
9. D. Haraway, 'A Manifesto for Cyborgs: Science, Technology and Socialist Feminism in the 1980s', in *The Gendered Cyborg*, ed. G. Kirkup *et al.* (London: Routledge, 2000), pp.50–7.

10. J. González, 'Envisioning Cyborg Bodies: Notes from Current Research', in *The Gendered Cyborg*, ed. Kirkup et al., pp.58–73 (p.61).

11. Radclyffe Hall, *The Well of Loneliness* (London: Virago Press, 1982 [1928]), p.187.

12. J. Halberstam, *Female Masculinity* (Durham, NC: Duke University Press, 1998), p.268.

13. Ibid., p.45.

14. Elsinore, who did not in fact die as a child, later returns in a chance meeting with Eva in the American midwest and offers her a second chance to form an adult relationship with her. Eva refuses her, realizing that it is now too late – whether for this relationship or for Eva to have a fulfilling same-sex relationship, is not made clear.

15. P. Smith, '" And I Wondered if She Might Kiss Me": Lesbian Panic as Narrative Strategy in British Women's Fiction', *Modern Fiction Studies*, 41, 3, 4 (1995), pp.567–607.

16. Hoogland, *Elizabeth Bowen: A Reputation in Writing*, p.241.

17. M. Wittig, *Les Guerrillères* (Boston, MA: Beacon Press, 1985 [1969]), p.30.

18. M. Wittig, 'One is not Born a Woman', in *The Straight Mind and Other Essays*, ed. M. Wittig (Boston, MA: Beacon Press, 1992), p.16.

19. M. Wittig, 'On the Social Contract', in *Straight Mind*, p.40.

20. Ibid., p.39.

21. Wittig, 'One is not Born a Woman', p.18.

22. Braidotti, 'Signs of Wonder', p.295.

23. L. Irigarary, 'Sexual Difference', in *French Feminist Thought: A Reader*, ed. T. Moi (Oxford: Basil Blackwell, 1987), p.126.

CHAPTER TWELVE

Bowen: The Critical Response

JULIE ANNE STEVENS

In the twenty-first century Bowen criticism has arrived at a point where it is beginning to ask why her writing has provoked such a varied response.[1] The last decade of the twentieth century saw a flurry of publications that looked at the writer in a range of different ways: as a war novelist, or a lesbian-feminist, or a postmodernist. Her ranking as an Irish writer was placed under scrutiny by historians such as Roy Foster or Irish critics such as Declan Kiberd and Bill Mc Cormack. Also in the 1990s, Victoria Glendinning and Hermione Lee republished their critical biographies and studies. No longer was it a question of when Bowen's writing would be given its due regard. Now it was a matter of sorting through the criticism generated by her writing. Yet Bowen's ambivalent fiction eludes categories; it is a kind of writing that Hermione Lee describes as possessing an 'ambushing oddness' (she is a 'disturbing writer') and that Maud Ellmann finds 'profoundly disconcerting' (she is 'one of the strangest' of twentieth-century writers).[2] This chapter explores critical reactions to Bowen's strangeness, her way of looking at reality which I suggest emanates from an ironic vision. Such irony can be detected in the writer's use of form as well as her social comedy. An important question raised by this review of the impact of Bowen's disconcerting humour is whether or not recent studies such as feminist-lesbian analysis or psychoanalytic discussion neglect the multi-faceted nature of Bowen's fiction in pursuit of a particular agenda.

Bowen's amusing social commentary appears throughout her writing – think of Major Brutt's vain pursuit of an imagined notion of the Quayles' happy family life in The Death of the Heart.[3] Or look at her quirky character types, such as Constantine Ormeau in Eva Trout (every time we meet him he is on his way to lunch – he may not have much facial expression but he certainly possesses a stomach). Some characters verge on the grotesque, like Eva Trout, the 'monstrous heiress',[4] or demonic Madame Fisher in *The House in Paris*.[5] How ambiguous, then, are Bowen's destructive innocents (Portia and Eva are just as much victims as they are perpetrators) and how ironic are their fates. Humour also surfaces in what Hermione Lee speaks of as the 'comic confrontations' in Bowen's fiction between the 'romantic innocent' and the 'dispossessed or disenchanted' that indirectly reveal the writer's criticism of the modern world.[6] Lee also sees a 'consistent paradox' in Bowen's thought because while advocating objectivity and detachment in the handling of a particular subject the author cannot help but be attracted at the same time to sensation and romance (MT, p.6).

In her last piece of writing before her death that was published in *Pictures and Conversations*, Bowen describes how her work has been influenced by a specifically Irish or Anglo-Irish self-consciousness, a kind of showiness that one might equate with ironic self-awareness. Bowen says that much Irish writing possesses a bravado that she ascribes to an Irish history of belligerence: 'Bravado characterizes much Irish, all Anglo-Irish writing ... [and] we have an undertow to the showy'. There is a constant awareness of the fact of fiction: 'Art is for us inseparable from artifice'.[7] One could argue that such self-display and self-caricature reveal a deeply ironic sense of reality. Whatever the case, Bowen notes that certain forms of writing (drama especially) respond well to such artfulness. The compressed form of the short story has also flourished in Irish hands: 'We do not do badly with the short story, "that, in a spleen, unfolds both heaven and earth" – or should' (PC, p.23).

Bowen's short stories express most frequently her oddness, her flights of fancy: 'The short story ... allows for what is crazy about humanity: obstinacies, inordinate heroisms, "immortal longings"' (MT, p.130). Yet critical studies of Bowen are dominated by her novels. Phyllis Lassner's study of Bowen's short stories (1991) argues that the short fiction is a 'separate artistic achievement' and yet its criticism tends to be directed by the readings of the novels and falls into three basic categories: Bowen as 'social critic, a psychological realist, and a dramatist of moral truth'.[8] General studies of the short story, like Sean O'Faolain's early work *The Short Story* (1948), include commentary on the 'beautiful suggestibility' of Bowen's elliptical stories.[9] Or, in more recent studies, particular attention is given to Bowen's supernatural short fiction.[10]

Bowen distinguishes clearly between the short story and the novel. Short fiction possesses distinct attributes, and certain subject matter is fit for the abbreviated form.[11] Subject determines form. At the same time and as noted by Maud Ellmann, Bowen's fiction can incorporate multiple genres. Ellmann argues that the continual and often unreconciled allusions in Bowen's novels (fairy-tales, contemporary fiction, nineteenth-century poetry, for example) produce odd disparities. There is a 'collision between genres' that enacts a central Bowen theme: 'the resurgence of the infantile impulses of the unconscious in the midst of the complacencies of adult life'.[12] While Ellmann's psychoanalytic assessment reveals an interesting connection between Bowen's infantilism and her use of form, there is also the possibility that Bowen's shifting or unsteady fictional terrains follow in a tradition of Anglo-Irish literature. Just as Bowen was attracted, like her Irish contemporaries, to the short story, so too might her playful incorporation of different forms in longer works recall Irish literary influences. The pastiche-like nature of some of Bowen's writing reflects the 'discursive instability' and the 'stylistic hybridity' of much Irish fiction in the 1800s. Recent criticism on nineteenth-century Irish fiction in English has noted its resistance to modes of realism and the production of highly self-conscious novels noted for their 'discursive instability'.[13] Like earlier Anglo-Irish novels, Bowen's fiction self-consciously contains a mixture of forms.

Form in Bowen's writing might thus be considered an aspect of her ironic awareness as an Anglo-Irish writer. Moreover, she chooses the shorter form as a vehicle conducive to the strange and the peculiar. Her supernatural stories, as some critics point out, convey especially well the disorientation and sense of unreality conveyed by upheaval and war.[14]

W.J. McCormack's investigation of Bowen's use of the ghost story in his literary history, *Dissolute Characters: Irish Literary History through Balzac, Sheridan Le Fanu, Yeats and Bowen*, discusses some of Bowen's short fiction but concentrates on her wartime novel *The Heat of the Day* (1949). McCormack argues that the Second World War (and Irish neutrality) created a 'crisis of selfhood' in Irish writing. Bowen 'responded as a writer' to the war by 'reactivating an aspect of her literary inheritance'. McCormack points to the influence of Sheridan Le Fanu as Bowen 'adopted some of the stock-in-trade of the ghost story to investigate altered experiences of reality under the blitz'. He shows how the ghost story allowed her the opportunity to express in her fiction an altered notion of time caused by crisis, as well as the opportunity to subvert ideas about personality and character.[15]

A further attraction of the ghost story for Bowen may lie in its ability to disturb. The vague dimensions of the supernatural often provoke fear. Bowen's writing is frequently noted for its ability to suggest the undercurrents of fear that seethe dangerously beneath the fragile order of a given reality. This aspect of her work may contribute to its 'ambushing oddness'. A central paradox of Bowen's writing is created by the juxtaposition of order and disorder; an abyss seems to lie underneath the patterned lives of her characters. Lois in The Last September longs to be in a pattern, 'to be related; to have to be what I am. Just to be is so intransitive, so lonely'.[16] Pattern and habit keep fear at bay and create a place in unknown spaces. So Portia thinks in The Death of the Heart when she recalls how she and her mother would always find connections to things in the anonymous hotels they visited in order to create a sense of place:

> Habit is not mere subjugation, it is a tender tie: when one remembers habit it seems to have been happiness ... In unfamiliar places, [Portia and her mother] unconsciously looked for familiarity. It is not our exalted feelings, it is our sentiments that build the necessary home. The need to attach themselves makes wandering people strike roots in a day: where we unconsciously feel, we live. (DH, pp.168–9)

These wanderers or rootless people of Bowen's fiction are especially aware of the fragility of a surface order.

A discussion about English humour in The House in Paris (1935) distinguishes between different kinds of humour based on background and race. According to the Anglo-French Jew Max Ebhart (a modern-day wandering Jew), English humour is a kind of cheery bravado based on ignorance. It is '"ostrich courage"' (HP, p.121). In the modern world, the moderate and well-regulated perspective of the English humorist will no longer be possible. Max's hybrid background makes him more receptive to irony. Irony belongs to an outsider like him: '"Humour is being satisfied you are right; irony being satisfied that they should think you wrong. Humorous people know there is nothing they need dread"' (HP, p.120). It follows, then, that those with a sense of the ironic live with some kind of fear or dread. In Bowen's writing the threat of danger exists alongside the comic turns.

Max Ebhart and Karen Michaelis's discussion about humour originates in Max's awareness that the woman he desires comes from a stable English background. His criticism of English humour could be a way of masking his sense of undeservedness. However, his sharp comments also recall a distinction made in Anglo-Irish writing about the way the English see the world (and laugh at it) differently from other races. Writers that Bowen admired, Edith Somerville and Martin Ross, claimed at the beginning of the century that the dreary use of Irish stereotypes and the 'heavy-handed caricature' by the English was the result of an inability to comprehend Irish wit. English sensibilities had been dulled by complacency: 'One might safely say that this bare and still country carries an amount of good talk, nimble, trenchant, and humorous, to the square mile, that the fat and comfortable plains could never rival'.[17] In a similar way the hybrid Max claims that the well-cushioned life of Karen's people limits their appreciation of the darker side of the comic impulse.

Bowen's discomfiting sense of reality has been described in different ways by her critics. She is considered alternatively as 'complex' and down-to-earth. Spenser Curtis Brown, her advisor and friend, describes her personality as 'many-faceted': 'she could present to different people a different facet of the same personality'. Her writing, he says, showed a similar complexity; alongside 'high social comedy ... the Serpent was lying in wait' (PC, pp.xvi and xvii). Victoria Glendinning portrays an energetic and immensely charming woman, but one whose unsettled early life determined the ambiguities and evasions of her writing. She had a good sense of fun, however, and her literary leanings and inclusion in that group described by Cyril Connolly as the Mandarins – 'artists believing in the importance of their art, in grace and subtlety and sensuality and sensibility and romantic individualism', did not foreclose her appreciation of ordinary folk like her neighbour in Ireland, Jim Gates, 'extrovert, practical, a little coarse'.[18] Hermione Lee sees Bowen's humour as her 'most obvious Anglo-Irish trait', with leanings toward the violent and the grotesque and a 'playing to the gallery' that is found in Edgeworth, Le Fanu and Somerville and Ross.[19]

Like Somerville and Ross, Bowen's type of humour did not always strike the right note with her readers. Early criticism of Somerville and Ross's 1894 novel The Real Charlotte considered the authors' subject matter as vulgar, and in a similar way some of Bowen's initial critics resisted Bowen's tendency to write about 'vulgar people in banal situations'.[20] Yet this aspect of Bowen's writing attracts later readers (just as what was considered the nastiest of Somerville and Ross's writing – the least ladylike – has become the most intriguing). One might keep in mind, then, Bowen's comic depiction of a 'vulgar' character like Daphne Heccomb in The Death of the Heart. As an occupant of Waikiki villa in Seale, Daphne offers a vigorous alternative to Portia's innocence or Anna's sophistication. Ironically, she works as a librarian, who, incidentally, despises reading, yet she earns the respect of her elderly library subscribers because of her healthy disregard for the whole business of belles lettres and other such nonsense. When mild-mannered Mrs Adams attempts to prove her literary aspirations by poking through the classical works section of the library, Daphne swiftly dispatches her. She has no time for people 'messing the books about' (DH, p.222).

However vulgarly funny Daphne might be, she suggests a dimension in Bowen that might be aligned to what critics have noted as a kind of hardy and unsentimental practicality. For Glendinning, Bowen is a stoic romantic while Lee portrays a conservative sensibility that arises from the writer's Anglo-Irish background. Bowen recalls Edmund Burke with her 'belief in the moral effects of property, in benevolent imperialism, in tradition, in private ownership'.[21] Hermione Lee connects Bowen firmly to the land. Maud Ellmann, then, notes that despite the insidious pressures of the intense interior worlds of Bowen's characters, the author 'ultimately sides with the waking world of realism, as opposed to the hypnotic world of dreams'.[22] Bowen's attention to the concrete world (objects and places) has been linked to this practical world-view. Various critics are interested in what Ellmann describes as the 'verbal caressing' of objects in Bowen's writing.[23] Like Daphne Heccomb who is more interested in dancing and flirting than dusty books, so too do we find a determined physicality in Bowen's treatment of reality. 'Things behave like thoughts and thoughts like things, thus impugning the supremacy of consciousness', says Maud Ellmann.[24] Objects seem to have their own existence, even their own neuroses.[25]

Given the curious power of things in Bowen's writing, their ability to reveal repressed desire or an unconscious past – their animism – it is not surprising that the fiction has attracted psychoanalytic criticism like that employed recently by Maud Ellmann in *Elizabeth Bowen: The Shadow Across the Page* (2003). As early as 1975, Harriet Blodgett argued that Bowen was a 'psychological realist' who recalls Jung in her manner of 'constru[ing] libido and the unconscious'.[26] More recently, Ellmann applies Freudian models to Bowen's writing and follows upon post-modern studies, in particular Andrew Bennett and Nicholas Royle's *Elizabeth Bowen and the Dissolution of the Novel: Still Lives* (1994). Bennett and Royle, like McCormack in *Dissolute Characters*, argue that traditional concepts of realism cannot be successfully applied to Bowen's fiction. Character, for example, does not perform in the traditional manner in her writing: 'her novels derange the very grounds of "character"'.[27] Ellmann agrees with Bennett and Royle's observation on the tendency of Bowen's fiction to deconstruct itself, and she is especially interested in their use of psychoanalytic theories. For example, like them she uses the Freudian notion of cryptonomy developed by Nicholas Abraham and Maria Torok in her study of the power of the past in Bowen's *The House in Paris*. Ellmann argues that the novel's structure, the way the past is encased, or framed by the children's present, demonstrates the psychological significance of the story. The structure shows how the past can be concealed and, in a way, encased, as if in a crypt: 'The adults' story, enveloped in the children's, forms a crypt or "condemned passageway" within the text in which the secrets of the past are buried alive.'[28]

A significant difference, however, might be discerned when comparing Ellmann's psychoanalytic approach to that of Bennett and Royle. Ellmann's use of psychoanalytic thought in her study often displays the way the writer overturns or subverts Freudian ideas. Ellmann's feminist background becomes apparent when she shows how Bowen's writing 'challenges the patriarchal bias of Freud's theory'. For example, she looks at how Bowen replaces the male with the female in various Freudian models: the 'family romance' or the 'triadic structures of desire' that joke-telling reveals.[29] In the latter instance, 'female[s] ... are joined together by an absent male; this is the reversal of Freud's dirty joke, in which two men are joined by an absent female'.[30]

Ellmann's criticism is indebted to earlier feminist treatments of the writer by critics such as Phyllis Lassner, Rene Hoogland and Patricia Coughlan, who examine gender and sexuality in Bowen's writing. Some controversy has resulted from feminist-lesbian studies and discussion about Bowen's treatment of lesbianism. Before continuing a discussion of Ellmann's criticism, I want to consider more closely the disagreement amongst some critics over issues of gender and sexuality in Bowen's life and writings. I also wish to ask if feminist criticism neglects Bowen's ironic treatment of reality, as Hermione Lee suggests in her revised study:

> [Feminist] re-readings of Bowen present her, rightly, as a subversive writer with a passionate interest in women's lives, even if, for the purposes of argument, they have to underplay the social comedy, the unpredictable lack of formulae, and the surprising, ambushing oddness of much of her work, which doesn't lend itself to fixed agendas.[31]

The source of some of the disagreement regarding Bowen's treatment of women and sexuality in her fiction is a short biographical essay published by the American writer May Sarton in 1976, just after Bowen's death. A brief rehearsal of the facts of Sarton and Bowen's friendship is useful in this overview of the reaction to Bowen's brief lesbian affair.

Sarton first met Bowen when the American was 26 and Bowen was an established writer living in London. Their friendship intensified when Bowen visited Sarton in Rye (Radclyffe Hall's occasional home), where the younger writer had rented a house on Mermaid Street, just around the corner from Lamb House where Henry James had once resided. May Sarton does not hesitate to claim her sexual conquest: 'we slept together in my big bed after an exchange that had great tenderness in it'.[32] Perhaps Bowen's subsequent dismissal of Sarton as a lover and her later snubbing of her as a friend may have something to do with Sarton's revelations. The American's final visit to Bowen's Court after Alan Cameron's death in the 1950s did little to lessen the increasing distance between the women. Initially Sarton was the only guest but then a young woman suitably called Miss Lovelace arrived and Sarton was swiftly sidelined: 'for reasons I shall never now know, I had become a second-class citizen in Elizabeth's province'.[33]

Both Glendinning and Lee dismiss the question of Bowen's sexuality that May Sarton raised. However, although Virginia Woolf may have

described the American to Bowen as '"that goose"',[34] subsequent feminist critics believe an important clue is indicated by Sarton's story. These
critics have taken special interest in the representation of women in
Bowen's fiction and, in particular, a character type that might be
described as the hovering female figure. Powerful older females like
destructive Anna Quayle in The Death of the Heart, dying Madame Fisher in
The House in Paris, or dead Laura Naylor in The Last September are positioned
up high like avenging angels at different points in their novels. Portia
sees Anna looking out from her bedroom window, her face white like a
ghost, and Madame Fisher's presence seeps out from her room in the
top story of the house in Paris like some deathly substance: 'like smoke
coming under a door, the dead silence of Mme Fisher seemed to per-
vade everywhere' (HP, p.257). Of course, Laura Naylor's name scratched
on the upstairs window pane is not an actual presence and yet, at times
in the novel, she seems nearly to be there – certainly, she continues to
affect the living. Such women form complex relationships with younger
women and men; in some instances an indirect or 'oblique' sexual tension complicates these relationships even further.[35]

According to feminist and lesbian critics, the treatment of sexuality in
Bowen's fiction offers an opportunity to appreciate most fully the writer's
radical potential. Contemporary thought investigates dimensions of sexuality that make it suitable for a writer like Bowen, whose fiction often
explores the female libido. Patricia Coughlan, for example, speaks of
Glendinning's guarded approach to sexuality. She points out that developments in theory related to sexuality offer a more nuanced reading of
Bowen's representation of sexuality in her novels.[36] Rene Hoogland
argues that the 'traditional critical framework' of Hermione Lee's study of
Bowen precludes an appreciation of the writer's revolutionary qualities.
Lee's attention to the 'historical background of the author's critiques of
class convention and concomitant preoccupation with a declining civilization' make her less receptive to Bowen's later experimental novels.[37]
Hoogland believes that ignoring the suggestions of lesbian sexuality in
Bowen's work is also ignoring 'Bowen's subversive potential [that] resides
in precisely this area'. Earlier studies by Lee or Blodgett she sees as failing to 'recognize Bowen for what she also is: a truly radical, innovative,
and critically practising feminist', and while Phyllis Lassner's 1989 feminist study of Bowen serves as a useful starting point to examine the

writer's concern with the 'operations of gender',[38] a full appreciation of the writer's disruptive potential must examine more than gender and nationality. Sexuality is a vital aspect of her work and the 'fictions' underlying 'desire' contribute to the writer's radicalness.[39] A cautionary note, however, is sounded by Patricia Coughlan, who draws upon feminist-lesbian theory to assist her examination of women's relationships in Bowen but hesitates to offer straightforward lesbian readings of Bowen's fiction. Things are not so clear-cut with this complex writer because the 'subtle design and texture of Bowen's novels ... make them unsuitable objects for such simplifying upbeat readings'.[40]

Hermione Lee replies to Hoogland's criticisms in her revised study. She points out that Bowen rejected feminism and demonstrated a 'satirical attitude' to the one known lesbian lover in her life, May Sarton.[41] In so doing Lee asks how one can reconcile a feminist or a lesbian approach to Bowen the writer when Bowen the woman indicated her ambivalence (at least) to such practice and discourse. More convincingly she points out that Hoogland's approach is prescriptive and limiting; she claims that it is a 'flattening [and] intractable model for Bowen's slippery and complex fictions'.[42] Moreover and as already noted, she asserts that concentration on Bowen's representation of women by feminist writers leads to a neglect of other aspects of her writing, including its social comedy.[43]

Yet one could argue that feminist and lesbian theorists have shown how contemporary theoretical models respond to the elusive ambiguities of Bowen's writing. Such ambiguities issue from Bowen's ironic sensibility that determines the social comedy of the texts. Instead of ignoring the complexities and ambivalence of Bowen's writing, feminist theorists engage with them. For example, they point to the contradictions and paradoxes of the texts as possible instances of complex sexual motive. So though we may disagree with these critics' findings, we must note their determination to tackle the ambiguities of the material. Such criticism indicates that it is not enough to say that Bowen writes comic scenes; we need to ask why. These critics tease out possible reasons for the evasive nature of the text. At the same time, while acknowledging Bowen's ambivalent reaction to feminism or lesbianism, they maintain the importance of investigating a fiction that reveals a more complex sensibility than that displayed in public pronouncements by the private individual. Nonetheless, Hermione Lee's riposte to Hoogland's argument reminds us of the difficulty in reconciling the historical dimension of a writer's life and fiction with theoretical models of application. She returns us to those essential aspects of the writer's life while at the same time demonstrating her appreciation for the groundbreaking work of feminist critics who have made central in literary discourse the representation of women's experience.

An example of the development of feminist theory as it relates to Bowen's writing might be discovered in Maud Ellmann's study. The book is dedicated to her mother, Mary Ellmann, who wrote about Bowen but is better known for her 1968 debunking of female stereotypes in a book called Thinking About Women. The book might be seen as part of a feminist challenge to sexual stereotyping in both literature and psychoanalytic theory. Such work paved the way for later female critics to address women's writing in a more open manner, freed of such categorization. For instance and apropos our earlier discussion of Bowen's materiality, Mary Ellmann questions women's supposed closeness to the material world. She lightly ridicules the notion that 'woman feeds upon the fatness of things' and is so immersed in detail that she cannot discern grand abstract ideas that the less materialistic male eye perceives. Ellmann reveals how such thinking depends on binary oppositions and chauvinistic intent.[44] Her daughter's subsequent discussion of Bowen's treatment of objects has thus been liberated to look more closely at the powerful and varied significance that such dwelling on the material world might have. Maud Ellmann need not defend Bowen's attention to detail or her delight in furniture and chairs. Instead – and because the decks have been cleared by feminist writing such as that of her mother – the later critic studies how 'every object has a psyche' in Bowen's writing and how frequently 'consciousness escapes into the object'.[45] Her analysis of female relationships differs from earlier feminist studies, since she is not so much concerned with suggestions of lesbian sexuality as she is fascinated by the curious dynamic that has been created by absent others who make up various threesomes or foursomes with the characters in the fiction: 'in spite of innuendoes of lesbian desire, outing the heroine is not the point, for Bowen is more concerned with number than with gender'.[46]

Maud Ellmann's subtitle 'The Shadow Across the Page' refers to Bowen's 1937 article so titled and expressive of all that has not been said by the writer, the unwritten work that accrues as time passes: 'the silence of the worlds that Bowen never lived to rescue from the deep'.[47] Her first chapter, then, is called 'Shadowing Elizabeth Bowen' and refers to the critic's intent 'to shadow some of Bowen's most significant addictions through the cunning passageways of her imagination'.[48] But Ellmann is also interested in other kinds of shadows. As mentioned above, she explores the 'shadowy third' that haunts so many relationships in Bowen's fiction (indeed, the shadowy fourths and fifths who can press with such insistence on Bowen's lovers). She also studies the shadows of the writing that alternatively conceal and reveal the 'haunted chambers of the mind',[49] and she notes the absences that act as shadows on the present living worlds of Bowen's fiction.

In the end, Ellmann's study may reveal as much about her own pre-occupations as it does about those of Bowen. Certainly, her omissions in the text suggest a curious reflection of her subject's sensibility. The critic admits to this possibility early in her book: 'Prying into Bowen's secrets we are likely to betray our own. Her fiction interprets its interpreters, shaking our assumptions, undermining our defences, and penetrating deep into the haunted chambers of the mind.'[50]

The elusive nature of Bowen's writing continues to fascinate her critics. Her ironic vision responds to a range of critical theories while her mixed background allows for different angles of approach. Despite the recent interest in her writing that new critical studies indicate, one suspects a continued examination of both her short fiction and novels.

NOTES

1. Hermione Lee sums up the approaches to Bowen as 'a social realist, a Jamesian stylist, a comic satirist of manners, a historian of the Anglo-Irish, a lesbian sensibility, an anti-romantic but passionate analyst of fatal love, a civilian war correspondent, or an elegist for lost innocence'. 'Psychic Furniture: Ellmann's Elizabeth Bowen', Body Parts: Essays on Life Writing (London: Chatto and Windus, 2005), pp.187–93 (pp.187–8).

2. Hermione Lee, Elizabeth Bowen, revised edition (London: Vintage, 1999 [1981]), p.12; Maud Ellmann, Elizabeth Bowen: The Shadow Across the Page (Edinburgh: Edinburgh University Press, 2003), p.x.

3. Elizabeth Bowen, The Death of the Heart (London: Jonathan Cape, 1948 [1938]), here-after referred to in the text as DH.

4. Elizabeth Bowen, Eva Trout, or Changing Scenes (London: Vintage, 1999 [1968]), p.63, hereafter referred to in the text as ET.

5. Elizabeth Bowen, *The House in Paris* (New York: Anchor, 2002 [1935]), hereafter referred to in the text as HP.

6. Hermione Lee, Preface, in Elizabeth Bowen, *The Mulberry Tree: Writings of Elizabeth Bowen*, ed. Hermione Lee (London: Vintage, 1999 [1986]), p.1, hereafter referred to in the text as MT.

7. Elizabeth Bowen, *Pictures and Conversations*, Foreword by Spencer Curtis Brown, September 1973 (New York: Alfred A. Knopf, 1975), p.23, hereafter referred to in the text as PC.

8. Phyllis Lassner, *Elizabeth Bowen: A Study of the Short Fiction* (New York: Twayne, 1991), pp.xi, 157.

9. Sean O'Faolain, *The Short Story* (Cork: Mercier Press, 1972 [1948]), p.240.

10. See Valerie Shaw, *The Short Story: A Critical Introduction* (Harlow: Longman, 1983), p.258.

11. See Bowen's discussion of aspects of the short story in her introduction to her collected stories of 1959, 'Stories by Elizabeth Bowen', *The Mulberry Tree*, pp.128–9.

12. Ellmann, *Elizabeth Bowen*, p.4.

13. For further discussion, see Sean Ryder's summing up of a recent study of nineteenth-century Irish writing in English and his commentary on a particular interest in the open-endedness and 'stylistic hybridity' of the Irish novel in English in 'Literature in English', *Nineteenth-Century Ireland: A Guide to Recent Research*, ed. Laurence M. Geary and Margaret Kelleher (Dublin: University College Dublin Press, 2005), pp.118–35 (p.123).

14. Shaw *Short Story*, p.260.

15. William McCormack, *Dissolute Characters: Irish Literary History through Balzac, Sheridan Le Fanu, Yeats and Bowen* (Manchester: Manchester University Press, 1993), p.209.

16. Elizabeth Bowen, *The Last September* (Harmondsworth: Penguin, 1987 [1929]), p.98, hereafter referred to in the text as LS.

17. Edith Somerville and Martin Ross, 'Children of the Captivity', in *Some Irish Yesterdays* (London: T. Nelson and Sons, 1906), pp.269–81 (pp.277 and 272).

18. Victoria Glendinning, *Elizabeth Bowen: Portrait of a Writer* (London: Phoenix, 1993 [1977]), pp.169 and 110.

19. Lee, *Elizabeth Bowen*, pp.24–5.

20. Glendinning, *Elizabeth Bowen*, p.126.

21. Lee, *Elizabeth Bowen*, p.26.

22. Ellmann, *Elizabeth Bowen*, p.5.

23. Ibid., p.8. For instance, Hilary Pyle speaks of the 'cool abbreviate manner' in which Bowen depicts objects in her writing while Victoria Glendinning speaks of Bowen's 'painterly sensitivity' in her representation of gardens. See 'A Portrait of Elizabeth Bowen by Patrick Hennessy' and 'Gardens and Gardening in the Writings of Elizabeth Bowen', in *Elizabeth Bowen Remembered: The Farahy Addresses*, ed. Eibhear Walshe (Dublin: Four Courts Press, 1998), pp.57 and 30. Most recently, Elizabeth Inglesby examines Bowen's treatment of objects in '"Expressive Objects": Elizabeth Bowen's Narrative Materializes', *Modern Fiction Studies*, Special Issue: Elizabeth Bowen, 53, 2 (Summer 2007), pp.306–33.

24. Ellmann, *Elizabeth Bowen*, p.5.

25. Ibid., p.6.

26. Harriet Blodgett, *Patterns of Reality: Elizabeth Bowen's Novels* (The Hague: Mouton, 1975), pp.8 and 15.

27. Andrew Bennett and Nicholas Royle, *Elizabeth Bowen and the Dissolution of the Novel: Still Lives* (Basingstoke: Macmillan, 1994), p.xvii. Mc Cormack, *Dissolute Characters*, p.210.

28. Ellmann, *Elizabeth Bowen*, p.121.

29. Ibid., note 32, pp.174 and 71.

30. Ibid., p.72.

31. Lee, *Elizabeth Bowen*, p.12.

32. May Sarton, 'Elizabeth Bowen', in *A World of Light: Portraits and Celebrations* (New York: W.W. Norton and Co., 1976), pp.191–213 (p.197).

33. Ibid., p.209.

34. Quoted in Hermione Lee, *Virginia Woolf* (London: Chatto and Windus, 1996), p.701.

35. Bowen speaks of Somerville and Ross's terrain of 'obliquity, unsavoury tragedy, sexual no less than ambitious passion' in *The Real Charlotte*. I think such indirect and oblique behaviour is evident in many of Bowen's characters. See 'The Irish Cousins by Violet Powell', *The Mulberry Tree*, p.187.

36. Patricia Coughlan, 'Woman and Desire in the Work of Elizabeth Bowen', in *Sex, Nation and Dissent in Irish Writing*, ed. Eibhear Walshe (Cork: Cork University Press, 1997), pp.103–34 (pp.108–9).

37. Rene C. Hoogland, *Elizabeth Bowen: A Reputation in Writing* (New York: New York University Press, 1994), p.19.

38. Ibid., p.20. Phyllis Lassner, *Elizabeth Bowen* (Totowa, NJ: Barnes and Noble, 1989).

39. Ibid., p.301.

40. Coughlan, 'Woman and Desire in the Work of Bowen', p.125.

41. Lee, *Elizabeth Bowen*, p.10.

42. Ibid., p.11.

43. Ibid., p.12.

44. Mary Ellmann, *Thinking About Women* (London: Virago, 1979 [1968]), p.97.

45. Ellmann, *Elizabeth Bowen*, pp.6 and 7.

46. Ibid., p.70.

47. Ibid., p.224.

48. Ibid., p.3.

49. Ibid., p.5.

50. Ibid.

CHAPTER THIRTEEN

The 'Placing' and Politics of Bowen in Contemporary Irish Literary and Cultural Criticism

HEATHER LAIRD

When compared with other examples of single-author scholarship, the body of criticism concerned with Elizabeth Bowen's writing appears extremely fragmented. Amongst the Elizabeth Bowens figured in literary and cultural criticism is the 'Anglo-Irish Bowen', the 'modernist Bowen', the 'postmodernist Bowen', the 'bisexual Bowen', the 'woman writer', the 'British wartime author', and the 'writer of Irish Protestant Gothic'. Indeed a novice to Bowen's work, browsing through the book-shelves of an academic library or through the multitude of Bowen web-sites, could be forgiven for assuming that during the course of the twentieth century there had been a number of different authors called 'Elizabeth Bowen'. This chapter provides an overview and an analysis of writings about Elizabeth Bowen in contemporary Irish literary and cul-tural criticism. It suggests that questions concerning Bowen's national and ethnic identity (or identities) and affiliations, and of the manner and ways in which Bowen's Anglo-Irish heritage shaped her more overtly Irish writings, are now, as they were in her own day, a central and reoc-curring concern for critics who read Bowen's work in the context of Irish literature and culture. The chapter will examine the role assigned in writings from various critical and ideological perspectives to what is sometimes described as Bowen's lack of roots, but might perhaps more accurately be referred to as her profusion of roots, highlighting what I consider to be the more fruitful critical approaches to this aspect of her life and work. It will pinpoint what tends to be omitted, primarily issues of gender and sexuality, in analyses of Bowen as an Anglo-Irish writer. In the concluding paragraphs, it will suggest ways in which her in-between status can be most successfully linked to what might initially appear to be very different aspects of her writing, demonstrating the connections that exist between her literary writings set predominantly in Ireland and her other works of fiction.

Bowen was famously described by her erstwhile lover, Sean O'Faolain, as 'heart-cloven and split-minded ... consistently declaring herself born and reared Irish, residing mostly in England, writing in the full European tradition'.[1] This characterization of Bowen is echoed in the work of more recent commentators, many of whom make reference to Bowen's description of her childhood identity crisis in her autobiographical *Seven Winters* when embarking on a discussion of her in-between status and the divided loyalties engendered by such a hyphenated existence.[2]

With regard to the 'placing' of Elizabeth Bowen, the Irish revisionist historian, Roy Foster, and Jack Lane, a member of the nationalist Aubane Historical Society, are at opposite ends of the spectrum. Bowen's in-between status for Lane ensures that she cannot be categorized as Irish or as an Irish writer: 'Elizabeth Bowen has an attribute which it is difficult for an Irish writer to acquire – she was English. Her youth was spent between Dublin, the South of England, and North Cork – *correction*, Bowen's Court: not North Cork.'[3] For Foster, however, it is this same in-between status that qualifies Bowen as 'distinctively if uncomfortably Irish'.[4] In Foster's account of the connections in Irish and English history, *Paddy and Mr Punch*, 'cross-channel borrowings', too often dismissed as the 'historical consequence of exploitation', are implicit in Irish history ensuring that Irish culture is indelibly comprised of multiple and variant traditions.[5] Lane, who acknowledges connections between Ireland and England but suggests that in the case of Anglo-Irish families like the Bowens such connections were quintessentially 'predatory', asserts that Elizabeth Bowen should only be included in an anthology of North Cork writers under erasure.[6] In his introduction to a published volume of the espionage reports Bowen sent to the British Ministry of Information during the Second World War, Lane explains that while excerpts from *Seven Winters* and *The Last September* were included in the *North Cork Anthology* published by the Aubane Historical Society in 1993, a line was put through Bowen's name in the title to signify that 'though Ms Bowen had been physically connected with North Cork through Bowen's Court, she was not a North Cork writer'.[7] Bowen was included in the anthology in deleted form, Lane tells us, 'in order to explain why she does not belong to it'.[8]

While Foster and Lane situate Bowen at opposite ends of the Anglo-Irish hyphen, ethical evaluations of the nature of the historical relationship between Ireland and England, and between the Anglo-Irish and the 'native' Irish, are of fundamental importance to both commentators' delineations of Irishness. Foster, who as an Irish revisionist historian is far too wary of apportioning blame in an analysis of these relationships,[9] argues that those who believe that 'the "real" Irish experience is that of unrelieved pain' and who consequently focus exclusively on the exploitative nature of Anglo-Irish relations proffer too limited a definition of Irishness.[10] In contrast, Lane, whose sympathies are recognizably (and narrowly) nationalist, suggests that those who ignore the exploitative nature of Anglo-Irish relations and of the relationship between the Anglo-Irish and the 'native' Irish put forward too broad a definition of Irishness. Journalists and academics, some of whom, according to Lane, go on pilgrimages to the turnip field where Bowen's Court once stood, lamenting the loss of a house paid for and sustained through the exploitation of a local tenantry, 'are trying to redefine Irish culture in a way that makes it meaningless'.[11]

One of the principal focuses of interest (and anxiety) for commentators concerned with the geographical and ethnic placing of Bowen as a writer are the aforementioned confidential reports on political and civic life in Ireland that she compiled for the British Ministry of Information during the period of the Second World War. These reports, now accessible in the National Archives in Kew, were published by the Aubane Historical Society in 1999 as justification for their earlier included exclusion of Bowen in the North Cork Anthology. Sardonically suggesting in his introduction to these reports that the 'media opinion-formers and academics' who had been so critical of the North Cork Anthology demonstrate how highly they rate Elizabeth Bowen by unearthing further reports and making them generally available, Jack Lane is unequivocal in his assertion that Bowen's voluntary involvement in espionage amply demonstrates 'where her loyalties lay'.[12]

Contrary to what Lane anticipated, however, accounts in Irish literary and cultural criticism of Bowen's spying activities focus predominantly on mixed allegiances, her assumption of the role of spy being pitted against the actual content of the reports she sent to the British Ministry of Information.[13] Bowen spied for England, but, as numerous commentators point out, in her spy reports she contextualizes and, most notably in her earlier reports, justifies Irish neutrality. Moreover, while prone to condescending assessments of Irish people and their opinions, she is unabashedly critical of English attitudes towards Ireland. Drawing attention in her reports to anti-Irish feeling in England, Bowen points out that 'this assertion of her neutrality is Eire's first free self-assertion' and consequently the Irish people quite rightly view neutrality 'as positive, not merely negative'. Just prior to this, however, she states that 'the childishness and obtuseness of this country cannot fail to be irritating to the English mind'.[14]

The most recent commentary on Bowen's espionage activities is to be found in Clair Wills's *That Neutral Island*. In this ambitious cultural history of wartime Ireland, Bowen's involvement in clandestine information- and opinion-gathering work is interpreted in conflicting ways. In Wills's introduction, Bowen would appear to be numbered amongst the Irish intellectuals whose close links with the Allies should be viewed less in terms of mixed allegiances than in the context of a desire to see themselves, and be seen, as the 'voice of the nation's conscience'.[15] Later in the book, however, Wills, who points out that Irish neutrality was 'to increase the alienation of some Anglo-Irish, who felt forced to choose between England and Ireland', tells us that 'although [Bowen] claimed she always thought of herself as Irish, the war called forth her obligation towards England'.[16]

Bowen's mixed allegiances and the extent to which, and ways in which, these mixed allegiances shaped her literary writings have, in my opinion, best been explored within the Irish context by critics whose work is informed by post-colonial literary and cultural theory. This approach has to date been somewhat limited by a failure on the part of such critics to engage in potentially fruitful comparative work that reads Bowen alongside settler colonial writings from other geographical locations.[17] It has succeeded, however, in shifting the focus, in an analysis of Bowen's divided loyalties, from the personal to the structural, thereby allowing us to move beyond the aforementioned circular debates that have tended to dominate analyses of the 'Anglo-Irish Bowen'. Both Declan Kiberd and Margot Gayle Backus, for example, position Bowen as a descendant of a settler colonial elite. This elite, they tell us, was separated by class, education and religion from the majority of Irish citizens, but was equally estranged from an England in which they were invariably considered Irish or at least too Irish to be comfortably classified as English. In Kiberd's 'Elizabeth Bowen – The Dandy in Revolt', which, like the work of so many, perhaps too many, Irish literary critics, focuses almost exclusively on *The Last September*, Bowen is both a product of, and a commentator on, a planter community. This was a community, Kiberd states, that assumed a pose or, more specifically through the Big House, an 'exterior show of spaciousness and command' to mask an inner uncertainty that resulted from its contentious origins and its subsequent failure to naturalize its rule.[18]

Kiberd and Backus, in their writings on Bowen's fiction and on Anglo-Irish society in general, draw our attention to strained inter-generational relations. For Kiberd, it was the preservation of the aforementioned pose that placed inordinate pressure on the younger members of the settler familial system. For Backus, this pressure was, and still is, primarily the result of the perpetuation of specific patterns of loyalty and animosity. With reference to *The Last September*, Kiberd asserts that 'Lois is as much a victim of Danielstown values as the Irish rebel who crosses her path: for the Anglo-Irish are as guilty of ignoring the needs of the heirs within as the dependents without. In return for nothing, the young are compelled to adopt a time-honoured set of manners and attitudes, to be "sealed" and "finished", so that the social forms may survive the death of their contents.'[19] In *The Gothic Family Romance*, Backus acknowledges the toll elicited from the younger generation through the process of maintaining 'a time-honoured set of manners and attitudes' but chooses to foreground 'recurring narrative conventions testify[ing] to the continuing cost that is being exacted from children born within a settler colonial order that prioritizes loyalty to an abstract national identity above local cooperation and identification'.[20] When referring to the above-cited statement by Kiberd, Backus quite rightly points out that while 'all Big House children were "effectively told to embalm themselves alive, perform approved routines, and deny all feeling", only the female half were reduced to this living death ... "in return for nothing"'.[21]

While Backus's introduction of a gender dimension is an important addition to Kiberd's post-colonial analysis of the 'Anglo-Irish Bowen', an engagement with the writings of such internationally renowned scholars of settler colonialism as Daiva Stasiulis and Nira Yuval-Davis would have significantly enhanced her argument. In their introduction to *Unsettling Settler Societies*,[22] Stasiulis and Yuval-Davis locate the divided loyalties of settler women in a colonial system that they were part of and fundamental to but also separate from and, to some extent, restricted by. Settler women, it is stated, are fundamental to the colonial system in that they are the biological and cultural carriers of colonial communities, expected to propagate with members of their own grouping and to transmit the symbols and ways of life associated with that grouping to their children. This introduction also draws our attention to the extent to which settler women are constrained by their role in the perpetuation of the colonial system and the guarding of its ethnic and cultural boundaries.

Backus fails to refer to such international scholarship on the gender aspects of settler colonialism, but her commentary on the Anglo-Irish community in *The Gothic Family Romance* makes it clear how relevant this scholarship would be to an analysis of Anglo-Irish women. She draws our attention, for example, to the physical, psychological and sexual restrictions associated with the breeding and the ideological tasks of reproducing the Anglo-Irish settler community. She asks whether these restrictions may be why 'Anglo-Irish women often depict the burning of [the Big House] during the Troubles with an astonishing degree of complacency, if not enthusiasm'.[23] A prime example of the kind of depiction that Backus is referring to is to be found in Elizabeth Bowen's *The Last September*, which concludes, rather spectacularly, with the front door of the novel's Big House standing 'open hospitably upon a furnace'.[24]

The Last September, which records the demise of the Ascendancy and is considered by many to be the quintessential Big House novel,[25] is one of two out of the ten novels written by Bowen that is set exclusively in Ireland. *A World of Love*, the second of these two novels, was written twenty-six years after *The Last September* and is centred on a former Big House turned working farm which has grown so isolated that neighbours believe it to be uninhabited.[26] Two of Bowen's other novels, *The House in Paris*, which begins and ends in Paris, and *The Heat of the Day*, which is set principally in wartime London, make substantial detours to Ireland and a number of her short stories were republished in 1978 under the title *Elizabeth Bowen's Irish Stories*.[27] In *The Anglo-Irish Novel and the Big House*, Vera Kreilkamp offers a nuanced reading of the 'Anglo-Irish Bowen' that engages with these texts and other writings by Elizabeth Bowen.[28] In general, however, Bowen scholarship, in contemporary Irish literary and cultural criticism, focuses predominantly and too narrowly on *The Last September*, with analyses of this novel frequently accompanied by brief references to *Seven Winters*, an autobiographical description of Bowen's Dublin childhood, and *Bowen's Court*, a family chronicle that is also a history of Bowen's ancestral Cork home.[29]

The Last September, typically contextualized in Irish literary and cultural criticism in relation to the aforementioned life writings and the allegiances and loyalties expressed therein, has, since its publication, been read by critics in varying and conflicting ways. Most notably, it has sometimes been read as a memorial to, and sometimes as a condemnation of, the Ascendancy that was Bowen's heritage.[30] In recent years, it has been most commonly and, in my opinion, more accurately viewed as a curious combination of the two, censure and admiration. The interpretation of certain key passages in the novel suggests much about the individual critic's approach. One of these passages, already mentioned in my brief discussion of Margot Gayle Backus's work, describes the burning of the Big House. Two other pivotal passages tell of an encounter or, on one of these occasions, a near encounter, that takes place between Lois, a young inhabitant of the Big House, and an IRA man. On the first of these occasions - the near encounter - a member of the IRA, walking through demesne land, passes close to where Lois, the protagonist of the novel, is standing watching him:

> It must be because of Ireland he was in such a hurry; down from the mountains, making a short cut through their demesne. Here was something else that she could not share. She could not conceive of her country emotionally ... Quite still, she let him go past in contemptuous unawareness. His intentions burnt on the dark an almost visible trail; he might well have been a murderer he seemed so inspired. (*TLS*, p.34)

Later in the novel, Lois, accompanied by Marda, a female visitor to the Big House, happens upon a republican gunman in an uncanny ruined mill:

The man's eyes went from one to the other, and remained ironically between them. His face was metal-blue in the dusk and seemed numbed into immobility. 'It is time', he said, 'that yourselves gave up walking. If you have nothing better to do, you had better keep in the house while y'have it.' Marda, a hand on the frame of the doorway, remained unmoved, but Lois could not but agree with him. She felt quite ruled out, there was nothing at all for her here. (TLS, p.125)

In relation to these extracts, what tends to preoccupy critics is the level of affinity that is established between Lois and the IRA men she encounters and the extent to which her desire (often conflated with Bowen's own desire) to break free of the confines of the house is shown to correspond with their desire to burn it to the ground. Roy Foster, while acknowledging that elsewhere in the novel Anglo-Irish contempt for the English 'comes ironically close to national pride in their own revolutionaries', asserts that the first two of these passages – the burning of the house and the encounter on demesne land – are 'quintessential views from inside the demesne walls'. The destruction of Danielstown at the end of the novel is described by Foster as an enactment of Bowen's worst fears for Bowen's Court.[31] The more ideologically opposed critics of Bowen are to Foster's revisionist perspective, the more likely they tend to be to stress ties between Lois and the revolutionaries and to read the burning of the Big House as the register as much of authorial desire as of anxiety. In Declan Kiberd's analysis, tentative bonds are formed between Lois and the insurgents. Lois, we are told, 'feels a weird mixture of envy and terror' when she sees the IRA man on the demesne lands.[32] She is both fearful of what he is capable of doing in the name of Ireland and envious that in the process of resisting the very traditions that are having such a deadening effect on her, he has become so animated. The burning of the house, which by the end of the novel Lois is no longer present to comment on, 'means that at long last she can escape the cocoon: she is free now to enter a world of risk and growth rather than languish in one of fear and inexperience'.[33] Margot Gayle Backus establishes still closer and more active links between Lois and the anticolonial insurgents, reminding us that Lois and Marda make a secret pack with the gunman in the derelict mill and physically block Mr

Montmorency from entering the building to pursue him. Lois's pre-emptive flight of fancy in which she imagines the carpet in Marda's bed-room burning 'with the house in a scarlet night' is one of a number of passages cited by Backus when she writes of the 'unspeakable wish on the part of Ascendancy women [in *The Last September*] that the settler colo-nial system might disintegrate'.[34]

Bowen's Court, a microcosmic history of both the establishment and dis-integration of this system, has in recent years begun to be justly elevated to the status of a significant Bowen text in its own right. Though the focus of critics who engage with the text is still on Bowen's allegiances, this family chronicle no longer functions solely in Irish literary criticism as an indicator of how Bowen might have wanted us to read *The Last September*. Astute commentators, such as Raphael Ingelbien who reads *Bowen's Court* alongside Bram Stroker's *Dracula*,[35] draw our attention to Bowen's lapses in *Bowen's Court* into plural pronouns and to the corre-sponding extent to which her identity as a narrator repeatedly blends with that of her subjects: 'We north-east County Cork gentry began rather roughly, as settlers' (BC, p.17). Closely identifying herself in such pas-sages with her ancestors and the colonial community that they belonged to, Bowen also makes clear, through the chapter titles of her Ascendancy (auto)biography, her marginal position within this community and the marginal position of the Anglo-Irish women who preceded her. Most of the individual chapters are named after Bowen's male forebears with roman numerals attached, as if they were monarchs (Henry I, Robert III, and so on). The section of the book that tells of Bowen's own 'reign' is simply entitled 'Afterword', not 'Elizabeth I', which connects Bowen in terms of familial and linguistic importance to the pair of sisters men-tioned in 'John Bowen I' 'whose sex did not even allow them capital let-ters in their father's will' and whose lives Bowen can only speculate about since 'they were not important, and ... left little trace' (BC, pp.77, 78).

Perhaps the lives of these sisters were similar to the imagined lives of the living ghosts whose ghostly presence Stella senses in the drawing-room of the Irish Big House featured in Bowen's wartime novel *The Heat of the Day*:

> After all, was it not chiefly here in this room ... that Cousin Nettie Morris – and who now knew how many more before her? – had been pressed back, hour by hour, by the hours themselves, into

cloudland? Ladies had gone not quite mad, not quite even that, from in vain listening for meaning in the loudening ticking of the clock ... Therefore, her kind knew no choices, made no decisions – or, did they not? Everything spoke to them – the design in and out of which they drew their needles; the bird with its little claws drawn to its piteously smooth breast, dead; away in the woods the quickening strokes of the axes, then the fall of the tree; or the child upstairs crying out terrified in its sleep. No, knowledge was not to be kept from them; it sifted through to them, stole up behind them, reached them by intimations – they suspected what they refused to prove. That had been their decision ... And though seated together, hems of their skirts touching, each one of the ladies had not ceased in herself to reflect alone; their however candid and clear looks in each others' [sic] eyes were interchanged warnings; their conversation was a twinkling surface over their deep silence. Virtually they were never to speak at all – unless to the little bird lying big with death on the path, the child being comforted out of the nightmare without waking, the leaf plucked still quivering from the felled tree. (HD, pp.166–7)

The cousin referred to in the opening lines of this passage is the present 'lady of the house', who is so reluctant to reassume the role of Anglo-Irish wife and assume the role of Anglo-Irish mother that she feigns insanity and remains voluntarily incarcerated in Wisteria Lodge, a home for the mentally ill. Her life in this plush asylum is shown to be a living death, but it is also made clear to us that for Nettie Morris the living death she has chosen is vastly superior to the living death she has left behind at Mount Morris.

It is not always necessary, however, to search in Elizabeth Bowen's 'non-Irish' novels and short stories for passages set in Ireland or for an overtly Irish theme in order to form interesting connections between her writings set exclusively in Ireland and her other literary works. Inter-generational tensions of the sort that Declan Kiberd and Margot Gayle Backus discuss in relation to The Last September are also a focus of interest in a number of critical studies of Bowen that centre on her writings set in England and on the continent, and pay scant attention to her Irish origins and Anglo-Irish heritage. One such study is Elizabeth Bowen *and the Dissolution of the Novel* in which it is stated that Bowen's novels 'embrace the concerns of both modernism and postmodernism as well as engaging with the historical specificity of two world wars, the changing role of women and the nuclear age'.[36] Andrew Bennett and Nicholas Royle, in this book, make reference to the importance of strained intergenerational relationships to *The Death of the Heart*, *The House in Paris* and *To the North*.[37] *The House in Paris*, for example, is described as being 'centrally concerned with the terrifying pressures which adults impose on children as they grow' and with the 'haunting of children by their own, and, more importantly, by others' pasts'.[38] Bennett and Royle's psychoanalytic analysis of the damaging genealogical structures revealed in the 'non-Irish' components of this novel offers insights to those critics who read Bowen in the context of Irish settler colonialism, just as a greater knowledge and understanding of Bowen's Anglo-Irish heritage would be invaluable to critics interested in such seemingly 'non-Irish' elements of her work.[39]

Façades (and the forces that threaten to shatter them) is another aspect of her work that critics of Bowen who fail to take fully into consideration the Irish context and critics who view her primarily as an Anglo-Irish writer find equally compelling. Drawing attention to St Quentin's quasi-Shakespearean assertion in *The Death of the Heart* that 'the world's really a stage', Bennett and Royle astutely point out that in Bowen's writings '"original" feelings are always in advance "in imitation"; unwitting or unconscious caricature ... marks every identity; the theatrical and dramatic inscribes every social relation, every experience of the self'.[40] In Irish literary criticism, the façade explored in relation to Bowen's work is almost invariably the pose assumed by the Anglo-Irish Naylors who in *The Last September* organize dances and tennis parties while outside the demesne walls a war of liberation takes place. In recent years a number of commentators who are interested in surfaces and their disruption in Bowen's work have begun the necessary task of linking themes considered central to an analysis of Bowen as an Anglo-Irish writer to what might initially appear to be very different aspects of her writing. In *The Gothic Family Romance*, for example, Margot Gayle Backus reveals points of conjuncture between Bowen's representation of the forces that seek to rip through the façade of Anglo-Irish society and her representation of the sexual desires and practices that threaten to shatter what is often depicted in Bowen's writings as the cracked surface of heterosexuality.[41]

This chapter opened with the observation that Bowen scholarship is extremely fragmented. To some extent, the disjointed nature of this body of criticism is an understandable consequence of the range and complexity of Elizabeth Bowen's work, but it is also the result of a failure on the part of many Bowen scholars, including ones engaged in Irish literary criticism, to trace the threads that run through what might appear, at first glance, to be a fragmented body of work. One of these threads, as I have suggested, is a fascination with fragmentation itself, with fragile or cracked surfaces and the pressures they are seeking to contain. This fascination is at the core of many of the different themes running through her novels and, consequently, connects the 'Anglo-Irish Bowen' with other Elizabeth Bowens of literary criticism, most notably the 'bisexual Bowen'. As an Irish woman writer from a settler colonial community that adopted a grandiose style in an attempt to cover up the repressed stories denied by its official narrative, Bowen was more attuned than most to the unspoken and, for some, unspeakable sexual desires that challenge what Adrienne Rich has termed 'compulsory heterosexuality'.[42] Her status as an Irish woman writer from a settler colonial community and the divided loyalties that this engendered also ensured, however, that Bowen's work never fulfilled its radical potential. The burning of Danielstown at the end of The Last September may be depicted as a necessary release for the stifled Lois, but the reader is also encouraged to admire the nonchalance of the older Naylors whose tennis parties are part of an attempt to maintain a slipping façade.[43] Same-sex desire is acknowledged in much of her writing but it is often rejected by characters in her novels as a non-sustainable life choice in favour of heterosexuality.[44] If Bowen was conscious of the fragility of surfaces and of the forces within that struggled to be released, she also had a fondness for the surfaces themselves and for those who sought to maintain them.

NOTES

1. Sean O'Faolain, 'A Reading and Remembrance of Elizabeth Bowen', London Review of Books (4–17 March 1982), pp.15–16.

2. See, for example, Margo Gayle Backus, The Gothic Family Romance: Heterosexuality, Child Sacrifice, and the Anglo-Irish Colonial Order (Durham, NC and London: Duke University Press, 1999), p.75.

3. Jack Lane, 'Introduction', in Elizabeth Bowen: 'Notes on Eire', Espionage Reports to Winston Churchill, 1940–2; With a Review of Irish Neutrality in World War 2, by Jack Lane and Brendan Clifford (Aubane: Aubane Historical Society, 1999), pp.5–9 (pp.5–6).

4. Roy Foster, Paddy and Mr Punch: Connections in Irish and English History (Harmondsworth: Penguin, 1993), p.122.

5. Ibid., pp.xvi, xii.

6. Lane, 'Introduction', p.5.

7. Ibid.

8. Ibid., p.6.

9. See also the work of J.C. Beckett and F.S.L. Lyons.

10. Foster, Paddy and Mr Punch, p.xii.

11. Lane, 'Introduction', p.6.

12. Ibid., pp.6, 7. This volume also contains a somewhat biased account of the controversy generated in the Irish Times and other Irish newspapers by the publication of the North Cork Anthology.

13. See Foster, Paddy and Mr Punch, p.113. See also Neil Corcoran, Elizabeth Bowen: The Enforced Return (Oxford: Oxford University Press, 2004), pp.184–5. Reminding us of a belligerent speech made by Churchill in the House of Commons shortly before Bowen's first report, Corcoran points out that Bowen's earlier overwhelmingly sympathetic reports on Irish neutrality were compiled at a time when Churchill was considering a possible re-conquest of sovereign Irish territory in order to access certain Irish ports.

14. Lane and Clifford, Elizabeth Bowen: 'Notes on Eire', p.12.

15. Clair Wills, That Neutral Island: A Cultural History of Ireland During the Second World War (London: Faber & Faber, 2007), p.12.

16. Ibid., pp.61, 80.

17. An example of such comparative work would be an essay that explores the points of conjuncture between Elizabeth Bowen's The Last September and Nadine Gordimer's South African female Bildungsroman, The Lying Days (1953).

18. Declan Kiberd, 'Elizabeth Bowen – The Dandy in Revolt', in Inventing Ireland: The Literature of the Modern Nation (London: Jonathan Cape, 1995), pp.364–79 (p.367).

19. Ibid., p.370.

20. Backus, Gothic Family Romance, pp.172, 19.

21. Ibid., p.172.

22. Daiva Stasiulis and Nira Yuval-Davis, 'Introduction: Beyond Dichotomies – Gender, Race, Ethnicity and Class in Settler Societies', in Unsettling Settler Societies: Articulations of

Gender, Race, Ethnicity and Class, ed. D. Stasiulis and N. Yuval-Davis (London: Sage, 1995), pp. 1–38.

23. Ibid., p. 214.

24. Elizabeth Bowen, *The Last September* (London: Vintage, 1998 [1929]), p. 206, hereafter referred to in the text as TLS.

25. For a concise historical overview of the Big House novel, see Seamus Deane, *A Short History of Irish Literature* (Notre Dame, IN: University of Notre Dame Press, 1994 [1986]), pp. 203–6. Bowen's *The Last September* is aptly referred to in this overview as the novel in which the Sheridan Le Fanu and the Somerville and Ross literary heritage is combined (p. 205).

26. Elizabeth Bowen, *A World of Love* (London: Vintage, 1999 [1955]).

27. Elizabeth Bowen, *The House in Paris* (London: Vintage, 1998 [1935]); *The Heat of the Day* (London: Jonathan Cape, 1949), hereafter referred to in the text as HD; *Elizabeth Bowen's Irish Stories* (Dublin: Poolbeg, 1986 [1978]).

28. Vera Kreilkamp, 'Stages of disloyalty in Elizabeth Bowen's Irish Fiction', in *The Anglo-Irish Novel and the Big House* (Syracuse, NY: Syracuse University Press, 1998), pp. 141–73.

29. Elizabeth Bowen, *Seven Winters: Memories of a Dublin Childhood* (London: Longmans, Green and Co., 1943 [1942]); *Bowen's Court* (Cork: Collins Press, 1998 [1942]), hereafter referred to in the text as BC.

30. See, for example, Hermione Lee's description of the novel as a 'form of elegy' that nostalgically marks the passing of the Ascendancy in *Elizabeth Bowen: An Estimation* (Totowa, NJ: Barnes and Noble, 1981), p. 51, and Edwin Kenney's assertion that the novel reveals the 'guilty void at the center' of the Anglo-Irish community in *Elizabeth Bowen*, Irish Writers Series (Lewisburg, PA: Bucknell University Press, 1975), p. 34.

31. Foster, *Paddy and Mr Punch*, p. 106. See also Heather Bryant Jordan's assertion that the final scene of *The Last September* is best interpreted in the context to Bowen's claim in *Bowen's Court* that she survived the instability of Bowen's Court's tenure during the period of the 1920s by teaching herself to imagine the house in flames, in *How Will the Heart Endure? Elizabeth Bowen and the Landscape of War* (Ann Arbor, MI: University of Michigan Press, 1992), p. 59.

32. Kiberd, *Inventing Ireland*, p. 369.

33. Ibid., p. 372.

34. Backus, *Gothic Family Romance*, p. 180. In *Heathcliff and the Great Famine: Studies in Irish Culture* (London: Verso, 1995), Terry Eagleton expresses a marked degree of understandable skepticism when discussing the kinds of alignments and connections that Kiberd and Backus draw our attention to in their analyses of *The Last September*: 'There is a spurious kind of fellowship between oppressor and oppressed: if the exploiter is an outcast, then so are those on whom he battens; if they have no identity, then neither has he. What this conveniently overlooks is that if the ruler bears the mark of Cain it is because of his own actions, which is why the oppressed are outcast too; but in Ireland this symmetry can pass as plausible, since the governing class really does have good reason to feel paranoid. Their sense of persecution, in part at least, is a dread of the vengeance of those they have persecuted. Estranged from the populace

by culture and religion, the elite can easily mistake itself for the marginal, and so misperceive itself as a mirror image of the people themselves' (p.191).

35. Raphael Ingelbien, 'Gothic Genealogies: *Dracula, Bowen's Court*, and Anglo-Irish Psychology', *English Literary History*, 70, 4 (2003), pp.1089–1105.

36. Andrew Bennett and Nicholas Royle, *Elizabeth Bowen and the Dissolution of the Novel: Still Lives* (Basingstoke: Macmillan, 1994), p.xiv.

37. Elizabeth Bowen, *The Death of the Heart* (London: Vintage, 1998 [1938]); *To the North* (London: Penguin, 1986 [1932]).

38. Bennett and Royle, *Elizabeth Bowen and the Dissolution of the Novel*, p.43.

39. Rare examples of how Bowen's 'non-Irish' writings can be effectively interpreted in relation to her Anglo-Irish heritage include Claire Connolly's fascinating reading of the 'uneasy textualization of belonging' in *Eva Trout*, a novel in which there is not a single mention of Ireland, in the context of 'Bowen's own near feudal understanding of the relation between people and property in her native Ireland'. See Claire Connolly, '(Be)longing – The Strange Place of Elizabeth Bowen's *Eva Trout*', in *Borderlands: Negotiating Boundaries in Post-Colonial Writing*, ed. Monika Reif Hülser (Amsterdam: Rodopi, 1999), pp.135–43 (p.139). See also Margo Gayle Backus' analysis of Bowen's celebrated short story, 'The Demon Lover', as a text which, notwithstanding its English wartime setting, 'displays a narrative logic that exhibits patterns of repetition and historical recurrence that are characteristic of Anglo-Irish narrative structure', in *Gothic Family Romance*, p.157.

40. Bennett and Royle, *Elizabeth Bowen and the Dissolution of the Novel*, p.73.

41. Backus, *Gothic Family Romance*, p.180.

42. Adrienne Rich, 'Compulsory Heterosexuality and Lesbian Existence', in *Blood, Bread, and Poetry: Selected Prose, 1979–1985* (New York: W.W. Norton, 1986), pp.23–75.

43. In 'The Big House' (1940), in *Collected Impressions* (London: Longmans, 1950), pp.195–202, Bowen expresses approval for the 'Big House people [who] concealed their struggles with such nonchalance and for so long continued to throw about what did not really amount to much weight. It is to their credit that, with grass almost up to their doors and hardly a sixpence to turn over, they continued to be resented by the rest of Ireland as being the heartless rich' (pp.197–8).

44. See Emmeline's assertion in *To the North* that 'houses shared with women are built on sand' (p.208).

Select Bibliography

WORKS BY ELIZABETH BOWEN

Encounters (London: Sidgwick and Jackson, 1923) (E)

Ann Lee's and Other Stories (London: Sidgwick and Jackson, 1926) (AL)

The Hotel (London: Constable, 1927) (TH)

Joining Charles and Other Stories (London: Constable, 1929) (JC)

The Last September (London: Constable, 1929) (LS)

Friends and Relations (London: Constable, 1931) (FR)

To the North (London: Gollancz, 1932) (TTN)

The Cat Jumps and Other Stories (London: Gollancz, 1934) (CJ)

The House in Paris (London: Gollancz, 1935) (HP)

The Death of the Heart (London: Gollancz, 1938) (DH)

Look At All Those Roses (London: Gollancz, 1941) (LR)

Bowen's Court (London: Longmans, Green and Co., 1942) (BC)

Seven Winters: Memories of a Dublin Childhood (Dublin: Cuala Press, 1942; London: Longmans, Green and Co., 1943) (SW)

English Novelists (London: Collins 1945) (EN)

The Demon Lover and Other Stories (London: Jonathan Cape, 1945) (DL)

The Heat of the Day (London: Jonathan Cape, 1949) (HD)

Collected Impressions (London: Longmans, Green and Co., 1950) (CI)

The Shelbourne (London: Harrap, 1951) (TSH)

A World of Love (London: Jonathan Cape, 1955) (WL)

A Time in Rome (London: Longmans, Green and Co., 1960) (ATR)

Afterthoughts (London: Longmans, Green and Co. 1962) (AFT)

The Little Girls (London: Jonathan Cape, 1964; New York: Alfred A. Knopf, 1964) (LG)

A Day in the Dark and Other Stories (London: Cape, 1965) (DD)

The Good Tiger (London: Jonathan Cape, 1965) (GT)

Eva Trout, or Changing Scenes (New York: Alfred A. Knopf, 1968; London: Jonathan Cape, 1969) (ET)

Pictures and Conversations, ed. Spenser Curtis Brown (London: Allen Lane, 1975) (PC)

Elizabeth Bowen's Irish Stories, intro. Victoria Glendinning (Dublin: Poolbeg, 1978/1986)

Collected Stories, ed. Angus Wilson(London: Jonathan Cape, 1980) (CT)

The Mulberry Tree: Writings of Elizabeth Bowen, ed. Hermione Lee (London: Virago, 1986; San Diego: Harcourt Brace, 1986) (MT)

Other Writings by Elizabeth Bowen

'The Big House' (1940), *Collected Impressions* (London: Longmans, Green and Co., 1950), pp.195–202 (BH)

'The Cult of Nostalgia', *The Listener*, 9 August 1951, p.225

SELECTED WORKS ON ELIZABETH BOWEN.

Backus, Margot, *The Gothic Family Romance: Heterosexuality, Child Sacrifice, and the Anglo-Irish Colonial Order* (Durham, NC: Duke University Press, 1999).

Bennett, Andrew and Nicholas Royle, *Elizabeth Bowen and the Dissolution of the Novel: Still Lives* (Basingstoke: Macmillan, 1994).

Christensen, Liz, *Elizabeth Bowen The Later Fiction* (Copenhagen: Museum Tusculanum Press, University of Copenhagen, 2001).

Coates, John, *Social Discontinuity in the Novels of Elizabeth Bowen: The Conservative Quest* (Lewiston: Edwin Mellen, 1998).

Connolly, Claire, '(Be) longing – The Strange Place of Elizabeth Bowen's *Eva Trout*', in *Borderlands: Negotiating Boundaries in Post-Colonial Writing*, ed. Monika Reif Hülser (Amsterdam: Rodopi, 1999), pp.135–43.

Corcoran, Neil, *Elizabeth Bowen: The Enforced Return* (Oxford: Oxford University Press, 2004).

Coughlan, Patricia, 'Women and Desire in the Work of Elizabeth Bowen', in *Sex, Nation and Dissent in Irish Writing*, ed. E. Walshe (Cork: Cork University Press, 1997).

Craig, Patricia, *Elizabeth Bowen* (Harmondsworth: Penguin, 1986).

Ellmann, Maud, *Elizabeth Bowen: The Shadow Across the Page* (Edinburgh: Edinburgh University Press, 2003).

Forster, Roy, *The Irish Story* (Harmondsworth: Penguin, 2001).

——, *Paddy and Mr Punch: Connections in Irish and English History* (Harmondsworth: Penguin, 1993).

Glendinning, Victoria, Elizabeth Bowen: Portrait of a Writer (London: Weidenfeld and Nicolson, 1977).

Hardwick, Elizabeth, 'Elizabeth Bowen's Fiction', Partisan Review, 16, 11 (November 1949), pp.1114–21.

Hoogland, Rene, Elizabeth Bowen: A Reputation in Writing (New York: New York University Press, 1994).

Inglesby, Elizabeth, '"Expressive Objects": Elizabeth Bowen's Narrative Materializes', Modern Fiction Studies, Special Issue: Elizabeth Bowen, 53, 2 (Summer 2007), pp.306–33.

Jordan, Heather Bryant, How Will the Heart Endure? Elizabeth Bowen and the Landscape of War (Ann Arbor, MI: University of Michigan Press, 1992).

Kreilkamp, Vera, The Anglo-Irish Novel and the Big House (Syracuse, NY: Syracuse University Press, 1998).

Lane, Jack and Brendan Clifford, Elizabeth Bowen: 'Notes on Eire', Espionage Reports to Winston Churchill, 1940-2; With a Review of Irish Neutrality in World War 2 (Aubane: Aubane Historical Society, 1999).

Lassner, Phyllis, Elizabeth Bowen (London: Macmillan, 1990).

—— Elizabeth Bowen: A Study of the Short Fiction (New York: Twayne, 1991).

Lee, Hermione, Elizabeth Bowen: An Estimation (Totowa, NJ: Barnes and Noble, 1981; London: Vision, 1981; London: Vintage, 1999).

—— 'Psychic Furniture: Ellmann's Elizabeth Bowen', Body Parts: Essays on Life Writing (London: Chatto and Windus, 2005), pp.187–93.

O'Faolain, Sean, 'A Reading and Remembrance of Elizabeth Bowen', London Review of Books (4–17 March 1982), pp.15–16.

Toomey, Deirdre, 'Bowen, Elizabeth Dorothea Cole (1899–1973)', Oxford Dictionary of National Biography (Oxford: Oxford University Press, 2004).

Walsh, Keri, 'Elizabeth Bowen, Surrealist', Éire-Ireland: An Interdisciplinary Journal of Irish Studies, 42, 3 and 4 (Fall/Winter 2007), pp.126–47.

Walshe, Eibhear (ed.), Elizabeth Bowen Remembered: The Farahy Addresses (Dublin: Four Courts Press, 1998).

Wills, Clair, That Neutral Island: A Cultural History of Ireland During the Second World War (London: Faber & Faber, 2007).

Index

INDEX